Contemporary Plays

CW00740251

Contemporary Plays by African Women

Niqabi Ninja

Not That Woman

I Want to Fly

Silent Voices

Unsettled

Mbuzeni

Bonganyi

Edited and introduced by

YVETTE HUTCHISON *and* AMY JEPHTA

methuen | drama

LONDON • NEW YORK • OXFORD • NEW DELHI • SYDNEY

METHUEN DRAMA
Bloomsbury Publishing Plc
50 Bedford Square, London, WC1B 3DP, UK
1385 Broadway, New York, NY 10018, USA

BLOOMSBURY, METHUEN DRAMA and the Methuen Drama logo are trademarks of
Bloomsbury Publishing Plc

First published in Great Britain 2019
Reprinted 2019

Niqabi Ninja copyright © Sara Shaarawi, 2019
Not That Woman copyright © 'Tosin Jobi-Tume, 2019
I Want to Fly copyright © Thembelihle Moyo, 2019
Silent Voices copyright © Adong Judith, 2019
Unsettled copyright © JC Niala, 2019
Mbuzeni copyright © Koleka Putuma, 2019
Bonganyi copyright © Sophia Mempuh Kwachuh, 2019

Introduction © Yvette Hutchison and Amy Jephta, 2019

The authors have asserted their right under the Copyright, Designs and Patents Act, 1988,
to be identified as authors of this work.

Cover design: Mzwandile Buthelezi

All rights reserved. No part of this publication may be reproduced or transmitted
in any form or by any means, electronic or mechanical, including photocopying,
recording, or any information storage or retrieval system, without prior permission
in writing from the publishers.

Bloomsbury Publishing Plc does not have any control over, or responsibility for, any
third-party websites referred to or in this book. All internet addresses given in this
book were correct at the time of going to press. The author and publisher regret
any inconvenience caused if addresses have changed or sites have ceased to exist,
but can accept no responsibility for any such changes.

No rights in incidental music or songs contained in the work are hereby granted
and performance rights for any performance/presentation whatsoever must be
obtained from the respective copyright owners.

All rights whatsoever in this play are strictly reserved and application for performance etc.
should be made before rehearsals by professionals and by amateurs to
Methuen Drama, Bloomsbury Publishing Plc, 50 Bedford Square, London,
WC1B 3DP (email: performance.permissions@bloomsbury.com).
No performance may be given unless a licence has been obtained.

A catalogue record for this book is available from the British Library.

Library of Congress Cataloging-in-Publication Data
Names: Hutchison, Yvette, editor. | Jeptha, Amy, editor. | Contains (work): Shaarawi,
Sara. Niqabi ninja. | Contains (work): Tume, Tosin. Not that woman. | Contains (work):
Moyo, Thembelihle. I want to fly. | Contains (work): Judith, Adong. Silent voices. |
Contains (work): Niala, J.C. Unsettled. | Contains (work): Putuma, Koleka.
Mbuzeni. | Contains (work): Mempuh, Sophia. Bonganyi.
Title: Contemporary plays by African women : Niqabi ninja, Not that woman, I want
to fly, Silent voices, Unsettled, Mbuzeni, Bonganyi / edited and introduced
by Yvette Hutchison and Amy Jephta.
Description: New York, NY : Methuen Drama, Bloomsbury Publishing Plc, 2019. |
Includes bibliographical references and index. Identifiers: LCCN 2018032010 |
ISBN 9781350034518 (pb) | ISBN 9781350034525 (hpod)
Subjects: LCSH: African drama (English)—Women authors. | African drama
(English)—21st century. | Women—Africa–Drama.

Classification: LCC PR9347 .C656 2019 | DDC 822.920809287—dc23 LC record
available at https://lccn.loc.gov/2018032010

ISBN: HB: 978-1-350-03452-5
        PB: 978-1-350-03451-8
        ePDF: 978-1-350-03453-2
        eBook: 978-1-350-03454-9

Typeset by RefineCatch Limited Bungay, Suffolk
Printed and bound in Great Britain

To find out more about our authors and books visit www.bloomsbury.com
and sign up for our newsletters.

Contents

Introduction

Yvette Hutchison and Amy Jephta

What do African women write about?

This impenetrable question is one we have been asked throughout the creation of this book, as scholars of African women's writing and as playwrights. *What do we write about?* Summarize it. Define it. Capture it in a sentence. What do these seven plays have in common?

The question is absurd mainly because it implies a homogeneity – that there is such a thing as a singular African Woman playwright, that such a person may be defined by her geography, by her cultural positioning, by her history, by the accident of being born on the continent – that it may be possible to define what 'we' write about based on who 'we' are. The reality is that such a categorization is not a given and is rarely neat. Impulses to tell stories bloom from contexts as much as they are borne from imagination, from the tangible realities of life as much as from the yearning for transcendence. The scope of subjects, themes, obsessions and impulses that frame these plays traverse a wide range of lived (and imagined) experiences. They are defined both by the coincidence of their shared geography and by the specificity of the lives presented therein. That the work is mostly political in nature is a given, in the way that a black woman putting pen to paper is almost always a political act, working as it does against the hegemonic canon of plays by white men. That the work is often tragic is similarly inescapable: these plays overwhelmingly reflect the inherited trauma of what it means to exist as a black woman, written between the lines or in the words themselves. That the work often – explicitly or otherwise – questions Africa's relation to the West or interrogates the post-colonial subject is true as well. Beyond that, however, lies a range of cultural specificities that make it difficult to speak for or on behalf of a 'we'. These works are playful, ironic, heartbreaking and funny, simultaneously bound to their environments while being universal. Some were written in the author's mother tongue and translated by her into English, while others include local languages in the English texts in songs, terms or proverbs.

Broadly, they fall into two thematic categories: The first engages directly with women's potential responses to gendered abuse: how they negotiate their desires and aspirations in a world where male control is often enforced through physical and/or sexual violence. Sara Shaarawi's *Niqabi Ninja* addresses Egyptian women's sense of shame regarding their bodies. This play fantasises about how the protagonist's sense of agency evolves through a comic superhero role model, from fearful defence to defiant offence. 'Tosin Jobi-Tume's *Not That Woman* considers the role of women in abuse, female solidarity and agency from a Nigerian perspective. Thembelihle Moyo's *I Want to Fly* (Zimbabwe) tells the story of an African girl who wants to be a pilot. It looks at how patriarchal society can limit female aspirations and shapes the thinking of men regarding *lobola* (bride price), how women are viewed as domestic or sexual commodities, why women endure abusive men, and the role society at large plays in these issues.

The second thematic thread in this collection considers the role of history in the experiences of women. Many historical periods of injustice, particularly colonialism and its legacies in the twentieth and twenty-first centuries, have not been acknowledged or critiqued to any great extent. The plays that follow explore aspects of how various disavowed collective histories and individual memories continue to resonate in the present, from a particularly female perspective. Adong Judith's memory play, *Silent Voices*, is based on interviews she conducted with the LRA Rebel Victims of Northern Uganda and how this conflict continues to affect Ugandans in the present. JC Niala's *Unsettled* explores gender violence across races, post-colonial issues and relationships between black and white Kenyans living in and out of the country. South African Koleka Putuma's *Mbuzeni* tells the stories of four orphaned girls, their sisterhood, and their fixation with death and burials. It suggests the unseen force that governs and dictate the laws by which the villagers live. Sophia Mempuh Kwachuh's *Bonganyi* draws on an old Cameroonian myth to suggest how the history of slavery continues to affect perceptions of women in their societies today. This play goes beyond the ghosts that haunt *Mbuzeni*, as it is told by a ghost at her funeral, on the eve of a dance competition she had hoped to win to free herself and her family from slavery, and thus achieve full personhood. These plays link ghosts and memory, the past and the present. They consider the complexities African youths face as they negotiate various complex and unjust pasts in order to make futures for themselves. The collection comes from the need to hear and read as many of these experiences as possible within the confines of a single book. These playwrights' names may be fresh to scholars and supporters of new writing from Africa, and many of these women are being published here for the first time, but they join the ranks of women who have led the movement of self-actualization among African female artists – writers like Fatima Dike and Gçina Mhlope (South Africa), Stella Oyedepo, Zulu Sofola, Julie Okoh and Irene Salami (Nigeria), earlier playwrights like Ama Ata Aidoo and Efua Sutherland (Ghana), Micere Mugo (Kenya), Rose Mbowa (Uganda), Penina Mlama and Amadina Lihamba (Tanzania), and so many more.

It would be ideal (if not feasible) to update this volume annually, based on the number of plays being written by South African women alone. That these plays often remain unproduced, are written without development funding or formal support structures and without a view to publication does little to curb the playwrights' irrepressible impulse to create. What this collection aims to do is widen the scope of new playwriting by a centimetre or two, to create a bit of room for these underrepresented voices, if only to hint at how many new writers have entered the conversation since such a collection was last published. If only to indicate how much legwork there is to be done to find similar spaces for other emerging and established female writers from the continent.

The context of the work

This collection emerges from material gathered for the Women's Playwriting International Conference 2015 and the AHRC-funded African Women Playwright's Network. In 2015, the Women Playwrights International Conference (WPIC) was held in Cape Town, South Africa – hosted on the African continent for the first time in its then twenty-seven-year history. Even though the continent has a long legacy of new writing, these works have often existed on the fringes of criticism, academic pursuit and production. It became clear during this conference, and in our subsequent work in this field, that the publication of new plays by women from Africa is still overwhelmingly scarce. Despite the UN recognizing and advocating gender equality and the empowerment of women, particularly with the appointment of Michelle Bachelet as the first Under-Secretary General and Executive Director of UN Women, African women continue to lack healthcare (more women die from complications giving birth than from war or cancer), education, and justice systems that will uphold their human rights and equal access to the means for economic empowerment or representation in cultural fora (cf. Mikell, 1997). Although women playwrights are very productive in creating new works for the stage and are active in many community projects, there is a significant imbalance in what is published by women on the continent. This is very noticeable when one compares published material on African-American women playwrights to their African counterparts. For example, Kathy Perkins's *Black South African Women* (1998), which reflects on women's experiences from both male and female perspectives, and *African Women Playwrights* (2009) constitute the anthologies of plays about or by African women. Although some African women playwrights have been published individually or in collections, these are vastly in the minority when compared with their male counterparts. The critical journal *African Theatre* engaged with women performance-makers in 2002 and 2014. When working on the last volume, journal editors Jane Plastow, Yvette Hutchison and Christine Matzke found that African women's work in performance cultures remains obscured, largely because of sexist inequalities. This volume traced the impact of domestic and state interference and discrimination, limited access to theatres and funding, and the tension between local and international audiences and its impact on African women creative artists. It led to questions regarding how the academy can facilitate wider engagement with the work of actresses, artists, writers and dancers who create from the front line, against the odds, and bring their knowledge and experiences to people in other contexts in Africa and beyond.

Later in 2015, we set up the African Women's Playwright Network (awpn.org), an AHRC-funded project, to respond to some of these challenges more directly. We created a virtual network through a mobile application that could be accessed on Wi-Fi enabled feature or smart mobile phones, and online via the web. This virtual community of African women creative practitioners are involved in poetry, playwriting and theatre making, in both mainstream and community-based contexts, and included researchers and others interested in engaging with literary or gender-based research in any part of the world. The project was born out of the urgency for African women to represent themselves: to speak for and about themselves, to see themselves in print and on-stage, for their own experiences to be reflected back at them in mainstream spaces. It is our hope that we can continue to address this critical gap and that this collection will enable African women, in some small way, to hear themselves: in their own voices.

Plays are, of course, created for performance and not necessarily for a reading audience. These written texts will never accurately capture the dynamism and energy of the live performance (in cases where the works were previously produced) or the nuances of the world in which the playwright situates herself. The peculiarities of language and regional dialects, the nuances of a performance style or a linguistic rhythm and having words spoken by an actor who possesses an embodied understanding of the text are all priviledges a reading audience forgoes. The play script as a tool of communication is especially difficult when the worlds presented are culturally encoded, translated into English, or exist as the result of a stage-to-page translation of a performance text. The playscripts presented here traverse a range of forms: some of them borne out of the stimulus of an individual writer with subsequent structured developmental support – as is the case with *Silent Voices* – others through workshop and collaborative processes that later led back to the final script, as is the case with *Mbuzeni*. While capturing these plays in their written form presents its own complications (arguments can be made against the need to find legitimacy through an English language publication, in cases where English is often a second or third language), the paradox is that the publication of plays by African women, in this form, is an essential part of the organization and archiving of these voices. And the grappling with them, as written texts, a necessary exercise. Each play is prefixed by a short biography by the author, the play's production history and the author's own critical contextualization of her work. We have added a short further bibliography of additional reading to accompany these new plays, to widen access to the debates and approaches to them. We hope that whether you are reading these plays out of general interest, or as part of a curriculum on theatre in the African context, or from a gender studies perspective, that this collection will stimulate further engagement with works by the many amazing women writing and creating theatre in Africa. Try to imagine them in performance as you read them. The text is, after all, only the skeleton of African story-telling.

General bibliography

Collections of plays by or about African women

Perkins, Kathy (ed.). 1998. *Black South African Women*. London and New York: Routledge.

Perkins, Kathy (ed.). 2009. *African Women Playwrights*. Urbana: University of Illinois Press.

Secondary reading

Bennett, Jane and Charmaine Pereira (eds). 2013. *Jacketed Women – Qualitative Research Methodologies on Sexualities and Gender in Africa*. Claremont: University of Cape Town Press.

Cole, Catherine, Takyiwaamanuh Manuh and Stephan F. Miescher (eds). 2007. *Africa after Gender?* Bloomington and Indianapolis: Indiana University Press.

DeLinda, Marzette. 2013. *Africana Women Writers: Performing Diaspora, Staging Healing*. New York: Peter Lang.

Farfan, Penny and Lesley Ferris. 2013. *Contemporary Women Playwrights into the Twenty-First Century*. Palgrave Macmillan.

Flockemann, Mikki. 1998. 'Women, Feminism and South African Theatre', in L. Goodman and J. De Gay (eds), *The Routledge Reader in Gender and Performance*. London: Routledge, 218–222.

Gouws, Amanda (ed.). 2005. *(Un)thinking Citizenship: Feminist Debates in Contemporary South Africa*. Aldershot/Burlington, VT: Ashgate Publishers.

Hutchison, Yvette. 2013. *South African Performance and the Archives of Memory*. Manchester: Manchester University Press.

James, Adeola. 1990. *In Their Own Voices: African Women Writers Talk*. Oxford: James Currey.

Mekgwe, Pinkie. 2007. 'Theorizing African feminism(s) – the Colonial Question', in Tobias Robert Klein, Ulrike Auga and Viola Prüschenk (eds), *Texts, Tasks, and Theories: Versions and Subversions in African Literatures*, Vol 3. Matatu 35, Amsterdam and New York: Rodopi, 165–214.

Mikell, Gwendolyn. 1997. *African Feminism*. University of Pennsylvania Press.

Nnaemeka, Obioma (ed.). 1988. *Sisterhood – Feminisms & Power from Africa to the Diaspora*. Trenton, NJ and Asmara: Africa World Press.

Plastow, Jane (ed.). 2002. *African Theatre: African Women*. Oxford: James Currey, Bloomington and Indianapolis: Indiana University Press, Johannesburg: Witwatersrand University Press.

Plastow, Jane, Yvette Hutchison and Christine Matzke (eds). 2015. *African Theatre 14: Contemporary Women*. Woodbridge: James Currey, New York: Boydell & Brewer.

Useful journals

Agenda
Research in African Literatures
South African Theatre Journal

Niqabi Ninja

Sara Shaarawi

Sara Shaarawi is a playwright, translator and performer from Cairo who is now based in Glasgow. She has had her work performed as various venues across Scotland including the Tron Theatre, The Traverse, Village Pub Theatre, Platform, and the CCA. Sara took part in the Playwrights Studio Scotland's 2015 Mentoring Programme and the National Theatre of Scotland's Breakthrough Writers programme in 2016 and Starter Programme in 2017. Other credits include the dramaturgy, performance and translation of *One Day in Spring* (Oran Mor/NTS) and *Here's the News from Over There* (Northern Stage). She is one of the recipients of the Playwrights' Studio Scotland's 2017 New Playwright's Awards and a founding member of The Workers Theatre, a theatre co-operative supporting radical art and performance in Glasgow and Leith. In early 2017 they ran a successful crowdfunder to raise money for a new theatre residency called Megaphone, aimed at supporting artists of colour based in Scotland. Her play in this collection, *Niqaba Ninja,* has been staged most recently at the Arts Admin Collective in Cape Town from 8–20 May 2017; see https://www.facebook.com/niqabininja/.

Production history

Niqabi Ninja first began as twenty-minute rapid response monologue in 2013, written specifically for Reclaim the F Word, a week-long festival centred around new writing about women and feminism curated by Julia Taudevin at the Tron Theatre in Glasgow. In 2014 it was developed into an hour-long two-hander, which had a reading at Mayfesto, a festival of political theatre at the Tron Theatre. In 2015, with support from Creative Scotland and Platform, *Niqabi Ninja* was developed further and performed as a work-in-progress at the Gender Programming event in Platform (Easterhouse). It was directed by Amanda Gaughan and performed by Nalini Chetty and Maryam Hamidi. In 2016, *Niqabi Ninja* was performed in Cape Town by Loren Loubser and Bianca Flanders under the direction of Megan Furniss. It has since then been performed in various venues across Cape Town.

Critical introduction

In 2013, I was asked by Julia Taudevin to write a piece about Arab women for a festival of new writing she was curating, dealing with themes around women and feminism. I decided to write a response to the mob sexual assaults against women that were happening during demonstrations in Tahrir Square; as well as a response to the rise in female superheroes in comics and cartoons (Burqa Avenger in Pakistan, Qahera in Egypt, Ms. Marvel . . . etc.). I wanted to look at rape culture beyond these specific assaults and how normalising seemingly 'harmless behaviour', such as catcalling, could escalate into such blatantly violent acts. This is the first play I ever wrote, and when I wrote it, I was angry. I was angry at the hopelessness I felt in fighting misogyny, not just in Egypt but the world over. When the play was developed in Glasgow in the spring of 2014, a series of rapes occurred in Queen's Park, which was situated about ten minutes away from where I lived. By then I had been living in Europe for almost three years, and I had discovered that the normalisation of violent sexual behaviour simply took another form in the West. This gave me the confidence to continue writing the play in English for a Western audience, perhaps in the hope that it would not only provide an alternative Arab story, but that they would also see their own story reflected in the experiences of Hana, from buying her first bra to receiving unsolicited sexual attention to being touched without consent. I was not interested in the 'man's point of view' or in exploring the reasons why men would choose to behave in such a way. I was angry, and I wanted to write a revenge fantasy, and so I focused the narrative on that anger. I didn't want to sugar-coat or compromise the horror of the experiences I was engaged with. I chose to present it in comic book form because comics are uncompromising in their violence, and fantastical in their storytelling. I thought this was the best form to communicate the strength all women must build within themselves to survive such violence. We learn at a very young age that we do not share the same comfort men experience in public and private spaces, we learn to build psychological defences against sexually aggressive comments, we learn how everyday objects can become weapons, we learn the quickest routes home, we know which streets are the darkest at night, we exchange advice and tips on how to protect ourselves. People often ask me if this piece is autobiographical, and my answer is always that it's fictional but that every experience expressed in the play is true. Hana doesn't represent me, but she is a dedication to every single woman I grew up with, every single woman who shared a story or called me in tears, every woman to whom I turned, every woman at those demonstrations, every woman who spoke out and every woman who didn't.

Characters

Hana, *a young Cairene woman.*
Niqabi Ninja, *Hana's alter ego*

Setting

A room in Cairo in the latter part of 2013.

We see the Cairo skyline, the citadel, the tower, the Nile, the Pyramids, the buildings that will never be fully constructed, rooftops, TV antennas and air conditioning fans, all covered in dust and haze. A figure appears. She's dressed in full niqab. She stands on a rooftop, looking out at the city. It's the **Niqabi Ninja**.

Hana Egypt. 2400 BCE. A goddess stands looking over the kingdom of Heliopolis. Her name is Isis. She and her husband, Osiris, had protected Egypt for thousands of years. But one day, Osiris is killed by his brother, Set, and his body is chopped up and scattered across the lands he was supposed to be protecting. Isis cried, her tears caused the Nile to overflow. She cried and cried until there were no more tears left. Set had underestimated her power. What Set doesn't know is that once the tears ended, Isis would rise as the hero of this tale.

Niqabi Ninja Every night I will hunt one of you down. Every night I will walk through the streets. I will take a mental picture of every piece of shit who dares to comment on my clothes, my breasts, my ass, my eyes, my mouth, my legs, my cunt. I will choose just one of you lucky bastards. I will rip you apart. And your screams will not be heard. I will make sure you pay for what you've done.

Hana Because Isis will find every single piece of her mutilated husband and she will put him back together. She will fix him. She will fix everything.

Niqabi Ninja Who am I?

We see **Hana**. *She's sketching, and she's not happy with how her comic is going.*

Hana Shit.

Niqabi Ninja You can't call me Isis.

Hana Chapter One: The Rise of a New . . .?

Niqabi Ninja Don't say goddess.

Hana Chapter One: The Beginning

A woman in a niqab stands over Cairo.

Niqabi Ninja Please don't give me a shit name. There are so many shit names out there.

Hana We see the skyline.

Niqabi Ninja   Burqa Avenger? Qahera? Those aren't names you'd say with a straight face.

Hana   We see the citadel –

Niqabi Ninja   Not that anyone would see my face anyway.

Hana   – the tower, the Nile, the Great Pyramids.

Niqabi Ninja   Even the one from the X-Men has an unoriginal name, what is it again?

Hana   We see buildings that will never be fully constructed, rooftops, TV antennas and air conditioning fans.

Niqabi Ninja   You know the one I'm talking about, the one that throws sand at people.

Hana   All covered in dust and haze.

Niqabi Ninja   And the sand eats their flesh.

Hana   Come on focus.

Niqabi Ninja   That part is cool. I like that. Do you think it's possible to create flesh eating sand?

Hana   The woman stands on a rooftop, looking out over the city.

Niqabi Ninja   Let's rip off that idea.

Hana   She is part human.

Niqabi Ninja   Why can't I remember her name?

Hana   Part goddess.

Niqabi Ninja   Hana?

Hana   She is –

Niqabi Ninja   HANA?

Hana   DUST!

Niqabi Ninja   What?

Hana   Dust! That's her name, Dust. Now can you please leave me alone?

Niqabi Ninja   Dust?

Hana   Yes.

Niqabi Ninja   That's her name?

Hana   Yes. Yes, that's what she's called, now please shut up.

Niqabi Ninja   Dust, the niqabi mutant from the desert, that's the best they could come up with? I mean, I guess it's better then like Sand or Storm. Storm is a stupid name. Why didn't they go with something Arabic?

Hana   She's Afghani.

Niqabi Ninja   No shit! Ok, I guess Dust is not that bad, now that I've given it some thought.

Hana   The woman has a design of wings on her abaya.

Niqabi Ninja   Seriously? We're back to Isis?

Hana   It's not pronounced Isis, it's Eezees.[1]

Niqabi Ninja   La' ya sheikha, fara'et awi. (No way! Makes a huge difference now!)

Hana   She's a goddess, she has powers.

Niqabi Ninja   Cairo needs more than powers.

Hana   Cairo needs a miracle.

Niqabi Ninja   What's all this talk about miracles and godly powers? Just give me some awesome weapons, and some killer skills, and a fucking badass costume!

Hana   I don't know how to start. I don't know where to start.

Niqabi Ninja   I like the rooftop/skyline thing.

Hana   I don't mean the comic, I mean . . . I don't know.

Niqabi Ninja   Tahrir?

Hana   No.

Niqabi Ninja   The UN report?

Hana   I don't know.

Niqabi Ninja   Why don't you start by giving me a name?

Hana   Would you stop focusing on yourself for a second?

Niqabi Ninja   No problem. I'm happy to move on. Let's focus on what we're going to do with these fuckers.

---

1 The Arabic pronunciation of Isis.

Hana   I don't want to think about that.

Niqabi Ninja   Fine. I'm done. No more ideas from me.

Hana   Finally.

Niqabi Ninja   . . . .

Both are quiet for a bit. We start to take in the bearings of the stage. It's a room that looks a bit like a storage room. Like an attic or a basement. There's some furniture. Some boxes and junk. There's a wall covered in sketches, paintings, drawings and stencils. There's also a camera but it's not set up. The room should look familiar but also it should not feel entirely 'real.' **Hana** *looks at the camera. She gets an idea.*

Hana   The woman turns a camera on. She presses record. She stands in front of the camera.

Niqabi Ninja *gets into position in front of the camera, which is still not set up.*

Niqabi Ninja   I don't care what size you are, what age, what class, whether you have a family who loves you or not.

Hana   Most women here are afraid to speak out. They don't want their families to know.

Niqabi Ninja   I don't care whether you are a good father, son, brother or husband.

Hana   They don't want to cause trouble. They don't want to be blamed.

Niqabi Ninja   I am coming after you.

Hana   Not her though.

Niqabi Ninja   I will chop you up.

Hana   She's gone beyond the fear.

Niqabi Ninja   And scatter your pieces far, far away.

Hana   No that's not it.

Niqabi Ninja   Why did you stop? I was enjoying that!

Hana   That's not how it should start.

Niqabi Ninja   How do you want it to start then?

'This is my message to Cairo and its people!'

Hana   I deleted that.

Niqabi Ninja   And thank fuck you did!

Hana   I just want it to be good.

Niqabi Ninja   Then start at the beginning.

Hana   Which beginning?

Niqabi Ninja   This is your story, it's your choice.

Hana   . . .

Niqabi Ninja   When did it start?

Hana   As soon as I hit puberty.

Niqabi Ninja   What age?

Hana   Twelve.

Niqabi Ninja   Sketch the frame.

Hana   Chapter Two: The Girl is not a Girl Anymore. Frame three.

Zamalek. Ismail Mohamed Street.

Cars. Beeps. Kids laughing and screaming.

Niqabi Ninja   Where exactly?

Hana   In between the dodgy hairdressers and the print shop.

A little shop.

Her first bra. She hated it. She hated buying it.

Her mother just stood there browsing calmly. As if she was shopping for fruit or something.

Niqabi Ninja   Because you're a woman now Hana.

We're not leaving until we buy you a bra.

Hana   Fine. This one.

Niqabi Ninja   Are you sure?

Hana   Yes mama, this one! Yalla let's go, please!

Niqabi Ninja   What about this one?

Hana   No, I don't want that one. It's gonna show!

Niqabi Ninja   But this is very cute, no?

Hana   No I don't want the metal thing. Or the round cups thing either.

Niqabi Ninja   Did you try it on at least?

Hana   La' I'll try it on at home.

Yalla, please mama, aayz a'mshi ba'a. (I just want to leave.)

Niqabi Ninja   Ok, as you like. Let's go.

Hana   As she walked with that bag beside her mother, all she could think was:

They all know.

They can see it, they all know I just bought one.

Yalla mama, walk quicker!

Niqabi Ninja   Pssst.

Hana   Oh no.

Niqabi Ninja   Ya aa'sal (hey beautiful).

Hana   Look down, don't look at them.

Niqabi Ninja   Aa'gebni el enti labsaa. (I like what you're wearing.)

Hana   Walk quicker.

Niqabi Ninja   Tab warini keda eshtarety eh? (Don't you wanna show me what you just bought?)

Hana   Stupid bra. Stupid bra. Stupid boobs!

Niqabi Ninja   That was when she learned her first rule.

Hana   The faster you walk, the faster it's all over.

We're back in the room.

Niqabi Ninja   See that wasn't so hard, was it?

Hana   Was it really that bad?

Niqabi Ninja   Of course it was.

Hana   But compared –

Niqabi Ninja   Don't do that.

Hana   . . .

Niqabi Ninja   Chapter Three: Discarded Clothes

Hana   Is that important?

Niqabi Ninja   It's all important. Come on Hana. The clothes.

Hana   Chapter Three. Our heroine grows up. She starts to throw away her clothes. At least one outfit per year. One comment a year is the most humiliating, the most upsetting, the scariest. She grows up and starts to drown out the noise. But sometimes the comments slip through.

Frame four.

Niqabi Ninja   Age 12 – Yellow T-shirt, jeans, brown sandals. No bra.

Hana   New frame.

Niqabi Ninja   Age 13. Long blue skirt, grey top, nike trainers, purple cardigan.

Hana   The school bus stop. A group of boys.

Niqabi Ninja   'Where are you going? You need to give me your number.'

Hana   One of them follows her for twenty minutes.

New frame.

Niqabi Ninja   Age 14. Black jeans, white shirt with a black sweater on top.

Hana   The koshk (kiosk) on her street. The street vendor.

Niqabi Ninja   'You've really grown, haven't you?'

Hana   She has to see him every day for four years on her way back from school.

New frame.

Niqabi Ninja   Age 15. Wide jeans, big Linkin Park sweatshirt.

Hana   Hassan Sabry street. The guy in the car.

Niqabi Ninja   'Want to go for a ride? I promise to make you smile.'

Hana   She looks at the ground and walks away quickly.

New frame.

Niqabi Ninja   Age 16. Jeans cut at the knees. Flowery, short sleeved shirt with a long, grey jacket on top, blue flats.

Hana   The guy in front of McDonald's.

Niqabi Ninja   'I'd fuck that.'

Hana   New frame.

Niqabi Ninja   Age 17. Beige pants, Beatles T-shirt with a black cardigan on top, breaking in first pair of DMs, black.

Hana   The boys getting stoned on the corner of her street.

Niqabi Ninja   'You look like you could take on more than one guy?'

Hana   They laugh. She marches home. She cries.

New frame.

Niqabi Ninja   Age 18. Black Leggings, patterned above the knee skirt, white T-shirt, dark red jacket, same black DMs.

Hana   The police officer.

Niqabi Ninja   'Those tits are begging for a good titty fuck.'

Hana   She never wore white again.

Niqabi Ninja   'Hey beautiful'.

Hana   She would never wear anything white again.

Niqabi Ninja   'You look delicious'.

Hana   Or yellow, or red, or blue or any colour.

Niqabi Ninja   'Nice ass'.

Hana   Just black.

Niqabi Ninja   'I would like a chance to rip –'

Hana   Stop!

Niqabi Ninja   . . .

Hana   . . .

Niqabi Ninja   I'm just trying to help.

Hana   . . .

Niqabi Ninja   Don't shy away from the details. It's the details that make all the difference.

Hana   . . .

Niqabi Ninja   Fine. I'm sorry. Better?

Hana   I'm not upset.

Niqabi Ninja   So what's the problem?

Hana   Chapter Four: The Woman is Devoured by Their Eyes

Frame eleven.

The woman walks down a street.

Frame twelve.

Eyes. Eyes everywhere.

Big round eyes, small squinty eyes, almond shaped eyes, lazy eyes, brown eyes, black eyes, hazel eyes, green eyes.

Thought bubbles.

Niqabi Ninja   They're eating me alive with their eyes.

Hana   They're penetrating her skin.

Niqabi Ninja   Without even touching me.

Hana   The clothes don't matter.

Niqabi Ninja   How I walk.

Hana   How she breathes.

Niqabi Ninja   How I look.

Hana   None of that matter.

Niqabi Ninja   Young eyes, old eyes, middle-aged eyes.

Hana   She senses the threats.

Niqabi Ninja   Relaxed eyes, bored eyes, nervous eyes.

Hana   And she walks on.

Niqabi Ninja   Staring at me. Just staring.

Hana   She used to blame her clothes.

Niqabi Ninja   Devouring me.

Hana   Now? Now she blames her body.

Niqabi Ninja   Enough! I'm bored of this.

Hana   I knew you wouldn't like that bit.

Niqabi Ninja   Stop giving them so much space. Cut to the chase, to the violence!

Hana   We can't skip ahead, everything needs its time.

Niqabi Ninja   Chapter Five, frame sixteen.

A woman stands over a tied up body.

Next frame, her hands tying a needle to a pencil with some string.

Next frame, she stands over the helpless body.

Speech bubble.

Are you frightened? Yeah, well you should be.

Do you know what this is?

Now, now, this will all be easier if you don't struggle.

I'm told you'll start to enjoy the sensation after a while.

It's to do with the adrenaline.

It kicks in with the pain. And the fear.

Who am I?

Hana   Chapter Five: Fear of the Masturbating Taxi Driver.

Niqabi Ninja   Why Hana? I was on to something!

Hana   Kasr el Nil Street. Downtown.

Niqabi Ninja   Always ruining my fun.

Hana   Frame sixteen. The woman puts her arm out to stop a taxi.

Niqabi Ninja   Where are you headed?

Hana   Dokki.

The woman gets into the taxi.

Niqabi Nina   Self-defence rules of being in a taxi alone include:

Hana   Not sitting in the front seat.

Niqabi Ninja   Avoid making eye contact.

Niqabi Ninja *tries to catch* **Hana***'s eyes, but* **Hana** *avoids them.*

Hana   If he asks: So how old are you?

Or

Niqabi Ninja   Are you married?

Hana   Then be alert.

Niqabi Ninja   Are you married?

Hana   Sorry? No, no I'm not.

Niqabi Ninja   Engaged?

Hana   La'

Niqabi Ninja   Seeing anyone?

Hana   No, not at all.

Niqabi Ninja   That's a shame, you seem like a very nice person.

Hana   Thank you.

She can sense his eyes on her through the rearview mirror.

Niqabi Ninja   Be very alert.

Hana   She focuses on looking out the window.

Niqabi Ninja   He's one of them isn't he?

Hana   Always have something sharp in your hand just in case.

Niqabi Ninja   Yes Hana.

Hana   He won't do it.

She just has ten more minutes to her journey. But then . . .

Niqabi Ninja   Traffic.

Hana   Cars everywhere, they are barely moving.

Niqabi Ninja   He's definitely gonna do it now.

Hana   She senses his arm moving, she keeps her eyes on the window.

Niqabi Ninja   If he goes for it then just walk out. Heels will slow you down, but they can be used as a weapon.

Hana   They're on a bridge, there isn't any space to walk.

Niqabi Ninja   Then scream. If he does it then scream.

Hana *starts to give him a quick glance.*

Don't look at him!

Hana   She takes out a pencil from her bag.

Niqabi Ninja   Aim for the eyes.

Hana   It hasn't happened to her yet.

But she's heard about it.

She knows all about this.

. . .

If this man unbuttons his trousers.

If this man begins touching himself.

She's ready.

She's ready for this.

Niqabi Ninja   So what do you do?

Hana   Sorry?

Niqabi Ninja   Are you working or a student or . . .?

Hana   Yes, I'm a student. Architecture.

Niqabi Ninja   No way! I did architecture in Helwan for a couple of years.

Hana   Yeah?

Niqabi Ninja   Yeah, I loved it, but I couldn't afford to keep going, and I had to take care of the family and all that, you know how it is sometimes.

Hana   Yes, yes I know.

Niqabi Ninja   I do miss it.

Hana   Do you think you'll ever get to finish it?

Niqabi Ninja   Inshallah. You never know!

Hana   Everything is ok. He's ok.

Not all taxi drivers are fuckers.

Niqabi Ninja   Taxi drivers are all fuckers.

Hana Not all men are fuckers/	**Niqabi Ninja** /Taxi drivers are
But they could be. We don't want to be afraid of every man we encounter in the streets. We	fuckers. Bus drivers are fuckers. People riding the bus are fuckers. Most men in the street

don't want to tense up every time we feel a man walking behind us. We don't want to assume every taxi driver will jerk off. We don't want to have to assess the level of threat every time. But we do. We have to. It's too risky otherwise. One miscalculation and . . .

are fuckers. Most men you encounter in the world are fuckers. Most women are also fuckers. Street vendors are fuckers. Schoolchildren are fuckers. High school students are fuckers. Teachers are fuckers. University professors are fuckers. The unemployed are fuckers. Your work colleagues are fuckers. Members of your own family are fuckers. Revolutionaries are fuckers. Religious people are fuckers. Religious leaders are definitely fuckers. The military are all fuckers. All politicians are the biggest fuckers. Policemen are massive fuckers.

Niqabi Ninja   And everyone in Egypt is either fucked over or fucked up.

Hana   It's so fucked up.

Niqabi Ninja   It's both. We're all fucked over and fucked up.

. . .

You should have made him masturbate.

Hana   But that's not what happened.

Niqabi Ninja   Who cares what actually happened? That was the scene, that was the moment where she should have grabbed that pencil and –

Hana   I want to tell the truth.

Niqabi Ninja   It's a fucking comic! No one cares about the truth.

Hana   I do.

Niqabi Ninja   Frame fourteen, Hana goes home and has a nice lunch. The end.

Hana   What about you?

Niqabi Ninja   What about me?

Hana   Do you go home and have a nice lunch?

Niqabi Ninja   I'm not the one in charge here though, am I?

Hana   No, you're not.

Niqabi Ninja   Lose the Everywoman speech at least. No one likes a preacher.

Hana   I'll edit it later.

Niqabi Ninja   When are we getting to the demonstrations bit?

Hana   There's still other episodes.

Niqabi Ninja   At least give her a proper weapon in the next bit.

Hana   Frame fourteen. Ramsis.

Niqabi Ninja   You've skipped London.

Hana   It's not the same in London.

Niqabi Ninja   You never felt scared in London.

Hana   . . .

Niqabi Ninja   It's the same thing.

Hana   No, it's not. They were drunk. People do stupid things when they're drunk.

Niqabi Ninja   Like wait until a woman is unconscious before raping her?

Hana   Look, London has nothing to do with –

Niqabi Ninja   Tell me Hana, do western hands feel any different?

Hana   I need there to be hope. There needs to be an escape. Maybe one day I can be somewhere else and I won't have to worry about . . . about my clothes and my skin and –

Niqabi Ninja   You'll still be worried. The rules might be different but they're still there.

Hana   I don't have to drink. I don't have to be around people who drink. I don't . . .

Niqabi Ninja   One outfit a year, right? For the scariest experience.

Hana   . . .

Niqabi Ninja   Do I need to remind you?

Age 20 – tight high waist trousers, sleeveless gold top, black jacket. Red flats.

Hana   . . .

Niqabi Ninja   Hana?

Hana   Chapter Seven: The Woman Visits London.

Niqabi Ninja   A club.

Hana   She thought she was tough. She grew up in Cairo, she could handle it.

Niqabi Ninja   1.30 am.

Hana   She doesn't recognise the usual threats.

Niqabi Ninja   It's very crowded.

Hana   But that doesn't mean the threats aren't there.

Niqabi Ninja   Rules to having a safe night out in the UK.

Club music comes on.

Hana   It was just too foreign for her to see them.

Niqabi Ninja   Be careful how much you drink.

Hana *drinks.*

Niqabi Ninja   Careful when you accept drinks from strangers. Try to make sure they get poured in front of you.

Hana *drinks more.*

Niqabi Ninja   Don't make eye contact. It encourages them.

Hana *feels people touching her. She gets uncomfortable but continues to try to dance.*

Niqabi Ninja   Men will touch you.

Hana   Hands . . .

Niqabi Ninja   Politely look at them and shake your head if you don't want them to. You can be slightly more aggressive if you feel you don't run the risk of being punched.

Hana   It's OK Hana.

Niqabi Ninja   Stay alert.

Hana   They're just flirting . . .

Niqabi Ninja   Often men won't leave you alone even if you tell them to.

Hana *is visibly drunker and barely dancing.*

Hana   Hands . . .

Niqabi Ninja   Don't drink too much. Don't flirt too much.

Hana   No . . . Sorry. No, I . . .

Niqabi Ninja   You will need to be able to take yourself home otherwise someone else will take you back to theirs.

Hana   No . . . Please don't touch me.

I need . . . I need to go . . .

Sorry no . . . I want to go home..

Niqabi Ninja   They will need a lot of convincing to believe that you don't want to fuck them.

Hana   No.. no.. Please don't . . .

Don't . . .

Stop . . . Stop it . . .

I want to go home . . .

Niqabi Ninja   Be careful.

Hana   No . . . I . . .

I want . . .

Niqabi Ninja   Otherwise you'll have no one to blame but yourself.

Hana   I WANT TO GO HOME!

Ninja/Hana   STOP!

Niqabi Ninja   I can't breathe in this thing!

They both breathe.

Niqabi Ninja   It wasn't your fault.

Hana   I shouldn't have had that much to drink. It was my fault.

Niqabi Ninja   Don't do that.

Hana   I can't remember what happened. I can't remember if something happened.

Niqabi Ninja   Let them do the blaming, but don't you do that. Let them talk shit.

Hana   I shouldn't have let that happen. I should not have gone on my own.

Niqabi Ninja   Don't go there on your own. Don't dress like that. Don't drink too much.

Hana   Chapter Seven: The Woman's Statement.

Niqabi Ninja   Don't wear too much makeup. Don't walk by yourself. Don't walk at night.

Hana   Frame twenty. The woman stares at the camera.

Niqabi Ninja   Don't look that way. Don't breathe like that. Look modest.

Hana   Next frame. The camera lens.

Niqabi Ninja   This would never happen to modest girls, good girls, decent girls. You must be asking for it. You are asking for it. You want it. You want it, don't you? Come on, say it. Say you want it!

Niqabi Ninja *smashes something in the room.* **Hana** *ignores her completely until the smash. She waits for her to calm down.*

Hana   Next frame. Speech bubble.

Niqabi Ninja   Do you know what it feels like to be so ashamed of your own body? Or to be so afraid of your own skin? So scared of that soft flesh under all those layers of clothes? Those absolutely useless clothes.

Hana   Terrified that someone would discover this?

She indicates her skin/body.

That someone would take it from you?

Niqabi Ninja   I do.

Hana   I know that fear.

Hana *begins to hang her more recent sketches to the wall.*

Niqabi Ninja   You know what I was thinking?

Hana   I probably do, yes.

Niqabi Ninja   I think I should have a theme tune as well.

Hana   You're not a cartoon series.

Niqabi Ninja   But I could be.

Hana   I don't know anything about music.

Niqabi Ninja   It doesn't need to be complicated, could be something like the Spiderman theme tune.

She hums the tune. **Hana** *laughs.*

Hana   I'll think about it.

Niqabi Ninja   Also, rethink the costume, I could look way cooler.

Hana   What's wrong with the costume?

Niqabi Ninja   A bit cliché. Even with the weird wing design that's on it now.

Hana   Are you serious?

Niqabi Ninja   I am. I swear. You can do better than this shit.
I preferred it when I looked more ninja and less niqabi.

Hana   But you've got all sorts of hidden pockets, and weapons.

Niqabi Ninja   Fein weapons dol?? (Where are these weapons?)

Ba'ali omr (waiting for these weapons that you speak of).

Hana *shows* **Niqabi Ninja** *a sketch. Suddenly* **Niqabi Ninja** *has a big stick seemingly out of thin air. She is very excited.*

SHUMA?!²

YAS HANA! THIS IS WHAT I'M TALKING ABOUT!

Now I can do some serious damage with this.

She swings it around a bit.

Hana   Glad you're happy with it.

Niqabi Ninja   Happy? I'm fucking delighted!

Imagine having this in Ramsis!

Hana   You can't.

Niqabi Ninja   You're no fun. Why does it have to be exactly as you remember it?

Hana   Because.

Niqabi Ninja   Leh Hana? Just say it.

---

2 'Shuma' is a popular weapon in rural Egypt; it's essentially a big stick that's thicker from one end. Used to bash people's head in.

Hana   Chapter Eight: The Motorcycle

The woman is visiting Kareem, her boyfriend.

Niqabi Ninja   . . .

Fine. But just because I don't have a choice, not because I want to.

Age 21 – Doc Martens, jeans, patterned top and a short-sleeved cardigan.

Hana   She needs to go home.

Niqabi Ninja   Ramsis, 9 pm.

Hana   She tells her boyfriend not to worry about taking her home. She can hail a taxi, the main road is just a five to ten minute walk.

Niqabi Ninja   Rules of walking alone in the street include:

Hana   Headphones.

Hana *puts on headphones.*

Niqabi Ninja   And loud music. To filter out the shit.

Hana *turns the volume up.*

Niqabi Ninja   Try to stay in big main roads, always look like you know exactly where you're going.

Hana   She recites the directions over and over in her head.

Straight.

Then right.

Second left.

Then right again.

Niqabi Ninja   Walk and dodge at the same time.

Hana   In time you learn to dodge people without thinking.

Niqabi Ninja   Motorcycle.

Hana *freezes, motorcycle passes, she breathes relief.*

Hana   It's gone.

Niqabi Ninja   Never stop walking.

Be aware of how much skin you're showing, how you move, how you breathe. Never make eye contact.

Hana   Look straight ahead.

Niqabi Ninja   Walk faster.

Hana   Lower the volume on the music.

Niqabi Ninja   Always have a perfume bottle or a sharp nail file on you. Always aim for the eyes.

Hana   Aim for the eyes.

Motorcycle.

Niqabi Ninja   It's coming back.

Hana   It's getting louder.

Niqabi Ninja   Walk faster.

If you choose to retaliate . . .

Hana   It's getting nearer.

Niqabi Ninja   . . . always be prepared to fight the battle on your own.

Hana   Louder.

Niqabi Ninja   Walk faster.

Hana   He's slowing down.

Niqabi Ninja   Walk faster.

Hana   Closer.

Niqabi Ninja   Faster!

Hana *freezes again, this time it is as if she is being grabbed.*

Hana   She feels his hand grabbing her from behind.

His finger in between her thighs.

Moving.

Motorcycle is still going.

He drags her a few steps.

It all happens so fast.

Niqabi Ninja   Scream.

Hana   Baaaaaaaaaaaaaas! (Stop/enough!)

Niqabi Ninja   He's driving off.

Ya aars! (Bastard!)

Say it!

Hana . . .

Niqabi Ninja   Cos omak! (Fuck you!)

Hana . . .

Niqabi Ninja   Yabn el ahhba, ya kazer! (Son of bitch, fucking piece of shit!)

SAY IT NOW!

Hana   He's gone.

Hana *lets out a frustrated scream.*

I hate this!

I hate him!

I hate his motorcycle!

I hate him for touching me!

I hate him for scaring me!

I hate that I couldn't call him a piece of shit!

Hana I hate this!	**Ninja** I hate this!
I fucking hate this!	I fucking hate this!
I hate walking!	I hate walking!
I hate this street!	I hate this street!
I hate this place!	I hate this place!
I hate this city!	I hate this city!

I hate myself for being scared.

Niqabi Ninja   Don't stop.

Hana   No . . .

Niqabi Ninja   Keep going Hana!

Hana   I CAN'T

Niqabi Ninja   Coward.

They both breathe.

Hana   Don't touch me.

Niqabi Ninja   'Mabrouk'.

Hana   Don't walk alone at night. Don't walk alone period. Don't move like that. Don't look like that.

Niqabi Ninja   'Mabrouk Hana, you've been officially baptized by the streets of Cairo lol'.

Hana   Don't look like that. Don't walk like that. Don't speak like that.

Niqabi Ninja   Who says that?

Hana   What did you expect Hana?

Niqabi Ninja   Baptized by the streets of Cairo?

Hana   What did you actually expect?

Niqabi Ninja   He did like to ram his Christian faith down your throat though, didn't he?

Hana   Did you expect to just walk down the road without someone grabbing you?

Hana *grabs the shuma and begins to smash things.*

Niqabi Ninja   Mind you, your Muslim exes weren't any better.

Hana   Without someone touching you?

Niqabi Ninja   You've always had a thing for such losers.

Hana   Without someone fingering you?

Hana *continues to smash things.*

Niqabi Ninja   Yes Hana!

Hana   They will not touch me.

Niqabi Ninja   This is exactly what I'm talking about!

Hana   They will not touch me.

Niqabi Ninja   Time to show those dickheads their own baptism.

Hana   They will not touch me!

Niqabi Ninja   Lol.

Hana *finishes, she has a new energy to her.*

Feeling better?

Hana   Chapter Nine: The Woman Decides to go to Tahrir.

Frame twenty-seven.

November 2012. Talaat Harb Square.

The woman sits with Kareem. It's late, she's drunk, she's in love. And he thought they could change the world.

Niqabi Ninja   This is where it began Hana! Right here, 1919. Men, women, Muslims, Christians, all uniting to finally tell the Brits to fuck off! Can't you feel that energy? You should have been there during the 18 days Hana, it was magic. Everyone respected one another, you know? Respected each other's opinions and life views, girls could walk around with no worries, it was like . . . it was like utopia! Tomorrow we have to go to Tahrir. In fact, we should take over every single fucking square in Cairo. If Morsi thinks he can proclaim himself pharaoh, then we sure as hell need to put him back in his place. He has no power without the people. WE are the people. WE are the power. WE own Tahrir. And if we can stand up to Mubarak and those wankers, then we can stand up to this cocksucker. Back in Tahrir where we belong. Everything about being there is simply, organic, you know? People just unite there, no weapons, no violence. Just bodies. The power of bodies. Just knowing that my body can make a difference. You need to feel it Hana, you need to feel that power. You need to feel how your body can make history.

Hana   That was a good speech.

Niqabi Ninja   Good speech. Shit guy.

Hana   He wasn't a bad guy.

Niqabi Ninja   I didn't say he was bad. I said he was shit. He was shit and whiny and made everything about himself.

Hana   He tried his best.

Niqabi Ninja   He was weak. When you needed support, he was weak.

Hana   He was revolutionary.

Niqabi Ninja   He wasn't revolutionary.

Hana   He wanted us to change the world.

Niqabi Ninja   Maybe. Chapter Nine: The Woman Decides to go to Tahrir.

Hana   Part One.

Frame thirty-one. The woman arrives at Tahrir, we see the back of her head, in front of her is one massive crowd.

Niqabi Ninja   Rules for walking into a crowd.

Hana   It's terrifying.

Niqabi Ninja   Put your arms in front of you.

Hana   Men everywhere.

Niqabi Ninja   Lead with your shoulders.

Hana   No space to move.

Niqabi Ninja   Don't be afraid to push.

Hana   No space to breathe.

Niqabi Ninja   Unfortunately, there's nothing you can do to protect your back.

Hana   She moves forward. Pushing into the people in front of her. People pushing into her.

Niqabi Ninja   If someone touches you, it'll be hard to tell who it is.

Hana   People groping and touching.

Niqabi Ninja   So focus on getting through the crowd.

Hana   Kareem holds her hand, pulling her through.

Niqabi Ninja   On getting out.

Hana   She pushes and pushes and . . .

Niqabi Ninja   Get out.

Hana   She's out. Shaken and scared but she's out.

Niqabi Ninja   Barely made it.

Hana   Holding Kareem's hand, he beams down at her. She smiles back. He doesn't notice the uneasiness in her eyes. She doesn't say anything.

Niqabi Ninja   She knew she was one of the lucky ones that day.

Hana   Chapter Ten: The Circle of Hell.

Niqabi Ninja   Good. Skip to the important part. No need to dwell on sad little Kareem, he doesn't need to take up any more space.

Hana   He didn't understand. He thought we were going to change the world. It wasn't his fault. What happened is not his fault.

Niqabi Ninja   He could have protected you. He could have tried. And the things he said to you when –

Hana   No one could have protected me.

Niqabi Ninja   But after you –

Hana   Enough.

Niqabi Ninja   Alright. But only because I don't want to think about his stupid little face.

Hana   Frame thirty-two. Eagle eye view of Tahrir Square.

That day in November, that day when she got out with just a grope and a grab, that was when the mob rapes of Tahrir began.

Next frame.

Niqabi Ninja   The circle of hell.

Hana   Next frame.

First, they separate a girl from the people she's with.

Niqabi Ninja   Next frame.

Hana   They crowd around her, they're usually around fifty or sixty men. And they form three circles.

Niqabi Ninja   Next frame.

Hana   The outermost circle is of men who try to shift the attention away from what's happening, usually shouting that there's nothing going on, or accusing the women of being spies or prostitutes.

Niqabi Ninja   Next frame.

Hana   The middle circle forms within this one, this circle is of men who pretend they are trying to get through to help her, but all they're doing is creating confusion and more importantly, they are creating a very difficult barrier to get through.

Niqabi Ninja   Next frame.

Hana   The innermost circle are the ones with their hands on the girl. They grab her, keep her in the middle, and form a tight circle around her. They undress her, and using just their hands, they rape her.

Next frame.

Eagle eye view of Tahrir Square, with three circles forming amidst the crowd.

Niqabi Ninja   Next chapter, our heroine leaves her pathetic boyfriend and decides to take matters into her own hands.

Hana   Chapter Eleven: Our Heroine is Not a Hero.

Niqabi Ninja   Fuck this bullshit.

Hana   She stays away from Tahrir Square.

Frame forty. Our heroine hides away behind a screen.

She volunteers for Operation Anti-Sexual Harassment.

Niqabi Ninja   Come on Hana.

Hana   She does their social media.

Niqabi Ninja   Why are you even mentioning any of this?

Hana   They need to raise awareness.

Niqabi Ninja   Write about your dreams Hana.

Hana   Visibility is the first step.

Niqabi Ninja   Tell them about her nightmares.

Hana   For a whole year, she helps document, translate and tweet all of Tahrir's mob rape stories.

Niqabi Ninja   Your nightmares.

Hana   Video. A girl is taken, screaming, into a subway station.

Niqabi Ninja   Alright, let's do it your way then.

According to a report published by UN Women in 2013, 99.3 per cent of women in Egypt have been sexually harassed in some form or another.

Hana   Video. A girl is taken, screaming, into a subway station.

Niqabi Ninja   91.6 per cent have received unwanted physical contact.

Hana   Video. The clearest documentation of the 'circle of hell' we have.

Niqabi Ninja   Over 90 per cent of the people participating in the survey, both male and female say that the harassment is caused by the indecent behaviour of women in public.

Hana   Article. A girl was penetrated with a knife.

Niqabi Ninja   97.3 per cent claimed women invited this type of behaviour.

Hana Article. A girl almost suffocated to death from men tugging at her scarf.

Niqabi Ninja 96.3 per cent blamed provocative clothing.

Hana Article. A girl drops to the ground, men park a car on top of her hair so she can't move.

Niqabi Ninja 95.2 per cent blamed enticing make-up.

Hana Article. An analysis of the 'circle of hell.' Organized sexual terrorism.

Niqabi Ninja 94.4 per cent blamed the way women talk.

Hana Testimony. I begged him, I implored him, told him I was a mother of two. I don't know what made this man turn from being my rapist to being my saviour.

Niqabi Ninja 93.3 per cent blamed the way women walk.

Hana Testimony. I was one of the operation anti-sexual harassment volunteers. I tried to help her, I couldn't even reach her.

Niqabi Ninja 86.2 per cent of women do not feel safe or secure walking in the streets of Egypt.

Hana Testimony. Hundreds and hundreds of hands everywhere. Stripping and violating my body. Fingers penetrating me everywhere.

Niqabi Ninja Statistics are never truly reliable.

Hana And my testimony.

Niqabi Ninja Most of these statistics are wrong.

Hana This is my testimony.

Niqabi Ninja The reality is 100 per cent of women in Egypt have experienced sexual harassment in some form or another.

Hana It happened to me.

Niqabi Ninja No matter what they wear, how they walk, how they talk or what they do.

Hana It happened to me.

Niqabi Ninja Time to tell the story.

Hana I can't.

Niqabi Ninja Tell the story Hana.

Hana   I can't do it.

Niqabi Ninja   Tell the story of why I exist.

Hana   I don't know.

Niqabi Ninja   Tell me why I'm here.

Hana   You're not.

Niqabi Ninja   I'm right here Hana, tell me why!

Hana   You don't exist.

Niqabi Ninja   Not yet.

Hana   You're not real.

Niqabi Ninja   Tell me why I'm standing right here!

Hana   Stop. Stop shouting.

Niqabi Ninja   NOT TILL YOU SAY IT!

Hana   STOP! YOU'RE NOT REAL!

They breathe. They are not in sync.

I'm losing my mind.

That's what's happening.

I can't do this. I can't fix anything.

I don't have superpowers.

I am not a hero.

Niqabi Ninja *sings to herself quietly while practising tattooing her ankle.*

Niqabi Ninja (*sings*)   Angry woman. Angry woman.

Hana   I am not a goddess.

Niqabi Ninja (*sings*)   Look out!

Hana   I don't need to do this.

Niqabi Ninja (*sings*)   Here comes an angry woman.

Hana   . . .

Niqabi Ninja   You're going to change the world.

There's just one part left.

Hana   Chapter Twelve: The Woman Decides to Return to Tahrir.

Niqabi Ninja   Chapter Twelve: Hana Returns to Tahrir.

This time no one convinces you to go.

Hana   I was tired of it all. I couldn't just sit there, being scared. I had to do something. I had to try. I had to fight it.

Niqabi Ninja   Who am I?

Hana   I had to give it one last shot.

Niqabi Ninja   I'm their new nightmare.

Hana   So I decide that in the next demonstration I'd go in with the rest of the volunteers. This time, I'm only there to help. To help the women. To help the girls.

Niqabi Ninja   To destroy the circle.

Hana   Time to get ready

Two pairs of underwear, a pair of spanks over that.

A corset.

Wrap my breasts.

Flatten them.

Make them disappear.

Sports bra on top.

Trousers with a belt.

Doc Martens.

Shoelaces in difficult knots.

Layers.

Undershirt.

Long-sleeved top.

T-shirt.

Buttoned up shirt.

Big sweatshirt.

Niqabi Ninja   Look as masculine as possible.

Hana   If I'm lucky they'll mistake me for a boy.

Niqabi Ninja   Now for the bag.

Hana   Change of clothes and shoes for the girls that are undressed.

An extra phone.

First aid supplies.

Water, two bottles.

Ok, I'm ready.

So I thought.

Niqabi Ninja   There are no rules to follow this time.

Hana   I can't hear anything but the chants and the launch of tear gas by the riot police.

The person I'm partnered up with, Omar, receives a call at exactly 2.57 pm.

We push through the crowd.

We pass KFC.

We pass Mohmmed Mahmoud street.

That's when I hear the screams.

They send a shattering chill down my spine.

I can't see her.

I don't know where the screams are coming from.

Omar signals to me which direction we're gonna move in next.

Niqabi Ninja   Hands.

Hana   Thousands of hands begin to touch my waist.

We push through.

The screams are much louder now.

I see her!

Niqabi Ninja   Push!

Hana   Omar's gentle eyes focus on her.

There's no hunger in them. Just determination.

Niqabi Ninja   Men.

Hana   The crowd.

Niqabi Ninja   Men everywhere.

Hana   I see her.

A man is clutching her long curly hair.

Another is pulling at her veil which is caught around her throat.

I can't see the rest of her body. But I can tell that her top has been ripped off.

They pull and thrash her across the ground.

With one final scream she disappears into the crowd.

I am being pushed back and forth.

I hold onto Omar's hand for dear life.

Omar is frozen.

His eyes wide in horror.

No!

We're in the middle of it.

We're in the circle of Hell.

The crowd suddenly surges.

They break me away from Omar.

Poor Omar.

Frozen in the chaos. In a moment he'll be helplessly beaten to the ground.

But I won't see it.

They have me now.

Niqabi Ninja   Hands.

Hana   Hundreds of hands.

That's all I feel.

I am pushed to the ground.

I feel several bodies fall on top on me, one or two thrusting themselves against me.

I feel people trying to take off my shoes, but they're on too tight.

Hana   Ha! Fuckers.   **Niqabi Ninja**   Ha! Fuckers.

They're trying to penetrate all the layers I have on.

All of these clothes.

Niqabi Ninja   Absolutely useless fucking clothes.

Hana   Fingers everywhere.

In between my thighs.

In my unbuttoned trousers.

In my hair.

Scratching me.

Someone is pulling at my bra straps.

All these hands.

It's only a matter of time.

They'll find a way through.

Some are saying they're here to help.

Once they get through to me, they simply join in.

Others are shouting to make it more organized.

To form a queue.

I can see people sitting on walls and fences.

Watching.

Sitting there. Watching.

I don't scream.

I freeze.

Like Omar.

I can't believe this is happening right now.

I can't believe this is happening to me.

Slowly the screaming and shouting around me starts to fade.

I look up at all the faces.

Who are all these people?

I can't even see the sky anymore.

I want to see the sky!

Please make it stop.

Please God make it stop.

Please let me see the sky.

Niqabi Ninja   Look up!

Hana   That's when I see you. Looking straight at me.

I always you knew you existed. But I had never seen you. Not like this. Not this clearly.

And in that moment, I hear a voice.

Niqabi Ninja   Fucking crush them!

Hana   I hear a guy screaming in pain beside me.

Niqabi Ninja   Harder!

Hana   My legs start thrashing. Kicking peoples' shins in. They fall over.

Niqabi Ninja   Aim for the sensitive spots.

Hana   I'm on my feet. I'm holding a nail file.

Niqabi Ninja   Groin, eyes, joints.

Hana   A man tries to grab my throat, his finger ends up in my mouth.

Niqabi Ninja   Bite down hard.

Hana   He screams and lets go.

Niqabi Ninja   Run!

Hana   I move down sheikh rihan street, right into the riot police.

Niqabi Ninja   Down this street!

Hana   The men I hurt are chasing me now.

They're angry.

I move into a building's entrance.

Niqabi Ninja   The chair.

Hana   It won't hold them for long.

Niqabi Ninja   Shout!

Hana   Help!

Help me!

Please open the door!

Nothing.

Niqabi Ninja   The roof.

Hana   I run up.

My clothes are ripped and I'm covered in blood.

Niqabi Ninja   They'll be up here soon.

Hana   Shit!

What do I do? What do I do? They're gonna kill me.

I walk to the edge of the roof.

The next building doesn't seem too far.

Niqabi Ninja   Do it!

Hana   No, no I can't.

Niqabi Ninja   You have to!

Hana   No I'm gonna kill myself like this.

Niqabi Ninja   You've been training.

Hana   No, I just wanted to knee some creep in the street not jump from buildings.

Niqabi Ninja   You need to do this!

Hana   No I can't!

I turn away.

Niqabi Ninja   They're gonna get you!

Hana   The doors burst open.

Niqabi Ninja   They're here.

Hana   I turn. I run.

Niqabi Ninja   JUMP!

Hana *turns and jumps. The world is still as we wait to see if she survives.*

Hana   I did it.

I fucking did it!   **Niqabi Ninja**   I fucking did it!

Hana   Chapter Thirteen: The Woman is Reborn a Goddess

Niqabi Ninja   Frame eight-five.

Hana   The goddess' feet. Chopped up bits at their side.

Once there was a goddess. She had no name and no purpose. Until one day, her world was ripped apart and torn to pieces. She doesn't know how that happened or why. She cried but it made no difference.

She was not Isis. She could not flood the Nile or revive the dead.

Her story is a different one.

Lights fade in and we see **Hana** *dressed all in black, without the niqab, the face veil, yet.* **Niqabi Ninja** *is dressed in* **Hana**'s *old clothes, without the niqab, she is familiar but not someone we recognize, like a ghost or an outline of someone we once knew.* **Hana** *is ripping down all the drawings and sketches.*

Hana   I saw you. On the roof. Looking straight at me.

Watching me.

Maybe you saved me.

Maybe I really am crazy.

Either way I'm here.

I'm real.

Hana *puts on the niqab. She takes her time. She is no longer unsure or hesitant.*

Niqabi Ninja   Final chapter.

Hana   Final Chapter: The First Victim.

A few days ago a man approached our heroine to inform her how he'd like to have his way with her ass one day.

So she started following him.

Little did he know that he's her very first choice.

Niqabi Ninja   Frame eighty-seven.

Hana   Name: Mostafa Hossam.

Age: 35.

Has a wife and two kids, lives in Manial and is a civil servant.

Likes to sit at a local 'ahwa after work. Likes to smoke shisha, drink Turkish coffee and devour girls with his eyes. Then he goes home to his wife just in time for dinner.

Following him wasn't easy.

Niqabi Ninja   It wasn't hard either.

Hana   Men aren't used to being followed by women. They don't have the sixth sense like we do. They don't know when there's a threat in someone's eyes.

Niqabi Ninja   Next frame.

Hana   Our heroine hunts him down, and knocks him out unconscious. She ties him to a table.

Niqabi Ninja   Next frame.

Hana   Close up on our heroine's cigarette.

We see the Cairo skyline.

Niqabi Ninja   How does it end?

Hana   With words.

She goes back inside to her victim.

She smiles.

She tattoos the words

'filthy pervert'   **Niqabi Ninja**   motaharesh wesekh

across his face.

She indicates on her own face, below her eyes, across her nose.

Then she tattoos his specific crime:

Touch   **Niqabi Ninja**   Lams

Filthy comments   **Niqabi Ninja**   Kalam wesekh

Harassment   **Niqabi Ninja**   Taharosh

Rape	**Niqabi Ninja**	Eghtesab
Mob rape	**Niqabi Ninja**	Eghtesab gamaai

Right in the middle of his face, for everyone to see. There's no way to hide it. Well, there is one way.

She indicates her outfit.

I want to mark him. So that everyone will know what he is.

I want him to have to live with what he's done for the rest of his life.

I want him to fear walking in the streets as I have.

I want him to be overwhelmed with the feeling of wanting to hide his body away.

Niqabi Ninja   To erase it.

To have it disappear.

Hana   Exactly.

That's the ending.

Niqabi Ninja   Ready?

Hana *doesn't answer. It's too late anyway,* **Niqabi Ninja** *has disappeared. The room suddenly looks very real and stark.* **Hana** *breathes.* **Hana** *then grabs the camera and sets it up. She takes a deep breath and presses record.*

Hana   Every night I will hunt one of you down. Every night I will walk through the streets. I will take a mental picture of every piece of shit who dares to comment my clothes, my breasts, my ass, my eyes, my mouth, my legs, my cunt. And I will choose just one of you lucky bastards. Tonight I've made my choice. And this is just the beginning. A warning to the streets of Cairo.

Who am I?

Pray you'll never have to find out.

Blackout.

The End.

Not That Woman

'Tosin Jobi-Tume

'Tosin Jobi-Tume holds BA and MA degrees in English and Theatre Arts from the University of Ilorin and University of Abuja, Nigeria, respectively, and she is currently on a PhD programme in the Performing Arts Department at the University of Ilorin, Nigeria. She teaches in the Theatre and Media Arts Department of Federal University Oye-Ekiti, Ekiti State, Nigeria. She is a playwright, director, choreographer, actor, dancer, singer, and a theatre scholar with experience spanning fifteen years. Jobi-Tume has participated in several theatrical productions, festivals, carnivals, workshops and conferences within and beyond the shores of Nigeria. As the Drama entry for the Nasarawa State Dance and Drama Troupe, her play *The Pact* won the first place at the NYSC Annual Cultural Festival in Bauchi, 2009. Her play, *Sweet Poison*, was among the selected scripts for the 2015 ASSITEJ SA New Writing for Young Audiences in Africa programme which was run in partnership with The Kennedy Center's New Visions New Voices project in Washington D.C., United States, and The Soweto Theatre in Guateng, South Africa. The play was performed at the ASSITEJ SA African Youth Theatre and Dance Festival held at the Artscape Theatre, Cape Town from 22–27 June 2015. She also has to her credit several published and unpublished plays, and dance scripts, including *The Pact* (2013), *Tribal Marks* (2014), *Mojogbayi* (2015), *Gimbiya, The Future is Now, Iyefemigha, Arodan, Roll Out the Drums, Blood on My Hands*, and *Man Pikin*.

Production history

The idea for this play came to the playwright during the Women Playwrights International Conference held in Cape Town, South Africa, in 2015. From the interactions and discussions with women from other climes, it became clear that violence against women is indeed a global issue, and a trend which must be curbed. Though the characters in the play are fictitious, the storyline is inspired by domestic violence stories in the media, personal experience, and experiences of friends and colleagues. An excerpt from the play was performed for the Fiwasaye Old Girls' Association (FOGA) Class of 1995 Reunion Event. It was directed by the playwright at the Fiwasaye Girls' Grammar School Akure, Ondo State, Nigeria, on the 28th April, 2018. The play has been read at one of the monthly play-reading sessions of the Association of Nigerian Authors (ANA), Ekiti State chapter, and has been billed for a reading at the Women Playwrights International Conference in Chile in October 2018.

Critical introduction

The issue of violence against women in Africa, and especially in Nigeria, has taken on epidemic dimensions. On a daily basis, the Nigerian media is filled with incessant reports of cases of rape, wife-battering, child-marriage, incest, child abuse, human trafficking and various other sexual assaults against women.[1] The various forms of violence meted out to women range from physical to psychological, sexual, and emotional abuse. Our observation is that plays considered to be 'feminist' in these climes mostly tilt towards blaming the woes of women solely on the patriarchal structure of the society. The position of this play is that, in as much as it is always easy to blame these vices solely on the menfolk in society, women are perhaps as culpable in the engineering and perpetuating of these ills; a classic case of undoing oneself.

The play seeks to debunk the myth of women being 'helpless victims' where issues of violence against women are concerned. The play generally addresses the conspiracy of silence which facilitates violence against women within Nigerian society. The play also identifies the numerous

---

1 See for example, Dibie Robert and Justina Sam Okere's report, 'Government and NGOs Performance with Respect to Women Empowerment in Nigeria' (2015, https://apsdpr.org/index.php/apsdpr/article/view/77) and Monica Agene's blog, 'The Reality Of Domestic Violence In Nigeria' (12 April 2017, http://www.womenforwomen.org/blog/reality-domestic-violence-nigeria), both of which provide background for the conditions explored in this play.

ways in which women engineer and perpetuate violence against women. The issues that are explored in the play as factors that hinder women from reporting domestic violence include poverty, financial dependence on the spouse and anxiety about the welfare of the children produced in such marriages, lack of proper knowledge about relationship and value systems, erroneous cultural, religious and societal beliefs, and societal stigmatization.

Not That Woman interrogates the Nigerian culture of stigmatizing female victims of sexual abuse, an act which is mostly perpetuated by women. The play urges women to organise more vibrant support groups as platforms to promote the empowerment and emancipation of women in general, while fostering rehabilitation and reintegration for abused women in particular. Research indicates that men who are raised in homes where domestic abuse occurs are more likely to grow into abusers themselves, while the women from such homes grow up to become psychologically disturbed and more likely to accept domestic abuse as normal. Thus, the vicious cycle continues. The play attempts to negotiate viable solutions to these issues.

Characters

Madam B, *the founder of the Succour for Women Refuge (SWR), and a philanthropist. She is 45 years old.*

Folake, *a reasonable, and very intelligent woman. She is a 38-year-old woman from the South Western region of Nigeria. She is second-in-command to* **Madam**.

Nkechi, *an outspoken woman who comes across as aggressive, but is actually soft and affectionate on the inside. She is from Eastern Nigeria, and a member of the SWR. She is 36 years old.*

Zainab, *a 25-year-old lady from Northern Nigeria, and a member of the SWR. Except for occasional outbursts, she is quiet and withdrawn. She also exhibits symptoms of passive aggression and depression.*

Joyce, *a friend to members of the SWR. She has a mousy demeanour, suffers low self-esteem, and is extremely needy. She is from the Southern region of Nigeria. She is 37 years old.*

Play-in-play characters

Madam Peace, *the founder of an illegal orphanage being run as a baby factory.*

Mandigo, *an employee of* **Madam Peace** *whose job is to have sex with and impregnate young girls living in the orphanage.*

Police Officer, *a very saucy and unprofessional middle-aged Nigerian female police officer.*

Larry's Mother, *an elderly woman with a no-nonsense attitude.*

Joyce's Mother, *an elderly woman with a subdued personality.*

Notes on staging

The director is at liberty to make whatever choices will be suitable for their production of the play, so long as the message of the playwright is not distorted.

Succour for Women Refuge (SWR): A sparsely furnished office with a desk and five chairs. Photographs of the Nigerian President and **Madam B** *are on the wall. Some books and award plaques are on display on a shelf.* **Folake,** **Zainab,** *and* **Nkechi** *are clad in black, and are in various degrees of grief.* **Folake** *is visibly agitated, she paces up and down the office. She obviously has a lot on her mind as she clenches and unclenches her fists.* **Zainab** *is quietly tidying up the office in a robotic manner, while* **Nkechi** *is seated, hugging and rocking herself. A dirge, 'Orin Aro', is sung softly by actors backstage.*

Nkechi   So, she is gone . . . she really is gone?

Folake (*stoically*)   Get a grip, Nkechi. It's been three days now . . . We all heard what the doctor said. Madam B is gone, never to return to us.

Nkechi   Why are we not allowed to see her corpse, though?

Folake (*mysteriously*)   Well, I'm sure they must have their reasons.

Nkechi   What reasons could that be?

Folake (*irritably*)   How am I supposed to know?

Nkechi   This is all so agonising . . . I don't understand it at all! (*Wails.*) My pillar is gone, my life is over . . . Who will replace Madam B in my life? How will Succour for Women Refuge cope without her?

Folake   SWR will be just fine. Nkechi. Please, get a hold of yourself.

All is quiet for a few seconds during which **Nkechi** *seems to pull herself together.*

Nkechi   How are we supposed to prepare for her burial?

Folake (*temporarily lost*)   Her burial?

Nkechi   Yes, her burial. (*Sarcastically.*) You know that little ceremony where a dead person is put six feet under the ground.

Folake (*irritably*)   Shut it, please. Of course, I do know what a burial is.

Nkechi (*sarcastically*)   Thank God for that. So any plans for Madam B's burial?

Folake   How do we organize a burial when there is no corpse?

Nkechi   Exactly my point. No burial, no closure.

Quiet. **Zainab** *mistakenly drops a box of files.* **Nkechi** *glances at* **Zainab**.

Nkechi (*gestures towards* **Zainab**)   And this one here says nothing, as usual. It's almost as if she is permanently dumbstruck.

Folake   Please, cut Zainab some slack. You know how she is. She's been through a lot.

Nkechi   Haven't we all?

Folake   Well, we respond to issues differently. We all have different capabilities and thresholds. You of all people should know that.

Nkechi *snorts. Quiet again.*

Nkechi   How about a wake-keep service, then?

Folake   Pardon me?

Nkechi   A wake-keep service.

Folake (*still lost*)   What?

Nkechi (*with deliberate slowness*)   I am suggesting that we organize a wake-keep service in Madam B's honour.

Folake   Oh . . . (*Reflectively.*) Yes, we could. But that may have to wait for now. We have so many other things to consider.

Nkechi   Other things like what?

Folake   Like clearing up her apartment, paying a visit to her mother, you know . . . stuff.

Nkechi   While we are at it, how about locating her killer husband's hideout as well?

Folake (*evasively*)   That too . . .

Becoming hysterical, **Nkechi** *moves to* **Folake**.

Nkechi   Folake, I need to know for sure, are you saying that we are never going to see Madam B again? Please make me understand . . . (*Yells.*) I refuse to believe this, this just can't be true . . .

Folake (*cuts her short*)   Will you keep quiet and allow me to think? If tears, wailings and shouts could bring the dead back, don't you think Madam B would be sitting right here with us? (*Softens.*) But alas, things don't work that way . . . They just don't. Believe it or not, Madam B is not coming back.

Zainab   Enough! Enough, I say!

Shocked silence.

Zainab   Madam B isn't dead . . . She has to come back. (*She stutters resignedly.*) She cannot . . . be dead. (**Zainab** *starts to sob.*)

Folake *goes over to* **Zainab** *to comfort her.*

Nkechi (*recovers from the shock*)   We are indeed the weaker sex. Madam B's husband is still at large, the man has practically disappeared into thin air . . . Our leader has been brutally murdered and all we can do is gather here to cry and moan, instead of hunting down her criminal husband who did this dastardly act. Oh my! The wicked man will end up enjoying all the wealth that Madam B toiled so hard to gather. This is no time for sentiments, we need to spring to action!

Folake (*calmly*)   So what do you propose we do now?

Nkechi   What sort of question is that? Of course, we search every nook and cranny for Madam B's husband, and when we eventually find him, we unleash untold terror upon him.

Zainab (*with quiet rage*)   That is it. We will slaughter him the exact way he slaughtered Madam B.

Nkechi   So what are we still waiting for? Let us move immediately!

Folake   Alright, we will go. But before we move, may I ask you both a question?

Zainab *and* **Nkechi**   Yes?

Folake   If and when we eventually find this man and slaughter him as you have so excitedly proposed, then what next?

Quiet.

Will this bring repose to the soul of our dear departed leader? I ask, will it grant her peace wherever she is?

Quiet.

And tell me, are you also prepared to bear the consequences of taking the law into your hands?

Quiet.

I didn't think so either. I must say that I am highly disappointed in you women. Have we forgotten so quickly all the values that our leader instilled in us? Has our tragedy so shortened our memory, that we forget the kind of person Madam B is . . . was? Do you think that this is what she expects from us; to go about unleashing terror?

Zainab *quietly goes back to her task of tidying up the office.*

Nkechi (*hesitantly*)   No, Folake . . . Madam B wouldn't have wanted that. But what do we do? Do we just fold our arms and allow her brute of a husband go scot free? We all know how porous our judicial system is. Even if Madam B's husband is found and taken to court, anything could still happen. By the time he greases the appropriate hands, the case could die a natural death and nothing will be heard of it again.

Folake   Nkechi, believe me I understand the rage that is tearing you apart. I feel it too, but as our elders say, 'you do not decapitate the head just to cure a mere headache'.

Nkechi   So you mean we are just going to sit here, sob, speak in proverbs, rationalise issues, and sob some more? Wow!

Folake   Nkechi, do you think I don't miss Madam B? I feel lost without her . . . it was her who gave my life a new meaning.

A sombre mood descends as spotlight picks **Folake**.

Folake   I know that you ladies don't know my story. Madam B took me in when my life had lost its purpose. See, I was born with the stiffest of wooden spoons; my parents were poorer than the church mice. They couldn't afford to keep my younger brother and I in school at the same time, most especially as I was just a girl and would definitely end up in the kitchen. (*Scoffs.*) My mother suggested that they keep only my brother in school, while I go and live with a distant uncle. My father agreed. My uncle was magnanimous enough to send me to school; however, he abused me sexually for ten horrid years. After I finished school, he seized my certificate and forced me to work in his shop while he paid me nothing. I was my uncle's sex slave until Madam B came along . . . she asked him to calculate all he had spent on my education, and she refunded it to him. Madam B rescued me, brought me to this refuge, and taught me how to live again.

Full light. **Folake** *turns to* **Nkechi** *and* **Zainab**.

Folake   Ladies, that woman opened our eyes to the values of life. Have we forgotten so soon?

Nkechi   You are right, Folake. Madam B gave us all reasons to live again.

Folake   What is it with the preference for male children, though?

Nkechi   Beats me . . . Even my father, the most irresponsible father and husband in the entire universe; an unrepentant wife-beater, and a die-hard drunkard, wouldn't forgive my mother for her inability to give him a male child. According to him he needed an heir to carry on the family name. (*Scoffs*.)

Folake (*laughs*)   And as if in a deliberate effort to spite him, your mother bore him seven beautiful daughters, right?

Nkechi (*smiles*)   Oh yes, she did. Sadly enough, she paid with her life. She died due to the incessant beatings from my father.

Folake   Poor woman. God rest her soul.

All   Amen.

Spotlight picks out **Nkechi**.

Nkechi   It was after my mother's death, that my nightmare really started. My father would drink himself to a standstill, beat me to a stupor, and then force himself on me. Oh yes, my own father took my virginity when I was just thirteen years old. There was no one I could talk to about the shameful and abominable thing he was doing to me, and so it continued until the day he gave me away in marriage to his drinking mate. Yes, in a bid to settle his drinking debts, my father married me off to his friend. When I got to my husband's house, my saga continued. My husband had no respect for me, he treated me very shabbily. One day, right in front of our house he beat me into a coma, left me unattended to and left for his drinking joint. Well, it so happened that a friendly woman named Madam Peace was passing by on that fateful day. She took pity on me and took me to a hospital where I was treated. And from there, she took me to an orphanage which she ran. Don't forget that I was still in my teens, an impressionable age . . . I thought I had met a saviour, little did I know that I was jumping straight from the frying pan into the fire.

Nkechi, **Zainab**, *and* **Folake** *all freeze for a few seconds. Then they dissolve to assume various characters in the unfolding dramatization.* **Folake** *plays* **Madam Peace**, **Zainab** *plays* **Mandigo**, *while* **Nkechi** *plays herself.*

Madam Peace   Mandigo, we have a new inmate. (*To* **Nkechi**.) Nkechi, meet Mandigo, and this is where you will be living from now henceforth. You will meet the other girls later.

Nkechi (*to* **Mandigo**)   Nice to meet you.

Mandigo *ignores* **Nkechi**, *eyes her appreciatively and smacks his lips.*

Madam Peace   Well, Nkechi. Your job here is to bear me children.

Nkechi (*shocked*)   Excuse me . . . Bear you children?

Madam Peace   Yes, your productive years as a woman will be put to judicious use while you are here. Don't worry, you shall be handsomely rewarded for your efforts. You will be paid fifty thousand Naira for every female child, and seventy thousand Naira for every male child you bear . . . all in cash, of course.

Nkechi *is dumbfounded.*

Madam Peace (*smiles sweetly at* **Nkechi**)   Don't worry, you will soon get used to the whole process. Mandigo here is the resident impregnator. He shall be working hard with you and the other girls to bear me healthy children. He impregnates you, you bear me marketable children, I reward you with good money, and everybody is happy. (*She smiles.*) I expect you to give him full cooperation.

Nkechi   No, I can't do that. I'm sorry, but I have to take my leave now.

Nkechi *makes to leave, but* **Mandigo** *stops her roughly.* **Madam Peace** *slaps* **Nkechi**, *and she falls into a corner sobbing quietly.*

Madam Peace   Don't be naive, my dear. You leave when I say you can leave. You must bear me five children before you leave this compound, and don't start getting any ideas, this house is well-guarded. If you try to escape, you will be gunned down. Dead girls tell no tales.

Nkechi *whimpers.*

Madam Peace (*suddenly business-like*)   Now listen up for this month's roaster. Mandigo will be taking Sandra on Mondays, Mary Jane on Tuesdays, Scholastica on Wednesdays, Phina on Thursdays, Falilat on Fridays, and Nkechi the newcomer on Saturdays. (*Smiles.*) Nkechi darling, we rest on Sundays, and keep the Sabbath day holy. Any questions?

Nkechi (*sorrowfully*)   Madam, I don't think I can do this . . . Please, let me go back to my family.

Madam Peace   Were you not listening to me? (*Softens.*) You want to go back to your family, right? Of course, you will . . . in due time. (*Hardens.*) After you have given me five healthy children. In fact, Mandigo will start with you today . . . consider it a bonus. (*To* **Mandigo**.) You start with her right away.

Mandigo *bundles her up forcefully as she screams wildly trying to break free.*

Madam Peace *(laughs loudly)*   Have a productive week!

Nkechi, Folake, *and* **Zainab** *dissolve into their former positions.*

Nkechi   I was in that hell hole for more than a year. I got pregnant the month after I got there. *(Smiles sadly.)* I had a bouncing baby boy . . . I was paid seventy thousand Naira for him, but I don't know who they sold him to . . . Madam Peace ensured that. I dreaded Mandigo's weekly visits, but mostly, I dreaded getting pregnant again . . . Thankfully, the home was raided a few months after I had my baby.

Folake   Yes, I remember Madam B said that someone had tipped her off about the shady dealings at that orphanage. Trust Madam B, she quickly alerted the security agencies.

Nkechi *(smiles)*   Madam B . . . a woman like no other. She rescued us, and took us to the hospital for treatment.

Folake   Was that how you discovered your status?

Nkechi *(sadly)*   Yes, three of us were discovered to be HIV positive.

Folake *goes to comfort* **Nkechi**.

Folake *(cheerfully)*   That's okay. You have been very faithful to your anti-retroviral drugs, and you are fit as a fiddle. Heck, with your boundless energy, you are going to outlive us all.

Nkechi   Yeah, yeah . . . My only pain is that I cannot trace my son, and I also lost contact with my six sisters. When I went back to look for them, I was told that my sisters all fled for their lives when my father started defiling them one after the other.

Folake   Oh dear . . . And your father?

Nkechi   Oh . . . He drank himself to death as expected.

Folake   What a life!

A sombre mood descends as lights dim. **Zainab** *sits at the centre stage. She starts to sing the melancholic 'wata rana' song in a trance-like mien.* **Folake** *and* **Nkechi** *turn to look at her. They move to flank her on both sides.* **Zainab** *hums as* **Folake** *and* **Nkechi** *render the next series of lines.*

Folake   She was only eleven years old when she was given in marriage to a sixty-three-year-old man. She had just reached puberty some few months before her wedding. She became pregnant almost immediately. People around her were jubilant, but she was clueless and couldn't fathom what the excitement was about. An eleven-year-old . . . she was only a child.

Nkechi She had no ante-natal care. She was oblivious to what was happening inside her body, and nobody cared enough to enlighten her. When it was time for her to put to bed, she suffered a two-week-long labour. Transferred back and forth between traditional birth attendants and native doctors, all to no avail.

Folake After fifteen days of hell, a long stick was forced into her abdomen. Her dead and decomposed baby was forcefully expelled. After the baby was buried, there was a fresh crisis; she had lost control of her bladder and rectum. Urine and faeces flowed out of her non-stop.

Nkechi Her co-wives mounted pressure on her illiterate husband to throw her out of the house. According to them, she had become a big embarrassment due to the unpleasant smell and the swarm of flies that trailed her. And on those grounds, Zainab's husband kindly gave her a divorce.

Folake No one wanted her, not even her family. She became a destitute until Madam B and the Succour for Women Refuge stepped in and took over. She was diagnosed with an extreme case of VVF. Her urethra, bladder and vaginal wall were completely eroded. Over four years, she had to undergo twenty repair operations to rehabilitate her.

Nkechi Madam B paid every cent of Zainab's medical bill. Today, Zainab no longer leaks urine or faeces, but sadly, she can never bear a child again.

Zainab *stops humming.* **Folake** *pulls* **Zainab** *up and holds her hands.*

Zainab You women are the only family I have . . .

Nkechi And we will always be here for you.

Folake We will always be here for one another. SWR is our fortress.

'Orin Aro' wafts in again as **Folake** *and* **Nkechi** *take turns to hug* **Zainab**.

Folake (*sighs*) These are really sad stories, but they are also stories of strength.

Nkechi Say that again.

Folake (*checks her watch*)   Could you ladies excuse me for a few hours? I have an appointment to keep.

Nkechi (*suspiciously*)   What appointment?

Folake (*briskly*)   Nothing important. What do you say we meet by this evening? Say 5 pm?

Nkechi (*shrugs*)   Whatever.

Folake *turns to* **Zainab**.

Folake   Zainab?

Zainab   5 pm is fine.

Nkechi   In the meantime, we should do something about the young ladies' resident here. I notice that they have become a little edgy since they heard of Madam B's demise.

Folake (*sighs*)   I noticed that too. What do you suggest we do?

Zainab (*solemnly*)   I can handle them.

Folake *and* **Nkechi** *exchange glances.*

Nkechi   Are you sure?

Zainab   Absolutely.

Folake   Well, that settles it then. Thank you, Zain. I'll be back in a few hours. I'm hoping that by then we will all be in a better frame of mind to take rational decisions. Good morning, ladies. We shall overcome.

Nkechi *and* **Zainab**   We shall overcome.

Folake *exits, and* **Zainab** *goes into the inner wing.*

Nkechi *makes to sit down, but then a visibly pregnant* **Joyce** *comes into the office.*

Nkechi   Joyce!

Joyce   Hello, Nkechi.

Nkechi   Good to see you. Wow . . . (*Poking a finger at* **Joyce**'s *baby bump*.) I see our tummy is no longer flat.

Nkechi *and* **Joyce** *share a smile.*

Joyce   Where is Folake? And Zainab?

Nkechi   Folake is out. Zainab is inside putting some things in order. How have you been?

Joyce   I'm fine.

Nkechi   That's good.

Joyce   And you? How are you?

Nkechi (*suddenly sober*)   Honestly, I don't know . . .

Joyce   Please accept my condolences on the death of Madam B. Who knew her husband was such a beast?

Nkechi   Indeed. Who knew?

Joyce   What a horrible way to die . . . My condolences, once again.

Nkechi   Thanks. We all are still in shock.

Joyce   May her soul rest in peace.

Nkechi   Amen. Meanwhile, I hope you are not cross with me for not checking on you as promised?

Joyce   No, not at all. I understand that you are a very busy woman.

Nkechi   My business gets more demanding by the day. I actually just got back from a business trip to China. And then Madam B dies . . . It's been really hectic.

Joyce   That's okay, I understand. At least your business is booming. That must feel great.

Nkechi   Yes, I'm grateful for that. Hmnn . . . (*Glances meaningfully at* **Joyce**'*s baby bump.*) I see you've been busy too.

Joyce (*smiles sheepishly*)   It is what it is . . .

Nkechi   I thought you wanted to leave him.

Joyce   Well . . .

Nkechi   After four poorly cared-for kids? Whatever happened to using contraceptives?

Joyce (*belligerently*)   God has commanded us to multiply and be fruitful. I am not averse to having more kids, and honestly I don't see how it concerns you.

Nkechi (*sarcastically*)   That escalated quickly . . . Has he at least stopped battering you?

Joyce (*subdued*)   Fat chance.

Nkechi (*in disbelief*)   You mean he still beats you in this condition? And you are still with him?

Joyce   What am I supposed to do? I am an African woman, and my place is with my husband. It is 'for better, for worse', remember?

Nkechi   You don't say . . .

Joyce (*defensive*)   Isn't it so everywhere? Any African woman that tells you otherwise is a liar.

Nkechi   I honestly can't believe what you are saying . . . An educated woman like you?

Joyce   And what has education got to do with marriage?

Nkechi   Everything!

Joyce (*tactically changing the topic*)   Meanwhile, let's talk about you; have you no plans to marry? You do realise that your biological clock is ticking fast, right? Pray tell, how do you cope without a man?

Nkechi (*dryly*)   Who says I don't have a man . . . or men, even.

Joyce (*snorts*)   How come you are not yet married then? You better hurry up, my friend. Time is not your friend, menopause beckons!

Nkechi   Marriage isn't for everyone. Frankly, I think I'm better off being single, than to be married to a man who sees me as a punching bag.

Joyce   You know something, Nkechi? If I didn't know better, I'd say you were jealous of me.

Nkechi   Jealous of you? What are you on about?

Joyce   Yes, you are jealous of my married status. You see, even though my husband abuses me, he is still my husband, and I am better off.

Nkechi   Incredible! You are right, this is none of my business, and I am deeply sorry for interfering.

Joyce (*primly*)   Apology accepted.

Nkechi   Fine.

Joyce   Fine.

Quiet.

Nkechi (*officiously*)   So what brings you here?

Joyce (*suddenly self-conscious*)   Err . . . (*Clears throat.*) Actually, I need a favour.

Nkechi (*dryly*)   Here we go.

Joyce   You see, school resumes soon and my kids will be sent out of school if their fees are not paid on time. Please, help a sister out.

Nkechi   Help? How? I don't understand.

Joyce   I need you to lend me some money.

Nkechi   Hmnn . . . How much are we talking about here?

Joyce   The fee is twenty-five thousand Naira per child. That makes a hundred thousand Naira in total for the four of them.

Nkechi   And where do you expect me to get that kind of money from?

Joyce   Come on, Nkechi. We both know that you have the money. Your fashion business is very successful. Please help me.

Nkechi   I'm sorry, I don't have that kind of money right now. And why can't your husband pay his children's school fees? After all, those are his kids, and he has a job.

Joyce   He has no money.

Nkechi   He has no money? Didn't he throw a lavish birthday party for his secretary just last week?

Joyce   Well, he says he doesn't have any money. What can I do? (*Confused.*) Wait a minute, did you just say that Larry threw a party for Paulina?

Nkechi   You heard me.

Joyce   You must be mistaken.

Nkechi   Well, believe whatever you will. But you must be the only one in this town who doesn't know that Larry is having an affair with Paulina.

Joyce   That's a lie.

Nkechi   Well, suit yourself then.

Joyce   Can we just leave the affair rumour aside, and address the issue which brought me here? If Larry has money and refuses to be responsible, what can I do? I can't allow my children to suffer for my poor choices.

Nkechi Oh, so now you admit that your husband is irresponsible, and that you made a poor choice? Yet you are willing to have more kids for him? Why bring more kids into an already sour marriage?

Joyce Nkechi, you can't understand.

Nkechi Anyway, that is your headache. You owe me no explanations. The bottom line is that, I cannot afford to lend you a hundred thousand Naira. You still owe me some money from last year, remember?

Joyce I promise to pay everything together, please help me.

Nkechi No, Joyce. I may be kind-hearted, but I am no fool.

Joyce Nkechi, please . . . You are my last resort.

Nkechi How about Folake? Why don't you ask her?

Joyce No, I can't. Folake paid the children's fees last term. I do not want to bother her again.

Nkechi Hmnn . . . (*She is silent for a few seconds.*) Okay. For the sake of the kids, what I can do is to give you eighty thousand Naira, and let go of the money which you owe me. Now, this is a gift, not a loan.

Joyce You'd do that for me? I'm so grateful, Nkechi. May God continue to bless you.

Nkechi (*bemused*)   That's okay. May God bless us all. You can come for the money tomorrow morning.

Joyce Thank you very much.

Nkechi But jokes aside, Joyce. When are you going to start doing something for yourself? Some small business that you can operate from home, perhaps? Since your husband is so irresponsible, and has refused to allow you practise your profession.

Joyce Well . . .

Nkechi Well, what? How you do you plan to take care of yourself, your four kids and your unborn baby? Borrowing money every now and then cannot sustain you, you know?

Joyce I hear you, Nkechi. I have also thought of it, but where will I get the capital to start a business?

Nkechi I have told you that here at SWR, we can give you a substantial loan to help you start your business.

Joyce   But you know I have no property to use as collateral.

Nkechi   Don't you worry. Folake and I will stand as surety for you. You only have to pay back in instalments every month, so that other women can also benefit from the scheme.

Joyce (*excitedly*)   Thank you so much my friend, I am really grateful.

Joyce *groans in pain as she gets up.*

Nkechi (*concerned*)   Are you okay?

Joyce   Cramps . . .

Nkechi   Maybe you need to see a doctor.

Joyce   No, it's not that serious.

Nkechi   Oh, I insist. You must see a doctor as soon as possible. Health is wealth, remember?

Joyce   Okay, I will. Thanks, once again. I really appreciate.

Nkechi   Nonsense. What are friends for?

Joyce's *phone rings, she looks at it and seems horrified. She signals to* **Nkechi** *to keep quiet. She takes the call.*

Joyce (*stammers*)   Hello, Larry . . . Fine . . . No, nothing . . . (*Alarmed.*) What?! You are on your way home already? Isn't that too early? (*Pause. Hastily.*) Of course everything is fine . . . I'm only surprised because it is unlike you to come home during the day. (*Pause.*) Oh, no problem . . . I can fix lunch quickly. No problem at all. (*Pause.*) All right, see you.

Joyce *hangs up.*

Nkechi   What was that about?

Joyce   That was Larry. He is coming home for lunch. I must be on my way now. He must not know that I left the house.

Nkechi   Really?

Joyce   Yes, really. I'll see you tomorrow. Give my love to Folake and Zainab. Bye.

Nkechi   Bye, dear.

They hug and **Joyce** *exits hurriedly.* **Nkechi** *stares after* **Joyce** *with concern.*

Folake *comes in looking forlorn.*

Nkechi   Oh, you are back. And early too. (*Checks her watch.*) I thought we agreed to meet by five o'clock?

Folake   Yeah . . . I'll still be going out. Just came here to check on things.

Nkechi (*sardonically*)   What things?

Folake *glares at* **Nkechi**.

Nkechi   Suit yourself. Did you meet Joyce on your way in? She just left.

Folake   No, I didn't. Oh, and I have been meaning to see her . . . Maybe, I'll drop by at her house tomorrow.

Nkechi   She will be here tomorrow. I had no idea she was pregnant again.

Folake   Now you know.

Nkechi   Meanwhile, I finally convinced her to come get a loan from SWR.

Folake   Really? That's great. At least then she will be able start some business and fend for herself and the kids.

Nkechi   Exactly what I told her.

Pause. **Folake** *seems to be lost in thought.*

Nkechi   Folake . . .

Folake (*jolted out of her reverie*)   Yes?

Nkechi   I am concerned about her health.

Folake   Whose health?

Nkechi   Joyce's health, stupid. Who else were we talking about?

Folake   Oh . . .

Nkechi   What is the problem with you, Folake? You thoughts are so far away. You are only present here in body, your mind and soul seem to be elsewhere.

Folake   There is absolutely nothing wrong with me. Your mind is over imagining things as usual. I'm fine.

Nkechi   If you say so. So about Joyce . . .

Folake   Yes, what exactly did you notice?

Nkechi   I think this particular pregnancy is putting a strain on her health. She seems to be in a lot of pain. Though, she tries to hide it.

Folake   Is that so? Then we need to get her to see a doctor as soon as possible.

Nkechi   And fast too, because her irresponsible husband would do nothing about it.

Folake   Actually, Larry's mother is the one who amazes me with her lack of empathy. She doesn't see anything wrong with her son's waywardness and irresponsibility.

Nkechi   Is it any wonder Larry is the way he is? It's obvious the woman did a poor job of raising him.

Folake   True. I still can't get over the way she behaved the last time we went to intervene in Larry and Joyce's squabbles. Remember how happy we were when she came around? We thought that she would be able to talk some sense into her son. How utterly wrong we were.

Nkechi *arranges herself and begins a mimicry of* **Larry**'s *mother, while* **Folake** *assumes* **Joyce**'s *persona.*

Nkechi (*in an affected accent*)   Joyce, I am highly disappointed in you. Why do you like involving your single friends in your marital problems? Have you no shame? What has my son done that no man has ever done before? Is he the first man to engage in little indiscretions? And you go about broadcasting to the entire world that he is cheating on you? Why won't he cheat on you? Just take a good look at yourself . . . you look like an old woman. My son certainly deserves better.

Folake   But Mama, Larry hits me all the time . . .

Nkechi   Oh, please! How big a deal is that? Are you the only woman to get a few beatings from her husband? Marriage is all about endurance and submission. Didn't your mother teach you so? (*Softens.*) Now, be a good wife and go prepare a sumptuous meal for my son. Don't forget that the way to a man's heart is through his stomach.

Folake (*quietly*)   Yes, Mama.

Nkechi *and* **Folake** *dissolve into laughter from the acting. They exhale together.*

Nkechi   Oh, how I itched to tell that woman a few home truths. Thank God you were there to restrain me.

Folake   I was just dumbfounded. Larry's mother is a fine kettle of fish. The peak however was when Joyce's own mother came.

Nkechi   Ohhh . . . Joyce's mother's perspective to the whole scenario takes the cake.

Nkechi *again arranges herself, walks with an exaggerated limp and begins a mimicry of* **Joyce**'s *mother, while* **Folake** *assumes* **Joyce**'s *persona again.*

Nkechi (*demurely*)   Joyce my dear daughter, a woman's place is with her husband. Let me tell you, a woman without a man is nothing. See, men only beat women they love. You have to stay in your husband's house and endure the beating for the sake of your children. That's what a virtuous woman does. That is how I endured with your father . . . and today I'm thankful. My children are my reward.

Folake (*wryly*)   I guess your permanently broken hip and the numerous scars on every part of your body are part of your reward.

Nkechi   Shut your mouth! How dare you talk to me like that?

Folake   I'm sorry, mother.

Nkechi (*firmly*)   Well, as I was saying, your place is here with Larry. If you should ever leave him, I will disown you as my daughter. I will not allow you to make me a laughing stock among my peers. No daughter of mine, I repeat, no daughter of mine will be a divorcee for whatever reason. Do you understand me?

Folake   Yes, mother.

Nkechi *and* **Folake** *dissolve into laughter from the acting.*

Nkechi   Phew! I died a thousand deaths that day.

Folake   So did I.

Zainab *enters.*

Folake   Zain, how is it going?

Zainab   Everything is fine . . . just fine.

Nkechi   The girls? How are they?

Zainab   I told you I could handle them.

Folake   So you did.

Zainab   I thought I heard Joyce's voice a while ago.

Nkechi   Yes, she was here, but she left a few minutes ago.

Zainab   Oh . . .

Folake   It's a good thing you are here, Zain. We need to put our heads together concerning Joyce's issue.

Zainab   What is it again this time?

Nkechi   The usual . . . abuse, infidelity, and irresponsibility on the part of Larry.

Folake   Joyce is in a really bad space, and we are the only ones who can help her.

Nkechi   Err . . . we tried that once, remember? When we tried to arrest Larry after he beat her up and raped her. You do remember what transpired, right?

Nkechi, **Folake** and **Zainab** *take positions in readiness to act out what transpired at the police station. Zainab assumes* **Joyce***'s persona,* **Nkechi** *plays the role of the* **Police Officer***, while* **Folake** *plays herself.* **Nkechi** *as the female police officer is busy picking her teeth noisily, while* **Folake** *and* **Zainab** *(as* **Joyce***) try to lay a complaint.*

Joyce   I really don't feel good about this . . .

Folake   Joyce, It's not about you feeling good, it's about doing the right thing. Larry belongs behind the bars.

The **Police Officer** *observes them with interest.*

Folake   Good evening, Officer.

Officer   Yes, Madam. What is the problem?

Folake *looks towards* **Joyce***, but* **Joyce** *remains silent.*

Officer (*impatiently*)   Yes? Yes? I don't have all day, please.

Folake   Joyce, aren't you going to speak up?

Joyce   Well, I'm embarrassed to say the least . . .

Folake   Are we going to make this report or not?

Silence.

Joyce, please talk to the officer.

Joyce (*hesitantly*)   Officer, my name is Joyce Baker . . . I live at plot 9, Shendam lane. I have come to report my husband. He . . . hit me.

Officer   Come again, please?

Folake   Officer, what she is trying to say is that her husband beat her up.

Officer   Oh. Is that all?

Folake   He raped her too.

Officer   Interesting. Anything else?

Joyce (*takes a deep breath*)   That's all, officer. My husband battered and raped me.

Officer *breaks into an uncontrollable laughter.*

Officer   I'm so sorry, madam . . . but you see, this is funny. Please, tell me, can a man steal his own property? Or can a man be questioned on how he chooses to treat his property? Didn't you just call him your husband?

Folake   Yes, he is her husband, officer. But are you saying that assault and spousal rape are not criminal offences?

Officer   How should it concern me how a man decides to run his home?

Folake   I don't understand what you mean.

Officer   Madam I'm sorry, but you see, we only attend to serious criminal offences here. Whenever your husband commits murder or armed robbery, you can come here to report him, and we'd be glad to be of service to you. But this . . . this is purely a domestic issue. We call it 'Domestic two fighting'.

Officer *chuckles some more.*

Folake   Officer, we are not joking here. That man battered and raped my friend, and he also threatened to kill her! He attacked her with a pestle, for crying out loud. Even though he is her husband, he has no right to do any of that. We demand justice!

Officer (*calmly*)   And you will get justice . . . but just not here. This is obviously a family matter, so I suggest you reach out to your family elders to settle the issue.

Folake   Can we see your DPO, please?

Officer   Whatever for? Madam, If you do not respect yourselves and make yourselves scarce right now, I will detain you for loitering and prowling.

Folake   You can't do that. It is illegal. We are learned people, and we know the law. Actually, my friend here is a trained lawyer. So, we are well aware of our constitutional rights as law abiding citizens of this country.

Officer (*with feigned surprise*)   Oh, I see . . . You are learned people? A lawyer? So, you know the law, right? No problem. If you don't mind, I am going to need you to answer a few questions.

Folake   That's okay.

Officer (*pretends to write with an exaggerated officiousness*)   So what is his name?

Silence. **Folake** *nudges* **Joyce**.

Joyce   His name is Larry Baker.

Officer   How old is he?

Joyce   Forty-four.

Officer   What does he do for a living?

Joyce   He is a businessman.

Officer   The exact time of rape?

Folake (*sarcastically*)   Officer, could she have remembered to check her watch while she was being raped?

Officer *gives* **Folake** *a withering look.*

Officer   Madam Complainant, you may please answer the question. What time were you raped exactly?

Joyce   I really can't say for sure, officer. But it happened this evening.

Officer   Okay. How many rounds? And how long did it last?

Folake   What?!

Officer (*with exaggerated patience*)   I need to document every single detail.

Folake   Officer! Aren't you a woman? Where is your empathy? How dare you ask her such an insensitive and irrelevant question?

Officer (*to* **Folake**)   By the way, how does this even concern you? Why are you so interested in this matter? Why don't you go ahead and arrest the man by yourself, then? A man decides to exercise his conjugal rights, and you are here making a song and a dance out of it. Nonsense!

Folake (*dazed*)   I can't believe this!

Officer   You better believe it!

Folake   Are you saying that being married, or anything for that matter justifies spousal rape? Officer, you mean you are just going to stand by and allow the man who perpetrated this evil act go scot free? Have you forgotten that your job is to protect people's rights, lives and properties? You are supposed to make us feel safe, and not the other way round.

Officer *guffaws.*

Joyce (*backing out*)   Folake, I knew this was a bad idea. Why don't we just leave?

Folake (*firmly*)   We will do no such thing. (*Changing tactics.*) Officer, please forgive my outburst. We need you to go and arrest that man immediately. Please . . .

Officer   Look here, madam or madams. Even if I were favourably disposed to your case, you still have two problems. Firstly; I'm the only one on duty, therefore I cannot leave this place. Secondly; there is fuel scarcity, therefore, no fuel in our vehicle. So you see, it is double jeopardy for you guys.

Folake (*despairingly*)   You really are not going to help us, right?

Officer *ignores her.*

Folake   Joyce, will you come and stay at my place for a few days? Or would you rather stay at the SWR?

Joyce (*stubbornly*)   As it is, I prefer to go back to my husband's house.

Folake   And you think that is a safe move?

Joyce   Yes, let me go back home. I'll be fine.

Officer   Are you people still here?

Folake (*to* **Joyce**)   Come on, then. Let's leave this place. (*To* **Officer.**) Thanks for nothing, Officer. Women like you are a disgrace to womanhood.

Folake *and* **Joyce** *make to exit.* **Officer** *hisses and laughs mockingly at them.*

Officer   Stupid and jobless women.

Zainab, Nkechi *and* **Folake** *dissolve from the acting.*

Folake   That was a horrible experience. I was mortified.

Nkechi   So was I.

Zainab   Let's face facts, Joyce does not want to be rescued.

Just then **Joyce** *comes in. She has bruises on her face and her dress is torn in a few places.*

Nkechi   Speak of the devil . . .

Folake   Joyce! We were just talking about you.

Joyce *silently sits.*

Nkechi (*notices her dishevelled appearance*)   Hey! What happened to you?

Joyce *is still silent. She sniffs as she wipes the corners of her eyes.*

Zainab   Are you okay, Joyce?

Silence from **Joyce** *still.* **Folake** *goes to her.*

Folake   Joyce, face me.

Joyce *avoids* **Folake**.

Folake   Joyce, let me see your face!

Joyce *reluctantly faces* **Folake** *as she breaks into body-wracking sobs.*

Folake   Oh goodness!

Nkechi   Larry has done it again, right? And in your condition? What sort of a man beats up his pregnant wife?

Joyce (*sobs*)   My life is a mess . . .

Folake   Oh dear . . . It will be alright. I'm so sorry, darling. What happened this time?

Folake *brings out a handkerchief from her purse, and she dries* **Joyce**'s *tears.*

Joyce (*amidst sobs*)   Earlier today, I was here to see Nkechi . . .

Folake   Yes . . .?

Joyce   Then Larry called to say he was on his way home. You know he doesn't like me to go out, so I hurriedly left.

Nkechi   And then . . .?

Joyce   Larry got home before me and discovered that I had gone out. When I got home, he went savage on me.

Nkechi   The man is insane!

Joyce (*sighs*)   Larry has made it abundantly clear that he doesn't want me keeping friends.

Nkechi   An insecure poor excuse of a man.

Joyce   Nkechi, the doctor you talked about? I think I'm ready. I don't feel good. That's why I came back.

Nkechi   That's no problem. We'll take you there.

Joyce   And to top it all, Larry is having an affair again.

Folake   What else is new? Does he ever stop?

Nkechi   Oh yeah? I thought you said it was a lie.

Joyce   I know he is . . . I've seen the tell-tale signs. Recently he has been having mood swings. One minute he is happy and ecstatically in love with me, the next minute he is angry, and nothing I ever do could bring him out of his foul mood. He'd receive a secretive call, jet out of the house and later he'd be back bearing gifts and professing his undying love for me. This emotional roller coaster has been going on for some time now.

Nkechi   The usual traits of a cheat.

Joyce   I know that the passion between him and this other woman would fizzle out, and the affair would pack up like so many others before it.

Nkechi   The news is all over town.

Folake (*to* **Joyce**)   Pay no attention to it.

Nkechi   Yes, of course. She should pay no attention. Until he infects her with STDs or worse still, HIV.

Folake glares at **Nkechi** balefully.

Nkechi   What? I'm only being realistic here.

Folake   Not now, Nkechi . . . Not now.

Joyce (*dolefully*)   He called me all sorts of names . . . ugly . . . good-for-nothing . . . He said that I have no substance or value . . . Please tell me the truth. Am I that ugly? Am I really good for nothing?

Nkechi   What nonsense! Of course, you are not. Don't you have a mirror? Or was he blindfolded when he courted and married you?

Folake   Joyce, how many times will I tell you that you are beautiful inside out? You are a masterpiece, and don't you ever forget that. You hear me? Don't you ever allow Larry, or anyone for that matter, to trample upon your self-worth and self-esteem.

Joyce (*helplessly*)   Then, why? Why does Larry treat me this way?

Folake (*exhales*)   You want the truth?

Joyce   Yes.

Folake   The bitter truth, or a sugar-coated version?

Joyce (*reluctantly*)   The bitter truth . . .

Folake   He treats you this way simply because you allow him. Now, don't get me wrong, there is nothing wrong with being a caring and selfless wife, but you need to retain your sense of self. It is very important! Why did you lose yourself, Joyce?

Joyce   I don't understand.

Folake   Tell me again, why on earth did you leave your job?

Nkechi   Larry!

Folake   Did I not warn you not to abandon your very successful law career for Larry?

Joyce (*groans*)   Oooh! Are we going to have this conversation again? I thought I explained to you guys that Larry said only fulltime housewives make good wives.

Nkechi   Of course, we remember! How could we forget that your male chauvinist of a husband 'decreed' that you stop working so you could be at his beck and call to cater to his every whim.

Joyce   Nkechi!

Folake   Joyce, please understand my point; I am all for selflessness in marriage, but to sacrifice your dreams and self-fulfilment at the altar of a man's ego in the name of 'making a marriage work' is just unfortunate.

Joyce (*weakly*)   It's because of the kids.

Nkechi   And don't you give me that crap about him wanting you to stay at home so you could take care of the kids. Your kids are relatively grown up, and they are all in the boarding school, meaning they are hardly home with you.

Folake   Joyce, we all know that it has never really been about you staying back home to take care of your kids. Larry has always wanted to have absolute control over your life.

Joyce (*protests feebly*)   Folake . . .

Folake   Deny it all you can, but you and I know that Larry purposely made you close down your thriving law firm for his own selfish interests. He was jealous of your success, and now that he has you right where he wants you, you have suddenly become 'ugly and good for nothing' to him.

Nkechi   Just look at yourself . . . See how he beats you black and blue. Your world revolves around a man to whom you mean nothing. I hope you find fulfilment in that.

Joyce   Well, it is not entirely his fault.

Folake (*surprised*)   Really? Enlighten us, please.

Joyce   I think I provoke him a lot. I know he is short-tempered, but I push him . . . To be honest, I think I deserve the way he beats me at times. See, Larry loves me, I'm very sure of it. Maybe this is just his own way of expressing love.

Nkechi   How novel! You should give yourself a round of applause.

Joyce   I can change him you know.

Nkechi (*turns to* **Folake**)   Can you believe this?

Joyce   I mean it . . . I only need to try harder.

Folake   And that is the mantra you've been chanting to yourself for the past fifteen years now. My dear friend, you cannot change people. You are neither a magician nor a miracle worker!

Joyce   My pastor says that I should intensify my prayer and fasting.

Nkechi (*groans*)   Oh . . . here we go again!

Joyce   He says divorce, for whatever reason, is a sin.

Nkechi   And if you believe that, you'll believe anything.

Folake   You know how we warned you when Larry first hit you during courtship. Remember what we told you then? We emphatically told you that if he hits you once, there is the likelihood that he will do it again and again and again.

Nkechi   I still remember how you replied us. (*Mimics* **Joyce.**) 'Larry loves me, he can't do without me. He will change for me . . .'

Joyce   You guys still remember that episode? That was just a few slaps, nothing serious.

Nkechi   Yes, darling. A few slaps and still counting. And at the rate at which this is going, Larry dearest intends to slap you into an early grave.

Joyce   That is not my portion in Jesus' name! (*Getting upset*.) Please, don't worry about me, I can handle Larry.

Nkechi (*dryly*)   Of course, you can.

Joyce   But seriously, what do you guys expect me to do? Leave him? You know I can't do that. Honestly, he loves me . . . He once told me that if he can't have me, no one else will.

Nkechi (*incredulously*)   And that to you is a symbol of love?! You must be more daft than I thought!

Joyce   Please, Nkechi! No need for insults.

Folake   Nkechi! That's okay, please. (*Contritely*.) Sorry, Joyce . . . We don't mean to insult you. We are just worried about you. (*To* **Nkechi**.) Please, apologise to her.

Nkechi (*reluctantly*)   I'm sorry . . . (*Softly*.) But seriously Joyce, you cannot continue like this. You may end up in a body bag. You need to take a break from this abusive marriage.

Joyce   And how will I take care of my children? I have no job, and no money of my own. My kids and I depend on Larry for everything.

Nkechi (*angrily*)   And I dare say that had been his plan all along! To make you dependent on him financially, emotionally and psychologically.

Folake   Listen, Joyce, we are not even saying you must divorce him, but you guys need to get some help.

Joyce   Get help, as in see a marriage counsellor?

Folake   Yes. Is that such a bad idea?

Joyce   No way! What will people say? You do know that we are a model couple, openly admired by our church members. I cannot afford for it to become public knowledge that I have marital problems. I can't expose myself in that manner.

Nkechi   Folake is right, Joyce. You guys should really see a counsellor. If you don't, one of these days Larry will just kick you six feet under.

Joyce   Stop being so dramatic, Nkechi. Things can never get that bad between Larry and me.

Folake   Joyce, may I ask you a quick question? Of what use do you think the image which you are protecting now would be to your children, your family, church, or the society, if Larry should succeed in killing you?

Joyce   God forbid! You guys should stop saying this, please. The Lord that I serve will never allow me to be so unfortunate. Evil will never befall me and my household.

Folake (*ignores her ranting*)   Another issue is that your kids are all boys and they are at an impressionable age. Raising them in a toxic environment such as this . . . Don't you worry that they will grow up thinking that it is normal for a man to hit or maltreat women?

Joyce (*primly*)   They won't. Please, stop blowing things out of proportion.

Folake   I'm just being realistic here, Joyce. These things happen.

Joyce   No. Larry is not that bad. It isn't as if he beats me every day, you know. He is just going through some sort of mid-life crisis, I'm positive he will overcome it.

Folake (*not convinced*)   Well, if you say so.

Joyce   Friends, I know you genuinely care about me, and I truly appreciate it, but this is my life! My marriage means everything to me, and I need you to respect that. Are we on the same page?

Nkechi (*drawls*)   We are not even reading the same book.

Joyce   Nkechi, Please . . .!

Nkechi (*surrenders*)   Okay, I will say no more. I am sorry for interfering again. It just breaks my heart to see you pine away needlessly like this . . . But, like you rightly pointed out, it's your life after all.

Quiet.

Folake (*to* **Joyce**)   So tell me, how are the boys?

Joyce (*grateful for the change of subject*)   They are fine. They are at my mother's place for the holiday. Talking about husbands killing wives . . . has Madam B's husband been found?

Folake (*sighs sadly*)   No. The police are still searching for him.

Joyce   I also hear that you guys are not allowed to see her corpse.

Folake   It is all for the best, I'm sure.

Joyce   How sad . . . Madam B was a wonderful woman. SWR will never be the same without her.

Nkechi   Yeah . . .

Zainab   Shall we take Joyce to the hospital now?

Joyce's phone rings.

Joyce   Shhhh . . . I need to take this, please. It's Larry calling again.

Folake   Of course.

Joyce picks up the call.

Joyce (*warily*)   Hello, Larry . . . (*Pause. Stiffly.*) I'm fine, Larry . . . (*Pause.*) I said I am fine . . . (*Pause. Relaxes a bit.*) Okay, okay . . . Just a little body pain, that's all . . . (*Pause.*) I'll take some painkillers, and I will be fine . . . Honestly you don't have to worry about me.

Nkechi *clears her throat loudly and shuffles feet.*

Joyce   What? Of course not. No one is here with me . . . (*Signals to* **Nkechi** *to sit still. Pause. Sighs.*) Larry, I said I am alone in the house. I'm not allowed to keep any friends, remember? So who would come visit me? (*Pause.*) You know that I always obey you, Larry . . . (*Pause. Disbelievingly.*) You went shopping for me? (*Pause.*) Why, thanks, Larry. That's really thoughtful and sweet of you . . . (*Pause.*) Okay, see you then. (*She hangs up the phone. Sighs.*) Ladies, I'm sorry . . . but I have to leave now. Larry is on his way home, and if he doesn't meet me at home, hell will be let loose again.

Nkechi *rolls eyes.*

Zainab   So, I guess the hospital visit is cancelled?

Joyce   I'm sorry.

Folake (*to* **Joyce**)   Promise us you'll be fine?

Joyce   Of course, I'll be fine. (*Excitedly*.) Guess what Larry told me on phone?

Nkechi (*dryly*)   No, we can't guess. But I'm sure you are going to tell us.

Joyce (*announces gleefully*)   He went shopping for me.

Folake   Hmnnn . . .

Nkechi   Oh dear . . .

Joyce   Aren't you happy for me?

Nkechi (*wryly*)   Why shouldn't I be? I can see that you lovebirds have kissed and made up on the phone. So, tell me why I wouldn't be happy for you.

Folake   You should be on your way now, Joyce. We wouldn't want a repeat of what happened earlier.

Joyce   Thanks, dear friends. Thanks for understanding . . . You do understand, don't you?

Folake   Of course, we do.

Zainab   We totally understand.

They hug. **Joyce** *exits.* **Nkechi** *exhales.*

Nkechi   And she goes again.

Zainab (*sagely*)   She will be back.

Folake (*checks her watch*)   Excuse me ladies, I need to quickly dash out. I'll be back soon.

Zainab   Again?

Nkechi   Remember we scheduled a meeting for five o'clock? It's almost time.

Folake   I'll be back before then. I promise.

Folake *exits. Suddenly a noise can be heard from outside. Female voices chant the solidarity song 'All we are saying, find the killer'.*

Nkechi   What is happening out there? Zainab, could you please check what the noise is about?

Zainab *doesn't move.*

Nkechi   Zain?

Zainab   I do not need to check. In fact, I masterminded it.

Nkechi   You masterminded what?

Zainab   A protest; a non-peaceful protest.

Nkechi   A non-peaceful protest? I am lost . . .

Zainab (*defiantly*)   I gathered all the other young women who have benefited from Madam B and this refuge in one way or the other, to stage a demonstration to express our displeasure concerning the brutal murder of our leader Madam B.

Nkechi   A demonstration, you say? But why have you brought it here? Or were you told that any of us here had a hand in Madam B's death? Are you blind to the fact that we also are in mourning?

Zainab   Well then, maybe we have different ways of expressing our grief. It has been days now since Madam B was brutally murdered, yet nothing is being done to fish out her killer. Sitting in a roundtable and weeping copiously the way we've been doing, is not my idea of showing grief. I believe in action.

Nkechi   I am speechless!

Zainab   We must fish out Madam B's husband, and kill him just as he killed Madam B!

The noise outside grows louder. Just then **Joyce** *enters with a big travelling bag. She looks forlorn.*

Nkechi   Joyce! What brings you here again?

Quiet.

Meanwhile, what's with the luggage?

Silence.

Is this about Larry?

Zainab   Is everything alright, Joyce?

Joyce *breaks down in tears.*

Zainab   Oh my . . .

Nkechi   What is it, Joyce? Please, tell me.

Joyce   I'm running for my dear life. Larry wants to kill me.

Nkechi   Surely you don't mean that?

Joyce Nkechi, look at me. I have never been more serious in my entire life. Larry is planning to kill me, so that he can be with his secretary.

Nkechi What?!

Nkechi Come, sit. Tell us everything. What exactly happened?

Joyce As promised Larry came home with gifts of clothes, shoes and bags. I was happy as I thought that everything would go back to normal, at least for now. Then I wanted to pick something from the bathroom, only to overhear Larry talking to his secretary on phone. I tiptoed to eavesdrop from near the door. That's how I got to know that Larry has actually been poisoning my meals for some time now.

Nkechi Oh my! That explains the pains you've been experiencing.

Joyce He plans to sell our house after my death and burial, and then relocate to Ghana with his secretary, so that they'd marry and live happily ever after.

Nkechi You've got to be kidding me.

Joyce I tiptoed quietly back to the sitting room, because I dreaded what he might do to me if he discovered that I had found out his evil plan.

Zainab Of course.

Joyce So immediately he left for the club, I packed a few of my things, and quietly eased myself out of the house, and out of his life. He has no idea where I am, and I intend to keep it that way.

Nkechi Wise move.

Joyce You know the most astonishing thing? While plotting my death with this woman, Larry never for once said anything about our four children, neither did he care that I am carrying his child. What would have happened to the poor kids? And to think that I remained in this horrible marriage all these years only because of them?

Nkechi Just imagine that?

Joyce Thank heavens they are still with my mother for the holidays. I decided there and then that I am more useful to my kids being alive than dead.

Nkechi I wish I didn't have to say 'I told you so'.

Joyce You did tell me so . . . What did I ever do to this man to deserve this? Why couldn't he just ask me for a divorce? Why plot to kill me?

Joyce *starts to weep.*

Zainab Don't worry Joyce, everything will be fine. The most important thing is that you are out of harm's way.

Nkechi Exactly. Where do you intend to go now, though? What are your plans?

Joyce I really don't know . . .

Zainab You do need to see a doctor as soon as possible. Who knows the extent of damage the poison must have done to your system and even the baby?

Nkechi Quite true. Will you go to your mother's place for a while?

Joyce That's out of the question. To start with she wouldn't believe that Larry could plan to kill me, and she would never approve of me leaving my husband.

Zainab You mean she would want you to remain with him even in the face of death? I find that very hard to believe.

Nkechi Then, you don't know Joyce's mother.

Zainab That is just awful. You still need to make a plan, though.

Joyce For now, my thoughts are still hazy. I need time to think and decide what I want to do with my life. One thing is sure though, I am never going back to Larry.

Nkechi I am happy your eyes are finally opened.

Joyce Can I stay here for a few days, please . . .?

Nkechi Of course, you are welcome here. SWR is always open to women seeking refuge from any form of abuse.

Zainab You can stay for as long as you like. This is why we are here.

Nkechi Joyce, oh Joyce . . . Poor you . . . Come here . . .

The protest song is raised again.

(*Exasperatedly.*) Zainab, please go tell your cronies to stop this madness.

Zainab *is silent.*

Nkechi What do I do now? Oh, how I miss Madam B . . . She would have known how to handle this situation. And where on earth is Folake when I need her . . .?

She is interrupted by a commotion outside. This noise is quite different from the previous chaos. Screams of 'Ghost!' can be heard.

What on earth is that again?

Zainab (*confused*)   Let me check what is going on out there.

Zainab *makes to go outside, but staggers back as she sees* **Folake** *entering in the company of* **Madam B. Zainab** *screams 'Madam B!' Pandemonium ensues.* **Madam B** *is wearing a bandage and a sling across her shoulder.*

Folake   It is alright, ladies. She is not a ghost.

Nkechi   Madam B, is this you? Or are my eyes deceiving me?

Folake (*smiles*)   It is our Madam B alright, she is not a ghost. She is alive. Come close. Touch her. Come on Nkechi, Zainab . . . Joyce . . .

Nkechi (*disbelievingly*)   Not so fast. I need to hear her talk. Madam B, if this is really you, then, please talk to us.

Madam B (*wearily*)   Yes, Nkechi . . . I am the one. Zainab, don't be afraid, I am not a ghost. Joyce dear, how are you?

They gingerly go close and touch her. **Madam B** *smiles at them. Jubilation as they try to hug her all at once.*

Folake   Careful, ladies. She is still very fragile.

Nkechi   Madam B, I am so happy to see you. In fact, words are not enough to express my joy.

Zainab   They told us you were dead, that your husband killed you.

Nkechi   What happened exactly?

Madam B   First of all, I want to thank God for sparing my life, and I am so grateful for the profound love and loyalty you women have shown. Yes, it is true, my husband tried to kill me. He actually left me for dead. If not for the timely intervention of Folake, I would be dead by now . . . I owe my life to her.

Folake   We all owe our lives to God. I merely did what any one would do for her sibling. You once saved me too, remember?

Nkechi   Folake, you mean you knew all along that Madam B was still alive, and you never let on?

Zainab   Folake, is this true?

Folake   Ladies, I am sorry I kept you in the dark all this while. I did it for Madam B's safety.

Zainab   How so?

Folake   A few months ago, I got a tip from a young lady who is one of Madam B's neighbours. She told me that Madam B was steadily undergoing domestic abuse from her husband. Since Madam B never discussed the issue with me, I decided to keep an eye on her.

Nkechi   How?

Folake   I told the young lady to watch over Madam B's apartment and alert me if any such thing happens again. On the fateful day of this unfortunate incident, the lady called me. She asked me to quickly go and check on Madam B as she could hear blood-curling screams from her apartment. I hurried down there, and happened upon Madam B's almost lifeless body in the pool of her own blood. Her husband had stabbed her and ran away.

Nkechi   What did you do then?

Folake   I called for help and rushed her to the hospital. Thankfully, she responded to treatment quickly, but because of the peculiarity of her case, the doctors and the police decided to allow the general public to believe that she didn't survive the attack.

Zainab   I'm short of words.

Nkechi   No wonder you've been so distracted. Why didn't you confide in us?

Folake   I couldn't. The police had to prevent the perpetrator from coming back to finish what he started, by making him believe that he had succeeded. When Madam B came to, she confirmed our suspicions – her husband had taken her cash, valuables and property documents, and left her for dead.

Nkechi (*to* **Madam B**)   I am a bit confused here. This doesn't add up. You've always made us believe that you had a perfect marriage. How then did this happen?

Joyce   Exactly! I always looked up to you guys as my model couple. I spent sleepless nights praying that Larry would love and treat me just the way your husband did you.

Madam B (*smiling sadly*)   That perhaps was the greatest mistake of my life. I wanted people to believe that all was well with my marriage, because I loved my husband dearly and I wanted to make it work. But the truth is that throughout my eighteen years of marriage to that man, he battered me in every possible way; verbally, emotionally, psychologically, physically, and even sexually.

Nkechi   You mean all those cuts and bruises we saw every once in a while weren't accidents as you claimed?

Madam B   No, darling. Those were injuries I suffered from domestic abuse.

Zainab   And you were always full of smiles and praises of your darling husband.

Madam B (*smiles sadly*)   My husband's maltreatment was a thing of shame to me. It made me feel less of a woman. Somehow I became convinced that there was something wrong with me to provoke such incessant anger in him. So, for every one of my husband's abuse, I always found a way to blame myself. Before I knew it, I had become an expert at conjuring up excuses for every one of his misbehaviours towards me. It was easier for me to cope that way.

Joyce   I can totally relate . . . I felt the same way with Larry too.

Folake (*turns to* **Joyce**)   Felt? What has happened between you and Larry?

Joyce   Long story . . . But the short version of it is that, I have left him, and I am alive.

Folake   Incredible!

Nkechi   She will fill you in later, Folake. (*To* **Madam B**.) I'm still trying to get my head round all you just told us.

Joyce   Really shocking. You were busy saving women from the exact thing you were suffering.

Madam B   Irony of life.

Folake   Unfortunately, there are lots of women out there in this same situation, but because they refuse to cry out for help, they die in silence.

Nkechi   And do you really blame them? What help can they get in a patriarchal society like ours where men hold all the cards.

Folake   That is not completely true. The people who helped me out with Madam B's case are all men. There are still some good men out there.

Nkechi (*snorts*)   And I'm the queen of England.

Folake   Now, Nkechi . . . Don't be so antagonistic towards men. Do not perceive all men to be bad. I personally know some men who are committed to making our society a place where women are gratefully accepted as deserving of equal rights with their male counterparts.

Nkechi (*snorts*)   Utopia!

Folake   There you go! This is actually part of the problem. In a situation where women expect every man to be a misogynist, when women cannot graciously accept chivalry from men without some sort of disbelief or distrust, then you have already written the script, and you leave the men no other choice than to play the roles you have assigned to their characters.

Nkechi   Well, well, well! Suddenly, Folake has become a mouthpiece for the men folk.

Madam B   Folake is right. We expect the worst behaviour from men and encourage them to treat us like dirt, but when they start living up to our expectations, we raise an alarm and then say that 'all men are bad'.

Nkechi (*grudgingly*)   That is not entirely true.

Folake   Nkechi, think about it. Do you really think that women are entirely blameless as far as these issues are concerned?

Nkechi   I'm not getting you . . .

Folake   Who raises the children?

Nkechi   Mostly women . . .

Folake   Visualize this; women raise their daughters to be good wives and to nurture male privilege. On the other hand, the same women raise their sons to act like 'men', and to lord it over their women. What then do you expect? I'm sorry, but I dare say that we women are our own worst enemies.

Zainab   Folake is making a valid point. Do you realize that for every woe that befalls a woman, another woman is involved, directly or indirectly?

Folake   True. These so-called patriarchal laws, who enforces them? Who is the madame who engages in girl trafficking? Who is the passive mother and the monster-in-law? Who tells the girl-child to keep mum after being raped for fear of stigmatization? Who stays with a man who violates her girl-child?

Madam B   Exactly. Who raises the wife-beaters? Who raises the female child to defer to every male in her life? Who makes sure the girl-child knows how to cook, wash, clean the house, and care for her brothers, while the boy-child is encouraged to go play football, watch action movies, and generally idle away?

Nkechi (*slowly*)   I am beginning to see sense in what you are saying . . .

Folake   Who advises her daughter to stay in an abusive marriage and pray? Who mocks single ladies of marriageable age as unwanted leftovers? Who mocks a woman who leaves her husband for whatever reason? Who is the other woman?

All   WOMEN!!!

Folake   Now, now, I am not saying that everything is entirely the fault of women. Of course, the men are culpable too. They are after all . . . men. But you see, we women need to start telling ourselves a few home truths. We run the society, so we should tactically position ourselves to not be victims.

Madam B   That's right! Right from birth we teach our daughters to be second-class citizens in their own world. We raise them to aspire to become wives to successful men, we don't give them the hope of becoming successful women in their own rights . . . It is saddening!

Folake   And why is it so difficult for women to raise their daughters to demand and enjoy respect from the men in their lives? Why are we so oblivious of our power? Don't we know that we determine how society treats us?

Madam B   Women lose their self-worth, self-esteem, joy and even life . . . just to stay with an abuser and please their families and society. When will this carnage stop? When?!

Folake   The time is now! We must begin to conscientize our society to develop zero tolerance for harmful socio-cultural practices and violence against women.

Zainab   And we must begin to raise our male children to respect and treat women right!

Nkechi   We must also raise our female children to respect themselves and know that they are deserving of respect!

Joyce   Women must begin to empower themselves, we must stop expecting men to do everything for us!

Madam B   Great! All these firebrand rants are music to the ears, but who will bell the cat? Who? It begins with you and me. I know that I am going to do my best to raise my only son to respect women as the mothers and the backbone of our society. But what about the other women out there? (*Turns to the other women*.) What about you? (*Turns to the audience*.) What about you?

Madam B *steps forward*.

Madam B   It begins with me! I will not be that woman who encourages her daughter to stay in an abusive relationship or marriage. A dead woman is neither a wife, nor a mother. At best, she is referred to as a late wife or mother.

Folake (*steps forward*)   It begins with me! I will encourage every female around me to dare to dream, nurture their self-esteem, and be the best they can be. I refuse to be an enabler of women's inequality with men.

Nkechi (*steps forward*)   It begins with me! I will not be that woman who mocks or judge any woman for being single, divorced, widowed or childless. A woman is a complete human being regardless of her marital status.

Zainab (*steps forward*)   It begins with me! I will not be a party to practices that stunt the development and well-being of women. I choose to support the cause of the girl child.

Joyce (*steps forward*)   It begins with me! I will not be a monster-in-law or a passive mother. My sons must know that it is unacceptable to bully or hit a woman. And no, I will not be the other woman, I refuse to be the reason for a fellow woman's heartache!

Madam B   That's the spirit ladies . . . That's the spirit.

Song 'We Shall Overcome' rents the air.

Curtain call.

The End

I Want to Fly

Thembelihle Moyo

Thembelihle Moyo is a Zimbabwean artist and mother of two girls in a family of eight people. Her passion for writing developed while she was at Magwegwe Secondary School, where she was acknowledged as the best student in creative writing and drama. After graduating from high school, Thembelihle taught at the school for four years, using her creativity to write dramas for students to perform during assemblies and prize giving days. At Amakhosi Arts Academy, she studied Journalism and Media, as there was no creative arts course. However, she enrolled in an evening course specialising in theatre, film, producing and directing, and so graduated with a Diploma in Creative Arts in 2005 and Diploma in Media Studies and Journalism in 2006. Currently, she is the founder and the creative director of Gitiz Arts Organisation which has developed Dance Zimbabwe and Dance Remedial Zimbabwe in collaboration with the Ministry of Primary and Secondary Education. This initiative suggests her other passion: to develop young performers.

Her plays include *Colour Blue* (2010), *Sibahle Nje, Nomhle* (2011), *Let It Out* (2014) and *Who Said I Don't Want to Dance*, which was selected for reading at the Women Playwrights International Conference in Santiago, Chile, in 2018. She has directed *Song of a Woman*, *It's Not Gold*, *Voices of Solo Women* and *Isipho Sami*, and has written two books: *Total Traditional Dances* and *Contemporary Dances Zimbabwe*.

Production history

I Want to Fly premiered on 27 March 2012 at Amakhosi Theatre Centre with an energetic cast. It was directed by Thembelihle Moyo, assisted by Mandla Moyo, and produced by Plays on Sunday. The script was edited by Naison Tfwala. Stage design was by Blessing Masora, props and make-up by Nomvuyiso Mabi, lights and sound by Thabani Trigger, and costume by Jeffrey Sibanda. The original cast included Qeqeshiwe Mntambo, Thulani Mbambo, Millicent Roberts, Nomvuyiso Mabi, Memory Muzondo, Kenneth Chikweza and Nhlanhla Ndlovu. It ran at the National Gallery in Bulawayo on 28 and 29 November 2012, at the Bulawayo Theatre on 27 March 2013, and was selected to represent Zimbabwe at the 10th Women Playwrights International Conference in Cape Town, South Africa in 2015. It was presented in reading by the CASA Awards on 27 March 2017 during World Theatre Week, as part of a campaign to fund a mid-career playwright for a year-long, full-time writing fellowship.

Critical introduction

I Want to Fly premiered in 2008, when a lot was happening in Zimbabwe's socio-political and economic context: the country had reached a melting point economically where it literally had no currency of its own. We depended largely on our neighbouring countries like South Africa, Botswana and Namibia for our food and fuel.

The gap between the rich and the poor was very wide. Poverty was a day to day topic and the country had no hope. The most affected group were women, especially peasant women based in the rural areas. As hunger dominated, most women could not travel long distances to access primary health care and family planning. As a result, more women had babies in 2008 compared to 2013. Mobile clinics were also inaccessible to many people as there was a shortage of fuel both to access rural areas, and for the people from these areas to come to the clinics. The increase in births together with an unstable economy made life very difficult. One of the consequences was an increase in child marriages. In 2008, while I was doing HIV awareness and prevention in the rural village of Lupane, Khazhane, I met many young girls between the ages of 13 and 15 who were already married. Most of these young girls told me that they had been married to older men who had a lot of cattle and could therefore look after the girls and their parents. Although most of them were coping day by day, they had dreams to achieve. From a distance, one might assume that only women and young girls were affected by this situation. However, young boys also were affected as most of them were forced to leave their homeland to support their families. These young boys were sent to work in nearby white-owned farms where they often faced sexual abuse by the older men. There was a rise in the number of pressure groups and non-governmental organizations who worked on child abuse, child rights and sexual reproductive health, and who lobbied political leaders and parties to find a solution to the country's situation.

As a writer, a mother and a citizen of my beloved country, Zimbabwe, I contributed by writing this play. I knew it would someday penetrate the media and the issues discussed in the play would reach the relevant authorities. Although it took more than two years to get it on stage, the year we premiered it, the play received many reviews in the media that highlighted the plight of the girl child. It played a bigger role in conscientizing the global world on what was going on in our country. We hope that the future generations will be able to tell our history using this play as one of their reference points. We are making our country a habitable nation with a stable socio-economic and political scene that supports the dreams of young men and women, whether they live in rural or urban areas of Zimbabwe.

Characters

Yinka, *18-year-old protagonist who is fighting for survival as she dreams of a better life. She is a hero to her brother* **Thusi**.

Aunt Sihle, *a woman in her late forties, a kind-hearted character who has many secrets from her past life. She loves to help her brother* **Nqwayi**, **Yinka**'s *father, even though she is going through tribulations, she remains a resilient character throughout the play.*

Shumba, *a wealthy, big man, in his late forties, who loves fashion and accumulating riches. He is a hypocrite who loves to flirt with women and threaten his wife by saying he will marry another woman. He has an eye for his niece* **Yinka** *and he is waiting for an opportunity to sleep with her.*

Mankwinji, *in her late forties, could be easily mistaken for a sixty-year-old because of the hardships she has faced. Giving birth to many children and raising them without her husband's support, her husband* **Nqwayi** *is never grateful for her hard work and makes a point of physically and mentally torturing her by saying that he will send her mother away.*

Mankwinji's Mother, *in her nineties, is a fragile a woman of peace who loves to sun bask and be with her grandchildren.*

Nqwayi, *in his fifties, is* **Yinka**'s *father. He sells everything he has, including his children.*

Yantonto, *an African traditional healer in her late fifties who is always dressed in black, and never smiles. Life to her is always about herbs and doing traditional rituals to appease the ancestors.*

Thusi, *a young adolescent around 12 years of age, is* **Yinka**'s *favourite brother and protégé. He loves looking after animals although he was heartbroken when his father* **Nqwayi** *sold the last goat they had at home.*

Mrs Manzini, *a teacher in her late thirties. She is a pillar of strength to* **Yinka**, *as she encourages* **Yinka** *to dream beyond her poverty-stricken life style.*

Note that the three minor roles may be played by one performer.

Setting

This play takes place around 2008 during one of Zimbabwe's great depressions in rural areas.

Props

Reed mat, old torn blanket, tooth paste, tooth brush, cup of water, Tonga smoking pipe, groundnuts, magazine, metal box, carrier bag full of groceries, a drum, herbs, a basket, knobkerrie, walking stick, a child's photo, opaque beer, a pack of clear beer, books, toy aeroplane.

Notes on staging

This play can be adapted to any setting in the world, the most important note is to have two settings that represent two social standings: one for the rich and the other for the poor. Painted canvas can be used as a backdrop depicting the set-up of the rich class and the poor class. An option of a tangible set up using furniture and other props which are in the play can also be utilized. Change of other settings like the school store room can be signalled by using removable furniture that can be easily taken off stage, while the original two sets still remain.

Prologue/Scene One

The story has two settings in juxtaposition, one represents the rich and the other the poor.

The poor area is depicted by a reed mat and a rolled up torn blanket. Traditional African huts are painted on canvas cloth, emphasizing the 2008 period where poor rural folks were still building their homes using mud.

The second area depicts a wealthier life-style – the painting on the canvas shows two quality chairs and a round table. Modern houses also add a touch of the rich lifestyle of these people in the canvas painting.

The curtains open and **Yinka** *is on the stage, miming flying like a bird, using her arms.*

Yinka (*recites the poem in a rich and strong voice*)

I want to fly like an eagle, fly high and far
Using my flamboyant wings and I will let
The winds blow me away. As far away from
Home as possible, I want to fly and visit those
Places I always dream of, I want to fly.

Yinka *looks in the direction of the wealthy setting as she picks up a handmade aeroplane from the ground where a magazine about aeroplanes is lying. She picks the magazine up, looks at it, and she pauses.*

Mankwinji, **Yinka**'s *mother, appears from the right wing limping slowly towards her daughter.*

Mankwinji   My daughter how far can you go?

The hunters have already laid a trap for you
You won't be able to fly high; your wings will be broken,
You are already destined to remain in this village and you shall plough
Back your fruits to this village not to any other.

She pauses and looks in her daughter's direction as **Yinka** *playfully flies her plane and* **Mankwinji** *swings into action. Shaking her head and moving towards her daughter.*

Mankwinji   How many times must I to tell you to stop dreaming, haa? You always want to irritate your father Nqwayi with small issues, throw away that gadget, will you?

Yinka *picks up her magazine and holds it tight in her arms, with her aeroplane.*

Yinka   No Mama I won't, this is my dream and it means so much to me.

Mankwinji *moves closer to her slowly but intentionally, eyeing* **Yinka***'s magazine.*

Mankwinji   Have you started preparing the evening meal, Yinka?

Yinka *frowns and shakes her head.* **Mankwinji** *grabs the miniature aeroplane and throws it to the far end of the stage.* **Yinka** *rushes to pick it up on the verge of screaming.*

Yinka   I made it Mama, it's my passion.

Mankwinji *breathes out loudly and paces up and down the room in confusion.*

Scene Two

Shumba, *a man in his late forties dressed in an expensive safari suit and sporting a hunter's hat, enters the stage and heads straight to two chairs that are placed near the rich canvas home. Lights up* Ndombola, *a Tonga smoking pipe, and puffs at it while leisurely tapping his foot in time to imaginary music.*

Aunt Sihle, *a buxom woman in her late forties enters stage left, carrying groundnuts in* (isitsha) *basket made of African* ilala *palm. She sits opposite her husband.*

Shumba   What are you doing? Toyi should be the one shelling those groundnuts.

Aunt Sihle   Fair enough, Toyi does most of the work here. It doesn't hurt the owner of the homestead to pitch in, once in a while.

Shumba *looks at her hard and shakes his head.*

Shumba   Why should I even be paying her, when you are doing most of the chores? With the baby on the way, you need to slow down. Let Toyi do the rest.

Aunt Sihle *looks at him puzzled.*

Aunt Sihle   A baby! Where from? Haven't we tried enough and failed?

Shumba   Don't worry, this time Yantonto is bringing very potent herbs.

Aunt Sihle *reluctantly puts down the* (isitsha) ilala *palm basket, stands up and paces around the room, confused.*

Aunt Sihle   I thought we understood each other on this matter. I won't be physically and mentally tortured by the old woman again.

Shumba *also stands up and faces her.*

Shumba   Sihle, you don't have a choice. I need a son, an heir to my wealth when I am no more, don't you get it?

Aunt Sihle   Each time I use the concoction, the pain and the heat become unbearable. Won't you feel for me Shumba? I am also a human being. Besides, we have a choice. My brother is blessed with so many children that he is willing to let us adopt two as our own.

Shumba   Eeh woman, hold it there! Listen to me very carefully; I need my biological son. Out there, other women are dying to make that baby for me if you can't.

Aunt Sihle *opens and closes her mouth but no words come.*

Shumba   Think positively woman, I am the man who gives you choices.

Shumba *turns and leaves after that bombshell.* **Aunt Sihle** *throws herself on the chair, finding it hard to accept what* **Shumba** *has just said. She holds her hands over her head, thinking hard. In the background soft drum beating is heard as different people throw in different thoughts going through her mind.*

Voice 1   Sihle, you have a choice. Throw open that closet. Prove to him that you are not as barren as he thinks. You know you gave birth to a little girl, why should you be tormented?

Voice 2   Oh! No, no that's not a great idea, you hoodwinked him into believing you were a virgin when you first met him ten years ago. You put up imaginary first time sexual pains. Of course you did.

Voice 1   So what do you suggest?

Voice 3   Both of you are silly and very wrong. This idiot is filthy rich. He wouldn't even notice if I looted his wealth, and started a new life. I know I am capable of having children.

One loud drum beat emphasizes the end of her thoughts as she goes off stage holding her head, confused.

Scene Three

Store room set up with desk and two chairs.

Mrs Manzi, Yinka's *chemistry teacher, in her early thirties, is seated in her store room, marking, when* **Yinka** *knocks on the door. She looks up and smiles at her.*

Mrs Manzi   Oh Yinka, you can come through, how was the Maths paper my dear?

Yinka   It was fine Ma'am; rumour has it that you are going away, in fact transferring to town.

Mrs Manzi   You are writing your finals and I hope you will pass, you are one of my top students and it was great to have you in my class.

Yinka *shyly smiles at her teacher.*

Mrs Manzi   If you do well in your Maths and Science subjects you might stand a chance to get a STEM bursary.

Yinka   What is STEM Ma'am?

Yinka *is little bit confused.*

Mrs Manzi   Science, Technology, Engineering and Mathematics. It is a new bursary which the government has introduced. You might stand a chance, considering your background and intelligence.

Mrs Manzi *says this with a smile on her face.*

Yinka   Who is going to help me with the application?

Mrs Manzi *scribbles something on the paper and hands it to* **Yinka**.

Yinka   What is this supposed to mean Ma'am?

Mrs Manzi   That is my home contact address; you could pay me a visit when you have collected your results. I have a feeling that you will be going to the air force college. I am sure you like flying, isn't it?

Yinka   Yes Ma'am, you guessed right. I have to go now, I am writing my chemistry paper this afternoon.

Mrs Manzi   You have my support all the way. Excuse me, I too have to go, I am invigilating the first formers.

She remarks as she follows **Yinka** *off stage.*

Scene Four

Yinka's father, **Nqwayi***, enters the stage calling* **Mankwinji***. Fear registers on her face,* **Mankwinji** *walks fast. She kneels in front of him as she says her greetings.*

Mankwinji Baba how was your day? I am here Nqwayi.

Nqwayi What are we having for lunch?

Mankwinji Sorry Baba, I couldn't prepare anything. I am saving the relish for the evening meal when everyone is home.

Nqwayi What might that be?

Mankwinji Dried vegetables, Baba.

Retracts slowly, fear written on her face, unsure what her husband might do to her.

Nqwayi Why are you moving away, are you scared of your husband? Come closer, all I need at this moment is food. We can discuss the rest when I am full. So, tell me Mankwinji, you are not serving your husband any beef today?

Nqwayi I couldn't join Aunty Sihle on a weeding programme. Jika wasn't feeling too well. Also, I had to attend a school consultation for Yinka.

Nqwayi I am sure we still have goats. How many are there?

Mankwinji One is ours, the rest belong to Aunt Sihle. One ewe is pregnant and should have kids any time soon.

He guffaws loudly and whistles a little bit.

Nqwayi Where is the goat? We need to sell it tomorrow.

Mankwinji This is our only goat Baba, please don't sell it. (*She begs her husband.*)

Nqwayi Don't even try stop me, you know the consequences. Jika, Jika! Where are you my boy?

Mankwinji *sobs while* **Nqwayi** *whistles, unperturbed at what is happening. A teenage boy appears from the other wing.*

Thusi Baba, here I am.

Nqwayi We are taking Mbelekazi to the Sale Pens. Find her now.

Thusi *stands still on the same spot, his father's face changes to anger and he takes steps towards his son.*

Nqwayi   Why are you still standing there? Get moving, unless you are challenging my authority. Don't forget that you are still my son.

Thusi   Baba, Mbelekazi isn't going anywhere. It is the only thing that is keeping this homestead stable. Everything else belongs to Aunt.

Nqwayi *raises the knobkerrie meaning to strike his son.* **Mankwinji** *steps between them. In a scared voice, she pleads with her husband.*

Mankwinji   Baba, please don't do that, you could kill him. (*She restrains the hand holding the knobkerrie.*)

Yinka *enters the stage carrying her books, humming a song. She stops abruptly when she sees the scene in the house.*

Yinka   Mama, Thusi what is the scene all about?

Nqwayi   At last! Your messiah is here. Thusi, I am not in the mood to fight. Woman! Simply do as I say. Prepare something for me to eat before we go.

Nqwayi *tries to dampen the confrontation that is taking place.*

Yinka   What is happening Thusi?

Angrily, **Nqwayi** *turns and faces* **Yinka**.

Nqwayi   *Ntombazana* (young woman), you think you have a right to question everything in this homestead. Is it the education the Catholics are giving you and paying for? I can't wait for the day you will be done with all this nonsense. You are going to kiss good bye to all this. Prospective husbands are eyeing you out there.

Yinka   No Baba, marriage can wait. I am going to college, to become a pilot.

Yinka *says it boldly.* **Nqwayi** *laughs loudly and shakes his head.*

Nqwayi   Keep on dreaming my girl, dreams can only be dreams. Thusi, let us go, it is getting late.

Thusi   Guess what Yinka! Father wants to sell Mbelekazi.

With pleading eyes, **Thusi** *asks her sister to intervene.*

Yinka   Don't prevent him from selling it. No harm will come out of it. If you do, he will continue abusing you for one goat.

Thusi   Yinka you are not serious.

Yinka *holds her brother's shoulders for reassurance.*

Yinka   You don't have to worry my brother.

Nqwayi   At least they are teaching you something wise.

Yinka *doesn't answer, she picks up her books and heads in the opposite direction.* **Thusi** *walks away and* **Nqwayi** *follows, asking* **Mankwinji** *to prepare food for him.*

The soft drum beat resumes. **Mankwinji** *continues to recite her sorrowful poem.*

Mankwinji   I am a mother, a wife and a breadwinner:
A punching bag when the need arises:
Who gives me babies every two years? How do
I run far away from this when the chain of six children will
Follow me? How do I remove these chains that are wound
Around me when I am a mother, a wife, and a
Punching bag, tell me how?

A loud drum beat ends her poem interlude as she walks away offstage.

Scene Five

Aunt Sihle *enters the stage carrying a metal box, sits down and opens it. She takes out a photo of a pretty toddler and looks at it hard and holds it close to her chest.*

Yinka *enters bringing a water melon for her Aunt,* **Sihle** *smiles as she sees her niece.*

Aunt Sihle   What brings you here Yinka my niece? I wasn't expecting you till the exams were over, look at how beautiful you are, is this the dress I brought you last year when I went shopping in the city?

Yinka   Yes Aunt, do I look pretty in it?

Aunt Sihle   Stunningly beautiful, no one will know that you are a village girl; you are a grown woman, now the men will kill each other for you.

Yinka *laughs heartily and proceeds to sit down; her Aunty follows her putting the photo on top of the table.* **Yinka** *picks it up and takes a look at the photo.*

Yinka   Who is she; she is so beautiful and innocent?

Aunt Sihle *sighs and snatches the photo away from her niece.*

Aunt Sihle   I was just remembering someone from the past.

Yinka   I understand you worked in the city; do you sometimes miss the city life? Oh! With all this wealth, I doubt if you do.

Aunt Sihle *stands up and paces the room unsure if she should tell her niece the truth.*

Aunt Sihle   Today's young people dwell on cash and wealth, but life is more than that, you can be rich and miserable at the same time.

Yinka *notices the dry humour and misery in her aunt's demeanour stands up and holds her shoulder whilst facing her.*

Yinka   What is the matter Aunty?

Aunt Sihle   Yantonto is the problem, I thought I was done and over with her. Shumba has asked her to come again. If only she knew what wounds she opens by coming.

Yinka   Please talk to uncle and try and persuade him . . .

Dressed in a printed expensive shirt, a straw hat and khaki trousers **Shumba** *enters. Doffs his hat and smiles at* **Yinka**. *Views her, bottom up.*

Shumba   Your Aunt doesn't need to persuade me to let you stay. You are welcome anytime.

Shumba *doesn't let go of* **Yinka**'*s soft hand.* **Yinka** *careful slides her hand from his grip.*

Yinka   That could tear mama into pieces if I left. Beats me how she is going to cope when I am gone to college.

Shumba   College! What college? The white men's education is filling your head. You have a cultural responsibility in the village which you shouldn't forget about. From time immemorial, a woman's place is in marriage. You may as well be my second wife.

Aunt Sihle   Come on Yinka! Aim for the stars; let no one tell you otherwise.

Yinka *brightens a little bit and smiles at her aunty.*

Yinka   A pilot, flying in the sky. Yes, I want to fly.

Shumba *guffaws loudly and shakes his head insanely.*

Shumba   Who is going to pay for your tuition? Beside, that is a male-only profession.

Aunt Sihle   Shumba stop being cruel to her. We both know that she is intelligent. Yinka does very well in science subjects. Money shouldn't be an issue. As family, we could also contribute.

Shumba *is irritated at* **Sihle**'s *defence of her niece, and he shows it by the change of his tone.*

Shumba   As far as I am concerned, it is my money that you are making plans for, without consulting me first. I am done with this conversation. Yantonto will be in early tomorrow morning. Be ready for her.

Shumba *turns and leaves the two staring at each other in pain.*

Yinka   I have exhausted all the candles that you last gave me Aunty, could I have some more?

Aunty Sihle *sighs and gives her a hug.*

Scene Six

Mankwinji *enters the stage, then kneels at her grinding stone and starts grinding groundnuts to make peanut butter. She hums a tune in vernacular.*

Nqwayi *follows, a calabash of traditional beer in hand, carries a wooden stool. Sits opposite his wife.* **Mankwinji** *continues doing her job unmoved.*

Nqwayi   I have been thinking hard Mankwinji.

Mankwinji *stops grinding and looks at him.*

Nqwayi   Thusi is lazing around; he has so much idle time on his hands.

Mankwinji *changes to a sitting position and sets aside the grinding stone, and listens to her husband.*

Mankwinji   You have all my support if you are sending him back to school. That is a brilliant idea Baba. Will you ask your sister for help? When he is grown up, he could repay the money. Or better still, we could use Yinka's (*lobola*) dowry to repay it.

Hands in his pockets, **Nqwayi** *is up and pacing around the stage. He removes them, unsure as to how to break his news to his wife.* **Mankwinji** *stands up and joins him.*

Mankwinji   We always have to do the best for our children Baba, don't we?

Nqwayi   You are right Mankwinji, we have to do that. So, Thusi isn't going back to school this time, but instead he will go to work.

Mankwinji   You hardly have any relatives in the city, young as Thusi is, where would he stay? Rather, let us send him back to school. With the best education, he could be a better man, like Nkabinde's children.

Nqwayi   End of discussion, Thusi is leaving to start a new life on the farms in Madojwa. White men pay well, period.

Mankwinji *shakes her head not believing her ears. Tears, sorrow engulf her.*

Mankwinji   You have the guts to sell my son, how dare you do that? You sold all your livestock and now you are selling my children?

Sorrow tears her apart, she sheds tears.

Nqwayi   Stop sulking over my livestock. They belong to me. You are aware that they are the legacy paid for by my sister's dowry. I have every right over them.

Mankwinji *moves abruptly and catches* **Nqwayi** *unawares. She manhandles him, holds him close to her by the shirt collar.*

Mankwinji   You will have to kill me first, before you cart my children away.

Nqwayi   Why would I even kill my dear wife? The choice is yours. I could send your old mother away, to die in the forest. Or you let the young man go.

Mankwinji   You are aware that my mother is an invalid, why do you give me living hell? There is going to be payback time, you will pay, Nqwayi. You would sell my son for cigarettes and alcohol? Nqwayi, how do you come by the money you are spending these days? Those people must have paid you advance monies against my minor son. Your parents made the biggest mistake when they left you this homestead. That set a bad precedent of your not being gainfully employed, Nqwayi.

Mankwinji *loses her temper kicks the calabash spilling the contents.*
Nqwayi *tries to save the contents. He strikes his wife.* **Mankwinji** *walks off stage. He shouts behind her.*

Nqwayi   Get lost, man. Have you forgotten your place in this house Mankwinji?

Nqwayi *leaves the stage.*

Scene Seven

When **Yinka** *sings 'Amazing Grace' on the right wing of the stage to her brother, on the left side,* **Aunt Sihle** *is showing emotions through the pain that she is feeling, its music and emotions.*

Thusi *runs in holding one of* **Yinka**'s *aeroplane books.* **Yinka** *follows behind teasing him in a sisterly manner.*

Yinka   Please bring back my book Thusi, will you? You must know how I cherish those books.

Thusi   Don't worry sister; I just want to have a look at the planes. It is in safe hands. I am not TJ who will tear the pages.

Thusi *stops,* **Yinka** *decides against taking the book from him. Both stare at each other.*

A scary, ominous drumming sound in the background is heard, **Yantonto** *the herbalist enters the stage. She mixes concoctions and burns some herbs for use on* **Aunt Sihle**.

Shumba's *face shows evil intent as he enters the stage holding* **Aunt Sihle**. **Yantonto** *stares at them, but doesn't stop what she is doing.*

Aunt Sihle   Please Shumba! Don't let her do it, this time the herbs will kill me, I am begging you. The pain is so unbearable.

Shumba   Sorry my wife, there is no turning back. I have already paid the medicine woman, endure it like a woman.

Yantonto   Set her free! (*She reprimands* **Shumba**.)

Shumba   She could escape.

Yantonto   Hey! I said, get out of this room and close the door behind you. These herbs are capable of stopping her from escaping; she is already under their spell.

Shumba *doubtfully leaves the room.* **Aunt Sihle** *stands hypnotized, she awaits* **Yantonto**'s *instructions.*

Yantonto   Woman! Lie down on the floor and stretch your legs wide, will you? Shake your body; I haven't got the whole day. I have other clients elsewhere, waiting for me.

Aunt Sihle *complies.*

Yantonto   Rule number one: No screaming, if you scream, you won't be able to conceive do you hear me? Any screams that you make will block the fallopian tubes. Endure the pain like a woman, not like a girlie.

Yantonto *administers her herbs into* **Aunt Sihle**'s *genitalia.* **Sihle** *screams.* **Yantonto** *gives her evil stares and maintains her composure.*

Yinka *and* **Thusi** *relax. They continue with their conversation.* **Thusi** *hands the book over to his sister.*

Thusi   I would love to fly with you some day.

Yinka   On one condition, that you go back to school. Sit for your Ordinary Levels and then Advanced Levels.

Thusi   You are aware that dropping out of school wasn't my choice. Father could no longer afford the fees. Anyway, enough of this, for memory's sake, please *sisi* sing the song 'Amazing Grace' for me.

Yinka   Going somewhere my young brother?

Thusi   Not me, but you. I can feel that you will be going to college soon.

Yinka *sings 'Amazing Grace'.* **Yantonto** *gives* **Aunt Sihle** *bitter herbs, she scowls. Everyone joins in, as* **Thusi** *and* **Yinka** *move off stage.*

Yantonto   Woman! Keep your fingers crossed, in no time, you will fall pregnant. Trust me.

Yantonto *puts her remaining herbs into her small bag. She leaves the stage.* **Aunt Sihle** *sobs silently; she reaches for her metal box and from it, takes the photo of her beloved girl. She painfully exits the stage.*

Scene Eight

Nqwayi *enters the stage calling* **Thusi**. **Thusi** *runs in.*

Thusi   Here I am father.

Nqwayi   Son! You are a grown man now, so I believe it's high time you started looking after the family. Show me your manhood.

Puzzled, **Thusi** *looks at his father.*

Thusi   I am already doing all those things Baba. You know I tend Aunt's livestock, help mother in the fields and I even look after my siblings if Yinka is away. What more do I need to be doing?

Nqwayi   Every Jack and Jill can do that. I mean real work. I got you a man's job on one of the farms across the river. You are leaving today.

Thusi   I thought you and Aunt agreed to send me back to school.

Nqwayi   I don't have time to babysit you Thusi. Mankwinji! Come and bid your son goodbye.

Instead **Yinka** *appears first before her mother;* **Mankwinji** *follows her with a small bag containing* **Thusi**'s *belongings.*

Yinka   Goodbye! Where is he supposed be going to Baba? Am I missing something?

Thusi *hides behind his sister for protection.*

Thusi   Baba is sending me to take up employment on the farms across the river.

Yinka   I thought your goat would be the last thing you sold. How can you then sell a minor like Thusi to those farms known for weird and strange things? You are stealing his childhood they will make him a woman sooner than he knows, most of the men on the farms have no wives, young innocent boys end up fulfilling their sexual cravings. Baba, this is very cruel? (*She turns to her mother.*) Mama, what is in that bag?

Mankwinji *stares at the floor, but doesn't answer her probing daughter.*

Nqwayi   Yinka, you are crossing the line. This is Nqwayi's home, and his word stands. You can only question his decision elsewhere, not in this home.

Yinka   Mama, can't you do something to stop Thusi going to the farms? Children his age are school going.

Mankwinji *lets the bag fall down.* **Nqwayi** *manhandles the struggling* **Thusi**. **Yinka** *tries to wrest* **Thusi** *from her father. Instead,* **Mankwinji** *holds* **Yinka** *tight.* **Thusi** *is forcefully taken away by his father, and screams as he leaves the stage.*

Yinka *looks at her mother with hostility.*

Mankwinji   Sooner or later my daughter, the day will come for me to claim my rightful place as a mother. It will surely come. (*She says this poetically.*)

Yinka   You are doing the exact opposite mama. How do you dare support father's selling my brother, your own son? I am not getting what is happening.

Mankwinji   Daughter, when last did you visit your grandmother?

Yinka   Today, why? What has that to do with grandma?

Mankwinji   Yinka, you are such a clever woman. Your grandma is capable of managing her life on her own?

Yinka   We can't pretend that we don't know that she is an invalid. These could easily be her last days.

Mankwinji *silences her daughter by putting the middle finger to her lips.*

Mankwinji   Being a man, Thusi could easily survive the jungle better than my mother. More often, life doesn't give us choices.

Yinka   Oh! So father blackmailed you? How could he use grandma's condition as an invalid as a weapon against you? I can't imagine that you believed him.

Mankwinji   You don't seem to know your father; he is capable of cruelty.

Yinka *sighs and paces around the stage not quite understanding her mother.* **Aunt Sihle** *enters the stage looking so tired and pale.* **Yinka** *smiles.* **Mankwinji** *stands at some distance fearful of what her sister-in-law would say.*

Yinka   Aunty, I am glad you have come just in time. There is a crisis in this home.

Aunt Sihle   What crisis? Right now, I am so tired. I need to ask a favour from your parents.

Yinka   Baba is sending Thusi away, to take up employment on the farms.

Mankwinji *moves in swiftly and intercepts* **Yinka** *before she explains the situation to her aunt.*

Mankwinji   Aunt Sihle, you look so tired, how can we help? You have been such a rock to us. Now is our turn to return that favour.

Aunt Sihle *puts up a subdued smile at* **Mankwinji** *and holds her shoulder grateful that she is willing to help out.*

Aunt Sihle   I need Yinka to come over to my place for a few days. Shumba needs looking after, while I am away. I am visiting the doctors in the city; I have a problem with my abdomen. Can Yinka come over and fill my shoes?

Mankwinji   It's alright, I don't think Nqwayi will object to that.

Aunt Sihle   You don't mind, Yinka my dear, do you?

Yinka   No Aunty, I will do anything for you.

Aunt Sihle   Then pack your things. Your mother will put your father in the picture when he comes home. Stop stressing about Thusi; I will sort it out when I am back from the doctors.

Mankwinji   Yes Yinka, go and pack, I will tell your father.

Yinka *gives her mother a hate filled countenance. She turns and exits the stage, leaving her mother pacing up and down, not so sure of what to say.*

Mankwinji   I real didn't want to send Thusi away, but I had no choice. He is still able bodied. I could have gone from him, but the children, who will look after them? And my mother is old and frail.

She sighs.

Aunt Sihle   Of course my brother didn't give you any choices, what with the brood of children that he has brought into this world. He is unable to clothe and even feed them. Let me check on Yinka, we have to go. I also need to do the packing.

Mankwinji *sighs, moves off stage relieved that* **Aunt Sihle** *is not probing further.*

Scene Nine

Nqwayi *walks on the stage holding clear beer and sits on the chair on the side.*

Dressed in a nice suit, **Shumba** *walks in. He holds a pack of six beers and smiles as he spots* **Nqwayi**. **Nqwayi** *stands up as* **Shumba** *approaches.*

Shumba   Look at Nqwayi drinking clear beer! How did you come by the money?

Nqwayi (*laughs ecstatically*)   Sibali, you are so full of yourself. You think that you are the only ones that can make money and spend it.

Shumba   If I were you, I would stick to the traditional beer and leave clear beer to those who have no responsibility. By the way, did you buy maize meal for the family?

Nqwayi *is irritated, he paces the stage.*

Nqwayi   Sibali, don't push your luck with me; I am not responsible for your impotency. Back off from my children. You haven't paid for this beer.

Shumba   Hold it there Sibali? Quite the opposite, your sister has issues. She is barren, not me.

Shumba *fumes with anger.*

Nqwayi   Get lost Sibali. Who told you I could get drunk with a single bottle of beer? Not clear beer for that matter. For the record, you have been bedding all sorts of women in this village. You take me for an idiot for not telling my sister about them. Now, prove to all and sundry, how many of them were impregnated by you?

Shumba   Stop it, will you? Enough of your rubbish, man. Never set foot in my homestead again begging for food. You are so ungrateful, how dare you say such hurtful things to your benefactor?

Nqwayi   Oh! I won't. My boy is taking up employment at a farm and Yinka has finished school. Soon, eligible men will be queuing at my gate, ready to pay dowry for her.

Shumba   Has Yinka found the right man?

Nqwayi   Blessed with such good looks, it won't be long before suitors flood my homestead, asking for her hand.

Shumba   Are you quite certain about that?

Nqwayi   Keep your jealousy, Sibali. I will not be sharing any dowry money with you, forget it.

Shumba Nqwayi, let me shed light about myself. I own enough livestock to last me the next hundred years. For all I know, your daughter wants to fly. How can you even bank on someone so unpredictable?

Nqwayi Fly, how?

Shumba You are such a fool, becoming a pilot takes more than ten years. Think again, she is not someone to bank on.

Nqwayi Every human being in this village has a dream, but most of them are never realized. This is one dream that won't come true. Listen here Sibali, I have to go now, and we shall meet again.

Nqwayi *picks up his chair and beer and leaves the stage.* **Shumba** *follows with his pack of beers.*

Scene Ten

Aunt Sihle *enters the stage carrying her bag full of clothes; she is followed by* **Yinka** *who is carrying her handbag.*

Yinka Hoping you will be fine when you get back from the doctors. Aunty, are you so sure you are not pregnant?

Aunt Sihle Right now my niece, the river is in flood and flowing.

They both giggle at this.

Make sure that Shumba doesn't drink himself silly, and that he eats well.

Yinka You know me well; I am good at following instructions.

Aunt Sihle *looks at her watch and sighs.* **Shumba** *appears from the other wing of the stage, before she says anything.*

Shumba You are still here. I thought you would be long gone, when I got back. Don't let the doctors harm my son. I know you are pregnant. Yinka, I am so excited. Very soon you will be coming here to help your Aunt look after the baby.

Yinka *and* **Aunt Sihle** *quizzically look at each other.*

Aunt Sihle I have to go now Shumba, transport doesn't wait for passengers.

Shumba   Oh! Go well my wife. Do you have enough money on you? I wouldn't want to see you and my son struggling to survive.

Aunty Sihle   Stop stressing Baba, I have quite a substantial amount. During my absence, Yinka will look after you. I know you dislike meals prepared by the maid. At least Yinka is your niece.

Yinka   Aunty, hurry up, I can hear the sound of a bus.

She touches **Yinka***'s shoulders and shakes hands with her husband.*

Shumba   So long my wife.

Aunt Sihle *walks out of the stage with* **Yinka** *handing her the handbag and she turns and faces her uncle.*

Shumba   It's the two of us now; I hope we will enjoy each other's company.

Stares at her, bottom up.

Your father was right Yinka. You are now a grown woman; you could be any man's dream.

Yinka *looks at her uncle hard, not so pleased about his comment.*

Yinka   To live harmoniously, we both need to respect each other's spaces, don't you think uncle? I am not interested in what my father said. As far as I am concerned, that cruel old man doesn't exist in my life. He sends my brother to work on the farms rather than going to school.

Shumba   Oh! That explains the source of the money he was spending the other day. So he hadn't sold any goats. I should have known.

Laughs heartily and **Yinka** *stares at him, not believing what he was saying.* **Shumba** *moves closer to* **Yinka***, who moves away from him.*

Shumba   What are we having for lunch Sibali?

Yinka   You are the boss, tell me what to cook, I will do the rest.

Yinka *answers sarcastically.*

Shumba   According to our culture, I am as good as your husband. You have the freedom to decide whatever you want to prepare. I am off to the beer garden.

Shumba *turns and heads in the opposite direction.* **Yinka** *sighs and picks up her head gear and goes off stage.*

Scene Eleven

Mankwinji *enters the stage helping her mother to a sitting position; nearest where there is enough sunlight.*

Mankwinji   Enjoy the sun before it gets dark mama.

Mankwinji *kneels on the floor, washing plates when* **Nqwayi** *enters leaning on his walking stick as an aid.* **Mankwinji**'s *mother is sitting next to her, basking in the sun.*

Mankwinji   Mother! Are you getting the right amount of sunlight?

Mankwinji's Mother   Yes, thank you for bringing me out to the sunlight my child.

Showing tiredness.

Nqwayi *stands up and watches his wife going about her daily chores, before he speaks.*

Nqwayi   Why don't you let the girls wash the plates while you take a rest? You will need the energy in the fields, when they leave for school.

Mankwinji   Yinka has gone to Aunt Sihle's place; Thabitha and Banele have gone to fetch firewood.

Stops washing the plates and talks to her husband.

Nqwayi   Yinka will not be here for long. You may as well stop worrying about her. She will be gone soon, so don't waste your breath over her Mankwinji.

Mankwinji   She has gone to her Aunt, who can pay her college tuition.

Nqwayi   Not in this homestead, the word 'college' makes me sick. It surprises me who taught you that word. You fail to pronounce the word 'school' in English, now you are saying 'college'.

Mankwinji   I am sorry, Baba, if she is not going there, where else is she going?

Nqwayi   Open your eyes and behold how beautiful she is. Yinka is getting married very soon.

Mankwinji   Marriage! Baba, no! That is totally out, is she aware of that?

Nqwayi   She doesn't need to know. I know she will listen to you, that is why I am asking you to persuade her to get married.

Mankwinji *holds her mouth intent to vomit, not believing her husband.*

Nqwayi   Do you know what is at stake?

Nqwayi *casts an evil eye on* **Mankwinji's Mother**.

Mankwinji   No Nqwayi, you are making a big mistake. Yinka is much stronger than I am. You won't be able to sell her like you did Thusi. Think again, Yinka is different. Don't underestimate that she can take risks and go far.

Nqwayi   Scared of her, hey? Think of your old mother. I am sure you wouldn't want her to spend her last days wandering in the forest.

He walks closer to the old woman and kneels in front of her.

Feeling cold Mama, can I help you go to your hut? I could make some fire for you.

Mankwinji's Mother   Yes my son, it's too cold out here, please take me inside.

Nqwayi *turns and smiles at his wife.*

Nqwayi   Can you see how fond of her hut she is? Think about my proposal dear wife.

Mankwinji   This is your end Nqwayi. You have gone too far.

She gathers her plates and goes off stage.

Scene Twelve

Yinka *is holding her blankets and she enters the stage to prepare her bed.* **Shumba** *enters from behind, putting on his pyjamas and sits on the edge of the chair.*

Yinka *turns and looks him.*

Yinka   I thought you were already in bed.

Shumba   Just came to check if you were comfortable. Aren't you scared of sleeping alone?

Yinka   Come on uncle, I am a grown-up girl, what do you expect?

Shumba   I know you are a brave girl, I was just checking on you.

Yinka   You are already missing your wife. If all goes well, she should be back by tomorrow.

Shumba   She hasn't told me the good news, I am hoping she is pregnant.

Yinka *shifts her gaze to the floor embarrassed. She isn't keen to divulge any information about the pregnancy.*

Yinka   Good night uncle.

Shumba   Feel free to call me, if you are scared of sleeping all by yourself.

Shumba *smiles and goes to lie down on the opposite side of the room. As soon as* **Yinka** *falls asleep and starts snoring, he tip-toes to her side and drools over her as she sleeps.*

He tip-toes back as soon as **Yinka** *turns her sleeping position. On the way out, he steps on a tin that makes a sound as it falls.* **Shumba** *runs off stage.* **Yinka** *wakes up, stands up and tries to locate where the disturbance might have come from.*

Yinka   These rats are disturbing my sleep. I had better use the other room.

She picks up her blankets and moves off stage.

Scene Thirteen

Aunt Sihle *enters the stage carrying her bags and some groceries and calls her niece.*

Yinka *enters the stage, running from the other direction.*

Yinka   Nice to see you back Aunty, how are you feeling now?

Aunt Sihle   After the doctors cleaned my womb, the medication seems to be working well. The pains I had have disappeared. Anyway, how was your stay? I bet Shumba didn't make unnecessary demands.

Yinka   Thanks Aunty, you have improved, you will be well soon. Unfortunately, I won't be staying to monitor your recovery. Something has just come up. Mother needs me urgently.

Shumba   Welcome home my wife; I am glad you are back. Tell me the good news.

Yinka   I have to rush home; you can discuss your family issues in the privacy of your home.

She squeezes her Aunty's hand.

Aunt Sihle   Take your pick of any of the grocery carrier bags and take it home. I will be seeing you soon dear.

Yinka *turns and picks up one carrier bag and exits on the opposite side leaving the two facing each other.*

Shumba   I can hardly wait my wife, what is the good news?

Aunt Sihle *sighs before she speaks.*

Aunt Sihle   There is no pregnancy Shumba. The doctors found the problem in my womb.

Shumba   What! Are you joking Sihle?

Aunt Sihle   Trying so hard to get pregnant is stressing me. You should be seeking that assistance from the doctors yourself. Give me a break.

Shumba   If that is the case, I am done. I am in no position to listen to anything you say again. A second wife to help you is coming. This chapter is now closed.

Shumba *turns and leaves her screaming.*

Aunt Sihle   Shumba! You can't do that! Not after I have done so much for this home over the past ten years. You cannot do this to me.

She screams and follows him.

Scene Fourteen

Yinka *enters the stage calling her mother to come and have a look.*
Mankwinji *enters the stage checking to see if there is anyone following her.*

Yinka   Mama come and take a look.

Mankwinji   Listen to me very carefully Yinka. You are aware of how much I care about you, apple of my life. You are justified for hating me after what happened to your brother Thusi, but this time, give me an ear. Please listen to me.

Yinka   Mother what is it?

Mankwinji *sighs desperately, unsure how to tell* **Yinka** *about her father's plans. She takes out a black cloth with a herb inside from her*

pocket. She hands it to **Yinka** *and brings out money from her other
pocket.*

Yinka   What is this for?

Mankwinji   Please take it, I won't find any other time to give it
to you.

Yinka   I don't understand why you are doing this mama. I am sure you
need the money more than I do.

Mankwinji   Your father is determined to marry you off. He is looking
out for such a man.

Yinka *opens and closes her mouth not quite believing her ears.*

Yinka   That can't be true mama. Baba is aware that I want to go to
college, to be a pilot.

Mankwinji   You can. You can go, only if you listen to me.

Yinka   Who is the stranger that he is marrying me off to?

Mankwinji   I am not certain, but by your beautiful looks, he could
marry you off to a rich man. If you got married, my plan will be realized,
because I need the cattle to start a new life with my children. I know that
your greedy father won't sell them all. I will take whatever he will not
sell off and leave. I could join my cousin Manyawu in the east. He
offered me a piece of land. Your father still believes he passed away a
long time ago.

Yinka   Enough of yours, and your children's future plans, Mama,
where do I fit in?

Mankwinji   Simple my daughter, you can use the money that I just
gave you, use it to go to town. Stay with my brother's children.

Yinka   My uncle's place isn't the safest, and besides, father wouldn't
hesitate to go looking for me there. Mrs Manzi my teacher could be my
saviour. I have her contact address; I could stay there with her instead.
He wouldn't find me there. What is this concoction for?

Mankwinji   This is (*manqoba*) black magic that Yantonto gave me.
You need to spike it in your husband's drinking water. This will
hypnotize him, putting him to sleep for maybe two to three days. This
will give you ample time to run for your dear life.

Yinka   How could father do that, how dare he do that to me?

Mankwinji *just holds her daughter's hand and they exit the stage.*

Scene Fifteen

Shumba *enters holding a bottle of clear beer, he paces the stage like one possessed.* **Nqwayi** *enters the stage in a jovial mood whistling, throwing caution to the wind.* **Nqwayi** *stands at a distance and watches and laughs hysterically.*

Shumba   How long have you been standing there?

Nqwayi   Long enough to see your disturbed mind, I thought I was the only one who frequented the bar in the morning, out with it brother-in-law.

Shumba   Your sister is back from hospital.

Nqwayi   Hawu! Is she pregnant?

Shumba   I would be celebrating if she was. She is not.

Nqwayi   Oh! Too bad, I see, what is your next plan of action brother-in-law?

Shumba   What do you suggest I do since you are her brother?

Nqwayi *smiles at* **Shumba** *as if he is his saviour.*

Nqwayi   Simple. Then marry my daughter.

Shumba   What? Are you mad? Sihle would kill me.

Nqwayi   Take it from me, she would be glad that you married someone she gets along with and loves.

Shumba   Yes, you could be right. Then persuade your daughter. I know that she can be as stubborn. Convince her that after all, I am saving her from the wolves of this world.

Nqwayi   I am the man, I will handle it.

Shumba   How many cattle is she worth?

Nqwayi   Ten will do, one she is educated, two she is a virgin, and three she is not barren.

Shumba   Do I have any reason to refuse the offer?

Nqwayi   Man! Bide your time, other potential suitors will not wait for you. They will snap her before you do.

Shumba *offers him his hand and they shake hands and go their separate ways.*

Scene Sixteen

Aunt Sihle *is seated on a chair knitting a woollen scarf.* **Shumba** *puts on a serious face as he enters stage.*

Aunt Sihle   Afternoon Baba, you are early today.

Shumba   Won't you congratulate me for finding a second wife?

Aunt Sihle   What? You are not serious, I am not barren, I swear for all I know.

Shumba   Then prove it with a brood of junior Shumbas. From now on Sihle, there won't be any more arguments with you. Hahaha. . . .! Yinka is coming here to give me children.

Aunt Sihle   No, no, no! You cannot trick her into this. Is she aware of all this? Yinka will break down if she finds out.

She cries out loudly.

Shumba   Nqwayi should have told her by now.

Aunt Sihle   Both of you are evil beings. How can you cut short Yinka's dreams? (*She remonstrates with* **Shumba**.) Please Shumba, don't do that to her, it will destroy her.

Shumba   Too late for that Sihle. The dowry has already been pegged. Two old men will accompany me to Nqwayi's home tomorrow.

Shumba *leaves stage.* **Sihle** *tries to stop him, but instead he pulls her off him.*

Scene Seventeen

Yinka *enters the stage shouting back at her father.*

Yinka   No absolutely, I am not getting married to that old man. Father, you have sold everything else. You have the guts to do that to us your children again? Forget it; I would rather go away and never come back.

Nqwayi   If you leave, make sure that you take your grandma, mama and the rest of the children with you. I will no longer be responsible for them.

Yinka   Grandma is an invalid; I can't take her with me. I better leave alone.

Nqwayi   All is well my daughter, you are free to go. Mankwinji! Come here.

Mankwinji *enters the stage running;* **Yinka** *is staring at her father not quite believing what is taking place.*

Nqwayi   You may as well pack your clothes, take your mother and the children along and go. I don't want to find any of you here when I come back.

Mankwinji   Why Baba, invalid as she is, how am I supposed to carry her? What have we done to deserve this?

Nqwayi   Ask Yinka your daughter; I don't have time to explain.

He turns as if he is leaving.

Mankwinji   Yinka, what is it child?

Yinka   Father I give up, don't send them away. I will do as you wish.

Nqwayi   That is being a good girl. It shows that you love your mother dearly, doesn't it?

Yinka   It is okay mama, come along; everything is going to be fine. We need to be going; the boys are waiting.

Yinka *puts on a brave face and leads her sobbing mother off the stage.*

Sound of a wedding song, 'Umakoti ngowethu' (Our Bride, a traditional isiXhosa wedding song, sung by the in-laws family at the wedding), is sung backstage as they change costume and the set.

Umakoti ngowethu
usengowethu ngempela bo
uzosiwashel'asiphekele
sithi helele helele siyavuma

Umakoti ngowethu
usengowethu ngempela bo
uzosiwashel'asiphekele
sithi helele helele siyavuma

Umakoti ngowethu
usengowethu ngempela bo
uzosiwashel'asiphekele
sithi helele helele siyavuma.

English translation
The bride is ours
She is truly ours
She will do washing and cook for us
yes, we cherish we cherish with pride

The bride is ours
She is truly ours
She will do washing and cook for us
yes, we cherish we cherish with pride

I'm so happy that you're my bride
I'll stand beside you with love and pride
because I know how much you care for me
I will cherish you, cherish you eternally.

The whole cast enters the stage as the community that accompanies **Yinka** *to* **Shumba***'s homestead.*

Scene Eighteen

Yinka *prepares her bed, on the table is a full glass of water, a tooth brush and a bucket.* **Aunt Sihle** *enters the room.*

Aunt Sihle   Hey dear! How are you coping?

Yinka   You know very well Aunty that I have dreams. They won't be destroyed here.

Aunt Sihle *kneels on the floor closer to her and holds her shoulders.*

Aunt Sihle   I want you to know that this wasn't my intention. I wasn't part of it, I promise to make it up to you and make your dream come true.

Yinka   You have been there for us. Now it is my turn to make your life bearable. Aunty, you have suffered long enough. I think it is him, coming to bed.

Shumba *coughs to attract their attention.*

Aunt Sihle   The first time hurts Yinka. I am feeling guilty though. I wish it was to someone you loved that you surrendered your virginity to.

Yinka   Goodnight Aunty, look after yourself.

She squeezes her thumb tenderly. **Sihle** *goes out of the room.* **Yinka** *gets ready for* **Shumba**.

Shumba *enters the room putting on a vest and underwear.*

Shumba   Young wife! Are you ready for your man?

Yinka   More than ready.

Shumba   Come to me woman, I hope that they schooled you in the basics of handling a man at initiation. Anyway, I don't mind teaching my young virgin one or two tricks.

Smiles mischievously at her.

Yinka   Have you brushed your teeth, Baba?

Shumba   Clever girl, the whites gave you the best education. Bring me the tools.

Yinka *hands him the toothpaste, toothbrush and water.* **Shumba** *brushes his teeth.*

Shumba   The water has a queer taste Yinka. Is this borehole water?

Yinka   No, my husband it is a pinch of *mvusankunzi*, an aphrodisiac to enhance your performance in bed.

Hypnosis sets in.

Shumba   Yinka help me, I can't move my feet and hands.

Yinka *stands up and helps him on to the bed. The cup and the tooth brush are lying on the floor.*

Yinka   You will be alright Shumba. There is no need to panic, Aunt Sihle will be there for you.

Shumba   And . . . you . . . too. (*His voice becomes slurred.*)

Yinka   Sshshh! Just take a rest. (*She stands up and takes her bag and goes off stage.*)

Shumba *remains in hypnotized position.*

Scene Nineteen

Mankwinji *enters the stage and removes everything from the stage and goes off.*

The hypnosis on **Shumba** *wears off. He calls* **Aunt Sihle** *to come to his side.*

Shumba   Sihle! Sihle!

Aunt Sihle *enters the stage walking towards him unsure.* **Shumba** *makes an effort to rise but fails.* **Aunt Sihle** *guffaws loudly.*

Aunt Sihle   The clever girl has done strange things to you, my boy. For the record's sake, let me show you something before I help you.

She goes to the metal box and removes the photo of the young girl and shoves it into **Shumba**'s *face.*

Aunt Sihle   The girl is my daughter. Barren! Me haa, haa, haaa! Bother me if you can.

Shumba   Water, please water.

Aunt Sihle   I will give you water if you agree that you won't bother me again.

Shumba *nods head in affirmative.* **Aunt Sihle** *helps him stand up and they exit.*

Scene Twenty

Mankwinji *enters the stage from the left wing, like a demented woman and removes everything, she exits using the right wing.*

Nqwayi *enters the stage, surprise showing on his face. He looks around for* **Mankwinji**, *and the children.*

Nqwayi   Mankwinji!, Mankwinji! Where are you and the children? Mankwinji! You cannot leave Mankwinji, I will find you, Yinka, Thusi, Oyea! Oyeah! Oyeah!

The End

Glossary of terms

Ilala – African reeds that grow in rivers used for making mats and baskets.

Isitsha – Is made out of reeds (*ilala*), usually used to carry dried products from the fields.

Mbelekazi – Names usual given to domestic animals like goats and cows.

Mvusankunzi – A strong herb used by some African men to enhance their sexual performances.

Manqoba – An African herb that is dangerous and can paralyze a person if drunk in excess.

Ngowethu – Ours.

Sibali – A dear word used by men, when addressing a sibling of their wives, or nieces.

Sisi – Sister.

Umakoti – Bride.

Silent Voices

Adong Judith

Adong Judith is an alumna of Sundance Theater Lab and the Royal Court Theatre International Playwrights Residency currently living in her home country Uganda. Adong is a theater/film director, writer and producer who creates captivating plays and films that provoke and promote dialogue on social issues affecting underprivileged groups. She is a Fulbright Scholar and 2015 graduate of the Temple University MFA Film and Media Arts program, where she also took MFA Theater Directing classes. She won the Margaret McNamara Memory Fund Education Grant USA/ Canada 2014 and was voted among the WHO IS WHO in American Universities and Colleges 2015. Play titles to her name include: *Silent Voices, Just Me, You and THE SILENCE, Ga-AD, A Time to Celebrate, Holy Maria* and *Blood*, none of which have been previously published. Her work has been presented in different theatres in New York, London, Toronto, Chicago, and Kampala and is or has been studied at Princeton University, Dartmouth College, and University of North Carolina, Chapel Hill, where she has been invited as a visiting artist. 'This is an important piece that deserves to be heard and we are pleased to be providing an opportunity for audiences to connect with its message', commented Kevin Spacey, Academy Award-winning actor and Artistic Director of the Old Vic Theater in London, on Adong's play *Just Me, You and THE SILENCE*. Adong has won a Prince Klaus Laureate award for 2018.

Production history

Partly developed at the Sundance Institute Theatre Program – East Africa Lab in 2010, from stories Adong had collected from her hometown of Gulu in 2006, *Silent Voices* has had three productions in Uganda and readings in Kenya and New York City. Directed by New York-based British director, Dennis Hilton-Reid, the play received an acclaimed world premiere in 2012 at the National Theatre of Uganda amidst fear of Adong's arrest for her portrayal of the government's role in northern Uganda war crimes. The play was described in Uganda as 'the spiritual rebirth of theatre in Uganda since the decline of critical theatre due to political persecution of artists during the Idi Amin Regime'. It brought victims and political, religious, cultural, Amnesty and Transitional Justice leaders together for critical, transformative conversations.

To access local communities, Adong returned to three towns in northern Uganda, Gulu, Kitgum and Lira in 2015 with an Acholi language production, which she directed and ran back-to-back in Kampala at the National Theatre of Uganda with the English production of the play.

Critical introduction

Silent Voices is a story that mirrors the views and emotions of victims of the Northern Ugandan War. It explores how victims have been ignored in the constant calls by Amnesty International, transitional justice projects, governments, NGOs and political leaders, to 'forgive' and 'reconcile' with perpetrators at the expense of justice. Through the protagonist, Mother, who is a symbolic representation of life and death, *Silent Voices* examines what ordinary citizens can be driven to by unhealthy policies.

In 2006, as a Teaching Assistant and Masters student of Makerere University's Department of Performing Arts and Film, I returned to my war-ravaged hometown of Gulu to study the use of theatre in the psychosocial therapy of the children who filled the ranks of Kony's army, one of the largest child armies in human history. My study was based at World Vision Children of War Rehabilitation Centre and Gulu Support the Children Organisation (GUSCO). I became intrigued by the religious angle of the support provided to the children by the organization. I wondered if the children truly forgave their captors, the LRA commanders, as the sessions seemed to indicate. In my discussions with the children they confessed that if there was no hell, there was no way in hell that they would forgive the commanders. This inspired me to begin interviewing the children, women and men who survived Kony's reign of terror, delving deep into the communities where some of the children had already been 'reintegrated'. I listened to the anger and frustration expressed by victims about the Amnesty Act, which they felt 'rewarded' perpetrators for confessing to often heinous crimes. There was a great feeling of betrayal, bitterness and the need for revenge. I knew then that a dissertation that would gather dust in the academic shelves of Makerere University would be an injustice to these stories. I felt so strongly that these stories – these war-weary yet defiant voices – needed to be heard and witnessed by the world. This is why I wrote *Silent Voices*. The title isn't a reference to the people of Northern Uganda, whose voices are powerful, raw and stunning. Rather, it speaks to the repressive silencing these victims feel their government is forcing on them in the name of forgiveness.

Ironically, I shelved the play in 2007 after rejections from renowned Ugandan theatre makers I had approached for a possible production collaboration, who suggested that the play was too ambitious and therefore destined to fail and/or that it preached revenge. In 2010, I submitted it to Sundance Institute Theatre Program – East Africa Lab and it was selected.

The attention the play received at the lab was a little confusing to me at the beginning because of all the previous rejections. It wasn't until Kenyan actress, Lillian Amimo, broke down in tears during the cold reading of the play that its power registered. I had written a play about Uganda, but it spoke to Kenya's post-election violence (2007), Rwanda's genocide (1994) and other post-conflict communities around the world.

A One-Act Play Based on Interviews with War Crimes Victims of the Northern Uganda War (1986–2006).

For the people of Northern Uganda, especially victims of the over two-decade Northern Uganda War.

Setting of the play

The play is set in Northern Uganda, years after the over two decades of war and subsequent peace talks that ended the war. The plays shifts from prison to bush to rehabilitation centre, court room, etc.

Characters in the play

The original production was staged with 30 performers as shown below because it was important for the playwright/producer to capture the communal essence of the Acholi people. However, recognizing financial challenges usually involved in productions, especially in a capitalistic world, producers and/or directors can choose to use the number of cast as per their discretion as long as it does not interfere with meaning of the play as intended.

Adult cast

Mother, *a former slave wife to a rebel commander now in her fifties. She is mother to* **Omony**.

Guard 1/Man, **Mother**'s *security guard in prison, who in Mother's unstable mental state becomes* **Man**, *the rebel leader.*

Guard 2/Boss, **Mother**'s *security guard in prison, who in Mother's unstable mental state becomes* **Boss**, *the* **President**.

CID/Mediator/LC5/Judge, *a pompous crime investigator, who in* **Mother**'s *unstable mental state becomes the peace talks* **Mediator**, **Local Council 5** *and* **Judge**.

Juma/Journalist/MP/Court Clerk, *a police officer who works closely with the CID, who in* **Mother**'s *unstable mental state becomes a* **News Anchor, Journalist, Member of Parliament** *and* **Court Clerk**.

Husband, *a young man in his early thirties, son of former rebel leader.*

Wife/Prosecutor, *a young woman in her thirties, married to* **Husband** *who in* **Mother**'s *unstable mental state becomes the* **Prosecutor**.

Margaret, *the granddaughter of former rebel leader and niece to* **Husband,** *who currently works as a former child soldiers' rehabilitation officer.*

Omony, *a young, likable man,* **Mother***'s son and boyfriend to* **Margaret.**

Bishop/Mother's Lawyer, *a Catholic Bishop, who in* **Mother***'s unstable mental state becomes her* **Lawyer.**

Child cast

Boy 1/Boy 4, *a 12-year-old former child soldier who is also Commander Man and Kadogo NoJoke.*

Boy 2/Cdr. Shooter/Kadogo NoJoke, *an 11-year-old former child soldier who is also Odokonyero Richard, Mother's brother, Kadogo Smiles and Commander Shooter.*

Boy 3, *a 10-year-old former child soldier who is also Commander Danger Hatari.*

Kadogo Action/Cdr. AK47/Kadogo Smiles, *an 8-year-old former child soldier who is also Kadogo Action and Commander AK 47.*

Boy 5/Kadogo Ninja/Cdr. Long Range, *a 9-year-old former child soldier who is also Kadogo Ninja, Commander Long Range and Mother's brother.*

Girl 1/Cdr. AK47's Bride/Cdr. Danger Hatari's Wife, *a 6-year-old former slave wife who is also Aber Flavia, Mother's sister and Commander Danger Hatari's wife.*

Girl 2, *an 8-year-old former slave wife whose name is Alal and is also young Mother/Commander Danger Hatari's bride.*

Girl 3/Cdr Shooter's Bride /Atuku /Scovia, *an 11-year-old former slave wife whose name is Abur, is also Commander Shooter's bride and Atuku, Commander Danger Hatari's senior wife.*

Girl 4/Cdr Long Range's Bride/Brenda/Cdr Danger Hatari's Wife, *a 10-year-old former slave wife who is also the bride to Commander Long Range, wife to Commander Danger Hatari and Brenda.*

Girl 5/Fiona/Cdr Man's Bride, *a 6-year-old former slave wife who is also Fiona and Commander Man's bride.*

Dancers

Dancer/Boss' Delegate/Woman/Crowd, *dancer who is also Boss' delegate in the peace talks, court witness woman and crowd member.*

Dancer/Amal/Crowd, *dancer who is also Amal, Mother's mother and crowd member.*

Dancer/Bride/Crowd, *dancer who is also the bride of the marriage ceremony at Mother's homestead and crowd member.*

Dancer/Waitress/Soldier 1 & 3/Crowd, *dancer who is Waitress at the peace talks hotel, government soldier 1 and 3 and crowd member.*

Dancer/Groom/Man's Delegate/Crowd, *dancer who is also the groom of the marriage ceremony at Mother's homestead, Man's peace talks delegate and crowd member.*

Dancer/Mediator's Asst./Man 2/Crowd, *dancer who is also Mediator's assistant at the peace talks hotel, court witness as Man 2 and crowd member.*

Dancer/Waiter/Soldier 5/Crowd, *dancer who is also Waiter at the peace talks hotel, government soldier 5 and crowd member.*

Dancer/Soldier 2/Man 1/Crowd, *dancer who is also government soldier 2, court witness Man 1 and crowd member.*

Dancer/Waiter/Soldier 4/Crowd, *dancer who is also Waiter at the peace talks hotel, government soldier 4 and crowd member.*

Dancer/Latigo/Crowd, *dancer who is also Latigo, Mother's father and crowd member.*

The entries, exits, scene transitions and position of characters on stage are merely suggestions, not in any way to limit directors' creativity. Directors are free to exercise their own creative liberties and/or discretion.

Prologue

Prison

Darkness reigns. Loud live Nanga of a sombre Acholi war song, Ubol
Muduku Piny *(Surrender the Gun), plays.*

*A spotlight reveals a live Nanga player/singer downstage right, who
continues playing and singing through the scene.*

*Rays of light from the small prison ventilation above reveal a silhouette
of* **Mother**. *She rocks a blanket that in her mind is a baby, which she
interacts with through mime in different ways. Her movement in Prison
must be limited, unable to go beyond the 'cage'.*

Lights flood up and reveals two male prison guards flank **Mother** *on either
side with guns in their hands;* **Guard 1** *right and* **Guard 2** *left, and a little
dirty old plastic bucket that stands close by and serves as* **Mother**'s *toilet.*

Moments later, the **CID** *walks in, closely followed by a policeman,*
Juma. *The* **CID** *holds a bunch of keys that he keeps rubbing with his
fingers.* **Juma** *carries a clipboard or notebook and pen.*

The **CID** *looks at* **Mother**, *who smiles at him, beckoning him to take the
'baby'. The* **CID** *sneers at her and continues, stopping next to* **Guard 2**.

Mother *realizes that what she is carrying is a blanket not a baby. She
quickly hurls it away*

The live 'nanga' dies down.

CID (*to* **Guard 2**)   Any change?

The guards shake their heads to indicate no change.

CID (*to* **Juma**)   The suspect hasn't exhibited any change.

Juma *notes.*

CID (*to* **Guard 1**)   Did she receive any visitors?

The guards shake their heads again.

CID (*to* **Juma**)   The suspect hasn't received any visitors.

As **Juma** *makes to write, his cell phone rings. It has the ring tune of a
baby laughing.*

In **Mother**'s *mind, this triggers the sound of laughter of her little sister,
Aber Flavia, who was killed by the rebel leader* **Man** *during their
journey, right after abduction.*

Juma *panics, afraid of the* **CID**. *He reaches for the phone and quickly turns it off and resumes taking notes.*

The laughter in **Mother***'s mind continues, now hauntingly turning into:*

Sister Voice   What about me?

She looks around wondering where the voice is coming from.

The **CID**, **Juma** *and the guards wonder what is going on.*

A dozen ghostly voices of the victims offstage.

Victim Voices   What about me?

What about me?

What about us?

Mother *is perturbed by the ghost voices.*

CID   What about me?

The voices go quiet. She stares hard into the audience but not specifically at the audience.

Mother   Why do you all look at me like so? Is it because of the chains? Or is it because of where I am right now? Do you find that curious? Well, if I were you I wouldn't. But then again who would listen to the advice of an old haggard woman like me? But you know something? The space between you and me is not that far. The distance is just . . . It was a full mist day. But the sun penetrated that mist and disappeared almost immediately. We were all happily hopeless with our full mist day. But the sun just sneaked in with promises. They called it peace talks.

A loud whistle goes off. Several prison doors open and close with a heavy bang. Sounds of prisoners getting out of their prison cells heard offstage.

The prison sounds trigger **Mother***'s memory. In her mind, all the characters on stage become characters from the peace talks. The two guards become* **Boss** *and* **Man** *in a peace talk session.* **Mother** *turns around to watch them, her back turned to the audience.*

Boss *is smartly dressed in a suit and* **Man** *in a long flowing white robe.*

The **CID** *becomes the* **Mediator**, *dressed like* **Boss**. *He stands and watches helplessly as* **Boss** *and* **Man** *argue.*

Mother *too watches them quietly, shocked at how self-absorbed they are.*

Juma *becomes the journalist. He captures the moment with his camera.*

In the far distance, sounds of an on-going battle between the rebel group and government can be heard.

Boss (*faces* **Man**)   You must surrender!

Man (*faces* **Boss**)   I'll not surrender!

Boss   I say surrender now!

Man   I will not surrender!

Boss   If you know what is good for you, you will surrender now before it's too late for you!

At this point they begin to sing their lines as they move towards **Mother** *still facing each other.*

Man   Who do you think you are to tell me what is good for me?

Boss   And who do you think you are, terrorizing my people?

Unable to hold back, **Mother** *makes to intervenes, but is stuck in her cage. She stretches out her hand(s) to them in a bid to stop them.*

Mother   Stop it! What kind of peace talk is this!

None of them hears or even notices **Mother***'s presence.*

Man   I am a freedom fighter!

Boss   Freedom fighters don't fight like you.

Man   I fight with divine powers! You're nothing but a terrorist!

Mother *tries again but still;* **Boss** *and* **Man** *ignore her. Their argument overlap* **Mother***'s lines, frustrating her effort.*

Mother   This is not about you two.

Boss   You are the terrorist . . . !

Mother   This is about the people of Uganda!

Boss   Living in the jungles of terrorists!

Mother   It's about people who have spent twenty years in fear, in camps, in captivity, in agony.

Man (*laughs loudly*)   But many years ago, when you were in my position and someone else in yours, you were called a terrorist! A bandit! If I were in your shoes and you in mine, you would be the terrorist!

Mother   This is about peace for all!

Man   So, don't use that word here!

Frustrated, **Mother** *signals the* **Mediator** *to intervene and drops down on the floor in frustration. The* **Mediator** *steps in between* **Boss** *and* **Man,** *trying to stop them. They halt standing right over* **Mother.**

Boss   Everybody knows you are fighting for nothing.

Man   I fight for a good cause. I fight with divine instruction. You fight for money.

Boss (*turns to the* **Mediator**)   Will you please tell this barbarian to civilize up?

The **Mediator** *pats* **Boss** *on the shoulders trying to calm him down, wearing a plastic smile that is almost genuine.*

Man   What did you just call me? (*To the* **Mediator.**) Will you tell him to stop calling me a barbarian?

The **Mediator** *pats* **Man** *on the shoulders too with the same plastic smile. The* **Mediator** *and* **Boss** *exchange a familiar look.*

Boss   Fine! I will stop and listen for the sake of the people!

Boss, *the* **Mediator** *and* **Mother** *all look at* **Man,** *waiting.*

Man   Alright for the sake of the people! (*To the* **Mediator.**) So let's start by telling him to take people out of the camps.

Boss   And tell him to stop abducting and killing them!

Man   I'm not an abductor! I'm not a murderer! I'm just a . . .

Mediator   Please.

Man   Am ready to . . . I will stop if he stops calling me a murderer and recognizes me as a true freedom fighter.

Boss   I will stop calling you a terrorist if you come out of the bush. Nobody will hurt you.

Mediator   Now you are talking.

Celebratory guitar plays, preferably a live guitar player, as the next sequence of events unfold in slow motion. The **Mediator** *notices something offstage. He approaches while* **Boss** *and* **Man** *look on eagerly. An attractive* **Waitress** *approaches with glasses of wine. They meet half-way all smiles.* **Mediator** *reaches out for two glasses of wine and* *hands one to* **Boss** *and the other to* **Man**. *He returns, picks up one glass for himself and turns back. They form a triangle around* **Mother**, *toast, spilling wine on her, and drink.*

Mediator   Let's find a better place to pursue the future, brothers. (*He raises his glass in the air.*) The future awaits!

They turn around walking upstage to where the guards stood guard earlier as the **Waitress** *exits.*

The **Journalist** *reports the news back to his home station in Kampala.*

Journalist   . . . Yes, thank you very much, Jacqueline Namazzi. I am reporting live from the Southern Sudan capital of Juba, where the peace talks between the rebel leader Man Kilama and the president, Boss Muherwe have started on a bumpy note. However, all is not bleak as the mediator, Wani Luate, seems to be doing a great job. I must admit Mr. Wani Luate has shown great mediation skills by getting both Man and Boss to stop the character attack and blame game in consideration for a peaceful chat. We can only hope that the peaceful chat will go smoothly. Jacqueline Namazzi, New Africa TV, Tonight.

Lights slowly black out as all return to their original characters and positions.

Mother   I was happily hopeless with my full mist day but the sun sneaked into my mist. The sun sneaked in, sounding all musical.

Mother's *silhouette figure as the rays of light slowly fade out.*

Jungle

Approaching authoritative voice of a boy commanding.

Boy 1 Voice   Move. Move it.

Several wasted children tied up in ropes attached to each other's waist, carrying heavy loads, enter the stage in one line.

A little girl in the middle is dragging herself along and slowing down the group.

Boy 1, *in neat army uniform and boots, walks ahead of the group and is well-guarded by two smaller boys, also in army gear. He halts the group.*

The audience must always be addressed as part of the different groups: rebels, community, public attendants at a court hearing . . .

Boy 1 (*authoritatively*)   Who is slowing us down?

The captives don't respond.

Boy 1   Don't make me ask again.

The captives still don't answer.

Boy 1 (*to his guards*)   Kadogos.

Kadogo Ninja/Action   Yes, Teacher Man.

Boy 1   100 canes each should warm them up to talk.

The children shudder in fear. Two of the front children, scared out of their wits cry out simultaneously pointing to the little girl in the middle.

Both   She is the one slowing us down.

Boy 1 *signals the* **Kadogos***. They go and untie the little girl bringing her to the front.*

Boy 1 *intimidatingly moves close to the little girl.*

Boy 1   Young girl, you will have to choose. You either walk fast or I send you home.

Girl 1 (*kicks him*)   I want to go home.

Boy 1 *is caught off-guard, torn between the pain of the kick and maintaining his authority.*

Boy 1 (*to the little girl*)   Your new home is with us.

He addresses all pacing from one end of the file to the other.

Boy 1   From today onwards, we are your mother, father, brother and sister. Do you hear me?

Girl 1   But I don't want a new home. I want to go back to my home. I want my mummy.

Boy 1 *contemplates for a moment and then begins to laugh scornfully.*

Boy 1   Very well then. You are slowing us down anyway. (*To his guards.*) Kadogos, send . . . (*To the girl.*) What is your name?

Girl 1   Aber Flavia.

Boy 1   Send Aber Flavia home. We have no time for her kind.

A slightly older boy from the back of the line speaks up.

Boy 2 (*fearfully*)   Sir, she's . . ./

Boy 1   I am not a sir. It's teacher.

Boy 2 (*even more scared*)   Teacher, she is too young to go back home alone. She will die alone in the wilderness.

Boy 1 *turns, looks at him and smiles.*

Boy 1 (*sweet*)   Do you want to take her home then?

Boy 2 (*eager*)   Yes Siii . . . Teacher.

Boy 1 *signals the* **Kadogos** *to untie* **Boy 2**. *They untie and bring him to the front, right hand side of* **Girl 1**. **Boy 1** *approaches him looking straight in the eyes.*

Boy 1   Can you take her home well?

Boy 2   Yes. Yes of course. She is my sister.

Boy 1   What is your name?

Boy 2   Odokonyero. Odokonyero Richard.

Boy 1   Good.

He turns to **Kadogo Action** *and signals him to give* **Boy 2** *the machete.*

Kadogo Action *quickly draws his machete and hands it to* **Boy 2**. *The boy looks at the machete puzzled.*

Boy 1   Go ahead and send your sister home.

The boy looks at the commander confused. A girl and boy at the back of the file are overly affected by this.

Boy 1   You offered to send her home. So, send her home now.

Odokonyero realizes what 'sending her home' means and drops the machete, bewildered.

Boy 2 (*shaking*)   But I thought . . . no, no. Please . . ./

Boy 1 *picks up the machete and firmly places it in his hands.*

Boy 1   Send her home or Kadogo Action and Kadogo Ninja here will send you both home.

Boy 2   But she is my sister . . ./

Boy 1 (*pats the* **Kadogos** *on the shoulders*)   We are your sisters and brothers.

The **Kadogos** *nod in agreement.* **Boy 1** *addresses all as he moves towards Aber.*

Boy 1   In our struggle, whoever does not cooperate is our enemy.

He caresses Aber on the cheek.

Boy 1   Right now, Aber is our enemy. (*To* **Boy 2**.) She has to be sent home.

Boy 2 (*falls to his knees*)   Please sir, she is only a child. She didn't know what she was saying.

Boy 1   There is no room to be a child in the struggle. We are the chosen ones, nurtured by the spirit of the struggle for liberation.

Boy 2 (*desperate*)   I will carry her on my back. That ways she won't slow us down.

Boy 1   And who will carry your load?

The girl at the back of the file who has been overly affected by this tries to step forward only to realize she is tied up.

Girl 2   I will.

Boy 1 *signals the Kadogos to untie* **Girl 2**. *They untie and bring her to the front, left hand side of* **Girl 1**.

Boy 1 (*turns around to see her*)   And who are you?

Girl 2   Cecilia. Cecilia Achan.

Boy 1   A sister?

Boy 2 *realizes what this means and tries to save his sister.*

Boy 2   No, I don't know her.

Boy 1 (*to* **Boy 2**)   Are you lying to us?

Boy 2   No.

Boy 1   Brothers and sisters do not lie to each other. Otherwise . . .

He makes the sign of chopping the head.

Boy 2   I am not lying, Teacher. Ask her.

Boy 1 (*to* **Girl 2**)   Are you their sister?

Boy 2 *stares hard at* **Girl 2**.

Girl 2   No. I just wanted to help.

Boy 2 *sighs, relieved.*

Boy 1 (*to* **Girl 1**)   Is she your sister?

Both **Boy 2** *and* **Girl 2** *quickly look at* **Girl 1**, *worried.*

Girl 1   I want to go home.

Boy 1   Very well then. We won't delay you any further. We have wasted enough time here as it is. Now, one last time, send your little sister home now or (*to* **Kadogo Ninja** *and* **Kadogo Action**) they will send you both home.

Boy 2 *looks at the commander, his eyes begging.*

Boy 1   I said now.

Boy 2 *raises his machete as if to strike* **Girl 1** *but halts unable to. He drops the machete down.*

Boy 1   Kadogos.

Kadogos   Yes, Teacher Man.

The **Kadogos** *take hold of* **Boy 2** *and* **Girl 1** *and lead them offstage.*

Boy 1 (*to the rest*)   The rest of you must watch as Aber and Odokonyero are sent home. This will serve as a reminder to all those who delay us or want to go home.

The children shudder.

Boy 1   Kadogos ready?

Kadogo Ninja/Action   Yes, Teacher Man.

Boy 1   Good. All of you look to the left.

The children turn looking to the left.

Boy 1   Okay. Kadogos, Now!

We hear screams of pain as the boy and girl are killed.

Live Acholi dirge song plays on the 'nanga' instrument until the two **Kadogos** *return wiping their bloody machetes.*

Boy 1   Does anyone else want to go home?

The children quickly chorus, 'No'.

Boy 1   Good. I am Commander Man and I will be your commander until we make it to the base. However, you will call me Teacher Man.

And so will you call all the commanders you will meet at the base. We are your teachers, sent by God to teach you and together we will rescue our people from oppression. Am I clear?

All   Yes, Teacher.

Boy 1   Teacher who?

All   Teacher Man Sir.

Boy 1   Teacher Man only will do. No need for a sir. I am not British. Now, in the military speed is of the essence. We must be at the base in exactly 45 minutes otherwise we risk an attack by the enemies. That said, I will not tolerate snails. Do you hear me?

All   Yes, Teacher Man.

Boy 1   Good. I like fast learners.

He signals **Girl 1** *and* **Boy 2**'s *load to* **Kadogo Ninja**.

Boy 1   Add that to Achan's load. (*To* **Achan**.) You said you wanted to help.

Kadogo Ninja *adds to* **Girl 2**'s *load. It over weighs her but she struggles not to let it show.*

Boy 1   Let's proceed. Like I said, we have exactly forty fi . . . (*looks at his watch*) forty-two minutes now to be at base.

Hand clapping emits from offstage. **Margaret**, *a young, beautiful and smartly dressed lady enters clapping, trying hard to hold back her tears from watching such an experience.*

Margaret   That was very good work Candano. Let's untie ourselves out of the rope.

Reveal

JuaKali Former Child Soldiers Rehabilitation Centre

Different expressionistic drawings of war experiences by children hang upon the wall.

The children struggle out of the rope and sit centre stage forming a circle. **Margaret** *joins the circle.*

Margaret   How many of us had a similar experience to that of Candano on the way to the base after abduction?

Almost all the children put up their hands.

Margaret   So, who is volunteering to pick up the story from where Candano has stopped? Let's say . . . what happened when you arrived at the base?

Girl 2 *and another girl put up their hand.*

Margaret   One of you will go first, then the other second.

Girl 2/3   I will go first.

Girl 2   But I had already even told Candano that I would go after him.

Girl 3   But Candano is not in charge here.

Girl 2   Neither are you.

Girl 3   Well, I am going next.

Girl 2   We are no longer in captivity where you used to be in charge of everything and everyone.

Margaret   Come on you two, let's not fight over this.

Girl 2   But Abur likes to bully others. (*To* **Girl 3**.) And yet considering what you did to us in captivity we shouldn't even be playing with you.

Children (*chorus*)   Yes, yes, yes.

Margaret   Okay, that's enough. Let's throw the ballot paper.

The school bell goes. All the children shout in unison, 'porridge time, porridge time.'

Children (*chorus*)   Porridge time. Porridge time.

Margaret (*excited*)   Okay. Okay. We will throw the ballot paper later.

The children run out excitedly. **Margaret** *follows them.*

Man's Ancestral Homestead

*A well-to-do couple's house. A woman (**Wife**) in a black dress and black head-tie sits quietly on the sofa. The first impression she gives is that she would win a quarreling contest.*

Live Acholi dirge plays mildly.

*A man (**Husband**) with a serious demeanour but very spirited enters carrying a **Little Girl** of about 7, playing tickle.*

He notices the quiet woman on the sofa and puts the girl down drawing closer to the woman as the girl runs to the bedroom.

Husband   You need to get out of that.

Wife   I am still in mourning.

Husband   For how long are you going to be in mourning?

Wife   For as long as I am still in mourning.

Husband   And how long would that be?

Wife   I don't get how you can be so calm in the middle of all this. Children are disappearing!

Husband   We don't know if these children are dead. And that's the reason why you should put away that black thing.

Wife   This black thing? What is wrong with you?

Husband   You can't mourn the dead more than the bereaved. The parents of the missing kids are up and about.

Wife   That's what I don't understand. It's like you don't care. It's like everyone doesn't care.

Husband   Of course, I care. We care.

Wife   I don't get it.

Husband   Of course, you don't get it. You are new here. You can't get it.

Wife   What do you mean?

Husband *doesn't answer.*

Wife   Do you know something I don't know?

Husband *still doesn't answer.*

Wife   Is that why only the children in this family are disappearing?

The little girl comes running back in with the 'Nanga' calling out to her dad.

Little Girl   Play it, Dad.

Husband   Not now, Fiona.

Fiona   Come on, Dad. Play it. Play it so I can teach mom how to dance. How I learned it from school.

Husband, *who sees this as the perfect opportunity to get* **Wife** *out of her sombre mood, takes the instrument and begins to play, singing an Acholi 'wife praise' song.*

Fiona *begins to dance, calling out to her mother to see. Unable to resist the child's charm,* **Wife** *smiles.* **Fiona** *reaches out to her, beckoning her to her feet.*

The two begin to dance, putting a smile on **Husband** *'s face as he takes a seat on the sofa. While* **Fiona** *dances on her toes,* **Wife** *dances with her feet stamped to the ground.*

Fiona   It's not like that, Mom.

Wife   How?

Fiona   Do this. Stand on your toes like this. Right toe before the left toe.

Wife *tries to follow struggling.*

Wife   It's difficult.

Fiona   It's not, Mom. I just learned it at school in a day.

Wife *does it staggeringly.*

Fiona   Yes, like that. Then move back and forth like this.

Fiona *dances showing her.* **Wife** *tries and fails miserably.* **Husband** *and* **Fiona** *laugh out loud.*

Wife   You two are such sadists.

Husband *and* **Fiona** *laugh even more.*

Wife   Okay, this is it. I am not doing this so you two can laugh at me.

Husband   Well, to become a true Acholi wife, you have to.

Fiona   It's hard at the beginning, Mom, but let's keep trying.

Husband   It's like learning how to ride a bike. You never learn without a fall at least.

He laughs.

Fiona   Just ignore Dad, Mom. Let's do it.

Husband *starts to play the instrument again and the two start to dance.*

Just then, **Margaret** *enters with some groceries. They are excited to see her,* **Wife** *more.*

Wife   Finally, someone I can team up with.

Margaret   Team up for what?

Wife   I am trying to learn the 'nanga' dance but I have the worst teachers ever.

Margaret (*puts the groceries down*)   I wish I could be of help but sorry, you are on your own.

Wife   Why won't you help me?

Margaret   Not won't, Aunt. Can't. Omony and I have something very important to do.

Wife (*curious*)   Something important like what?

Margaret   Just something important.

Wife   Important like a proposal?

Margaret   I am not telling.

Fiona   What's a proposal, Aunt Margaret?

Margaret *chuckles.* **Husband** *smiles.*

Margaret   That's a type of sweet, my dear. Like a lollipop.

Fiona *starts to jump up and down singing that she wants a proposal.* **Husband** *chuckles.* **Margaret** *and* **Wife** *are amused.* **Margaret** *playfully pinches* **Fiona**'*s cheek.*

Margaret   You will get plenty of proposals when the time is right.

She grabs one or two of the groceries leaving some behind.

Margaret   I have to go. You all enjoy your dance.

Fiona (*runs after* **Margaret**)   Mom, can I go with Aunt Margaret and have some proposals?

Wife (*grabs her back*)   No my dear, Aunt Margaret is already going to have some proposals with someone else. I will buy one for you later when I have time.

Fiona   I can buy it for myself.

Wife   No, you can't. Can we dance now and do sweets later?

Fiona   But I want it now, Mom.

Wife   What's wrong with you, Fiona? I said I will buy the sweets later. Do you want to go out there and disappear like all the other kids who are disappearing?

Fiona *cowers, scared.* **Husband** *rises, putting the instrument aside.*

Husband   Come on, don't talk to her like that.

Wife   And how should I talk to her?

Husband   Like a child.

Wife   You see. You are always spoiling her. She needs to know that there is danger out there.

She turns to **Fiona**, *who cowers even more.*

Wife   If you don't stop going out alone to buy your sweets, the ogre out there will eat you up.

Husband   Will you stop scaring the little thing?

Wife   Fine, knock yourself out.

She exits, grabbing the groceries left by **Margaret**. **Husband** *reaches for* **Fiona** *and hugs her.*

Husband   It's okay. Let's go buy your proposal.

Fiona   What of the ogre, Dad? What if it eats me up?

Husband   The ogre won't touch you when you are with me.

He lifts her up, exiting.

Mother's Ancestral Homestead

Mother *sits on an old dirty traditional Acholi papyrus mat on the floor of her empty house and winnows millet grains. By her side in a large sauce pan, 'ladod', used to hold clean grain and other things in Acholi culture. A small local tin-made oil lamp sits at a corner.*

A large painting of an Acholi homestead with a huge hen crowing right in front of it hangs up the back.

In the background, she hears voices of children playing and laughing in the nearby neighbourhood.

Mother   What is a family? When does a home become a home? It's so quiet. So still. The silence is deafening. It's so silent here you can hear the voice of silence.

She begins to winnow. As she winnows, she hums the melody of the Acholi song Bedo i Wilobo Yelo Wiya.

Mother (*sings*)   Hmm, bedo i wilobo yelo wiya lakonya peke
Maa atoo woko

Hmm, cwer cwinya man neka woko adoko gwok pa jii
Hmm, pur bene apuru kena lakonya peke
Maa atoo woko
Hmm, cwer cwinya man neka woko we adoko gwok Pa jii Maa tedo
bene atedo nono lacamo peke
Maa atoo woko
Hmm, cwer cwiny man neka woko adoko gwok pa jii.

[English translation:
Ooh living in this world haunts me, no one to help me
Mother, I wish I would die
Ooh this sadness kills me I have become other people's dog
Ooh even farming I farm alone, no one to help me
Mother, I wish I would die
Ooh this sadness kills me I have become other peoples' dog
Mother, even cooking I cook for nothing no one to eat it Mother, I wish I
would die
Ooh this sadness kills me I have become other peoples' dog.]

As **Mother** *pours a little of the clean grain into the saucepan,* **Omony**
enters all smiles closely followed by **Margaret** *holding some groceries.*
Mother *doesn't see her properly.*

Omony   I have brought you the visitor I talked about, Mother.

Mother *gets up, excited to receive them.*

Margaret   Good evening, Ma.

Mother   Good evening, my daughter.

Margaret *steps forward, handing her the groceries.* **Mother** *reaches for*
them but when **Mother** *sees* **Margaret** *clearly, she is bewildered, and*
lets the groceries drop on the floor.

Margaret *reaches down and picks them up.*

Mother (*to* **Omony***, wary*)   What is she doing here?

Omony   Mother! She is a good friend.

Mother   That's not what I asked you.

Mother *turns sharply to* **Margaret***, horrified by her presence.*

Mother   I think you should leave.

Omony   What!

Margaret *is confused.*

Mother   Just leave young lady and avoid trouble.

Omony   Mother you can't just. . ./

Margaret   It's okay, Omony.

Margaret *hands* **Omony** *the groceries and exits.* **Omony** *makes to follow her, calling out after her.*

Mother   Let her go!

Omony   Mother, what was that all about?

Mother   I said let her go!

Omony *is speechless. Amid the argument,* **Mother** *returns unconsciously to her winnowing.*

Mother   If you know what is good for you, you will start looking for another girl for a future wife.

Omony   What is wrong with this one?

Mother   Any girl Omony, but not from that family.

Omony   But she is not her family.

Mother   She is his granddaughter. I hope you are not thinking of marrying her.

Omony   Whose granddaughter and why can't I marry her? Mother is there something you're not telling me?

Mother   They messed up everything. And yet they were rewarded with big cars and big houses! Blood cars!

Omony   Who? Margaret's grandfather?

Mother   No, all of them. Those so-called liberators!

Omony   And what has that got to do with Margaret?

Mother   Just listen to your mother, Son.

Omony   Why are you so bitter, Mother?

Mother   You don't know what you are talking about.

Omony   I know what am talking about, Mother. She's a nice girl and yet you refuse to accept her.

Mother *only stares hard at him. He hands her the groceries.* **Mother** *ignores them.*

Mother   Take them away.

Omony   It's a gift, Mother.

Mother   I don't need blood things! So much destruction! So many lives lost! And all for what? Crumbs of sugar and salt?

Omony   It was a liberation, Mother. Certain sacrifices had to be made.

Mother   So, where is your liberation right now, Son? Where is your liberation? Selling little things in a village shop while they cruise in luxuries.

Omony   Things always don't work out as planned. We can't blame the leaders for that.

Mother   What leaders? You call those murderers leaders?

Omony   We will all be compensated.

Mother   When?

Omony   Their compensation came first. They say ours is coming soon.

Mother   Son, you call theirs compensation? No way! They have just been rewarded.

Omony   You don't understand.

Mother   What is there to understand? It is plain and clear.

Omony   It's amnesty, Mother.

Mother   Stop throwing around big words that you don't understand.

Omony   It's forgiveness and compensation, Mother. The surest way to peace. Don't you want peace?

Mother   And why start with them? Why start with the very perpetrators while their victims sprawl in poverty and more suffering? So much luxuries for so much destruction! They think they can get away with everything and we live happily thereafter?

Omony   And what does that even mean?

Mother   They can't just get away with it, Son!

Omony   I don't have time for this again, Mother. I have to go.

Omony *exits, taking the groceries with him.* **Mother** *calls out after him.*

Mother   Stay away from her, you hear me? Stay away!

JuaKali Former Child Soldiers Rehabilitation Centre

Margaret *gathers up the children.*

Margaret   Okay, Alal and Abur, let's see what you two have done.

Girl 2 *and* **3** *get up.*

Girl 2/3   Okay everyone, let's do this.

They smile at each other.

Margaret   You see how you two are working well together?

Girl 2 *and* **3** *nod in agreement and quickly exit, with the other children and* **Margaret**.

Jungle

The children, with **Girl 2**, *enter in a file and sit down in a circle.*

Boy 1 *enters wearing a long white robe and a big cross around his neck. He is guarded by his two* **Kadogos**. *He stands in the middle of the circle.*

Boy 1   Welcome to the base. This is a good time to get to know each other. First of all, the news will be on in a few seconds. They will be reading your names. So, when you hear your name read out, say 'present'.

Girl 2 (*excited*)   Like in school?

Boy 1   Exactly, like in school.

Boy 1 *nods to* **Kadogo Ninja**, *who turns on the small hand radio he carries, as the news signature tune comes to an end.*

Boy 1   Kadogo Action, note those who didn't make it.

Kadogo Action *nods in agreement.*

News Anchor Voice   . . . and now to our top story. The town woke up to the sad news of the abduction of about 20 children from the village of Atiak. Radio Paco managed to compile the names of the abducted, which we shall read to inform relatives, friends and in-laws.

As the **News Anchor** *reads the names, those who are present say so, and those absent* **Kadogo Action** *notes in a small note book as he says, 'Not Made it'.*

Achan Cecilia
Okeny Denis
Aber Flavia (Not made it)
Ayela Patrick
Odokonyero Richard (Not made it)
Olweny Mark (Not made it)
Otim Joseph
Abalo Gloria (Not made it)
Otema Julius (Not made it)
Lagum Jane . . .

News Anchor Voice   . . . Since their abduction last night, no news has reached our desk yet. But we will keep you updated. Our prayers go out to the families that God protect their abducted children. And in other news . . ./

Boy 1 *signals* **Kadogo Ninja** *to turn off the radio, which he does.*

Boy 1   Kadogo Action, report.

Kadogo Action   Five didn't make it, Teacher Man.

Boy 1   Not as bad as the past. Good. Very good.

He gives the children a long hard stare. And then begins to move around them intimidatingly as he addresses them.

Boy 1   For those of you who have made it here, congratulations and welcome to the future. Again, I am Commander Man, the chosen messiah of our people. And yes, we are the future. We are the future because we know our past. We know that our fathers' fathers' fathers' and fathers' fathers' and fathers' ruled these lands. We ruled this country. We commanded the 'opoko' boys. Those good for nothing weaklings, only good at herding our cattle.

Kadogo Action *and* **Ninja** *curse and spit.*

Boy 1   SU-PRE-MA-CY! That is what I am talking about here. We were the supreme power dominating over this land! But that was taken away from us. FROM US! And that is why I am here. That is why you are here. That is why we are here. We are here to take back our power! We are here to see our great men rule this country again! We are here to take back our supremacy!

He pounds his chest firmly with resolve. The **Kadogos** *raise their AK 47s in the air and fire as the children sit still in total fear.*

Boy 1   We were never slaves! We were never chicken! We were never prostitutes! But now our girls sell themselves to our enemies for cheap things like sugar, salt and soap! They turn against us for collaborations with the same men who raided our cattle and arrested our strong young, claiming they are rebels. The same men who raped our women and men, and killed the old! You are the chosen ones. The Chosen Ones to fight next to he who is chosen by the Lord Jesus himself to save the Acholi people. I am the word. The messenger of God to liberate and free our people! And that's why he has blessed me with supernatural powers. All we have to do is believe and we shall reign again! (*As he pounds his chest.*) I am talking about liberation, freedom and the restoration to supremacy! Can I hear everyone say these three powerful words?

All (*timidly*)   Liberation, Freedom and Supremacy.

Boy 1   I can't hear you.

All (*louder*)   Liberation, Freedom and Supremacy.

Boy 1   Kadogo Ninja, Kadogo Action.

Kadogo Ninja *and* **Action** *say it with utmost conviction.*

Boy 1   That's how we do it. Now can I hear you all again.

The children say it loudly, with conviction.

Boy 1   That's more like it. If we believe, miracles will happen.

He signals **Kadogo Action** *who bursts into a song.*

Kadogo Action   Lalar bin ilara.

They all join in the song in an accustomed way.

Group   Tita lok ma mit i kom Yecu lalar
Tita lok, ma mit ikom Yecu.

Kadogo Action   Lalar bin ilara.

Group   Tita lok mamit ikom Yecu lalar
Tita lok, lok mamit ikom Yesu.

As they sing, they walk and each pays allegiance by kissing the big cross around **Boy 1**'s *neck and form a line across centre stage left.*

*The singing should be militant and everything in the children's luggage
that can make a musical sound is used as accompaniment – water
jerrycans, washing basins, saucepans and others.*

Kadogo Action   Oloko pii odoko kongo.

Group   Tita lok mamit ikom Yecu lalar
Tita lok, lok mamit ikom Yecu.

Kadogo Action   Ocango wa luto-wang.

Group   Tita lok mamit ikom Yecu lalar
Tita lok, lok mamit ikom Yecu.

Kadogo Action   Oloko gweng odoko bom.

Group   Tita lok mamit ikom Yecu lalar
Tita lok, lok mamit ikom Yecu.

[English translation:
Kadogo Action   Saviour come and save me.

Group   Tell me the sweet words about Jesus the saviour
Tell me the sweet words, the sweet words about Jesus. (x2)

Kadogo Action   He changed water into wine.

Group   Tell me the sweet words about Jesus the saviour
Tell me the sweet words, the sweet words about Jesus.

Kadogo Action   He even healed the blind.

Group   Tell me the sweet words about Jesus the saviour
Tell me the sweet words, the sweet words about Jesus.

Kadogo Action   He changed rocks into bombs.

Group   Tell me the sweet words about Jesus the saviour
Tell me the sweet words, the sweet words about Jesus.]

Boy 1 *waves them to stop.*

Boy 1   Thank you, thank you.

Kadogo Ninja *gives him a piece of rock, which he takes and waves it in
the air.*

Boy 1   Yes, our Lord Jesus can turn the rocks into bombs for our cause.
All you have to do is believe. We have won lots of battles against our

enemies with the lord turning our rocks into bombs, against their man-made guns and bombs. So, do we believe?

All   Yes.

Boy 1   What?

All   Yes Teacher Man.

Boy 1   I said do we believe?

All   Yes, Teacher Man!

Boy 1   Do we believe?

All   Yes, Teacher Man!

Boy 1   Aleluyaaaaaa!

All   Ameeeeeeeeeeeeeen!

Boy 1   Good. Now, all boys to the left and all girls to the right.

The children hesitate not sure what it means to be on the left or right.

Boy 1   I will not repeat myself.

The children quickly do as commanded.

Boy 1   Now, who wants to be part of the chosen ones who will liberate of our people? Boys or girls?

Boys   Boys.

Girls   Girls.

Boy 1   And who wants to go home?

They make to answer in sharp competition between the boys and girls but on realizing what the question means, they all go silent.

Boy 1   Who wants to be a part of the chosen ones to liberate our people again?

Boys   Boys.

Girls   Girls.

Pauses to make the tense silence sink in.

Boy 1   Good. Kadogo Ninja, take all the boys with you.

*The boys hesitate, afraid that **Kadogo Ninja** is going to kill them.*

Boy 1   Come on, move. No one is going to be sent home, at least not now.

He laughs. No one else laughs.

Boy 1   Where is your sense of humour people? That was meant to be a joke.

He laughs. They force a laugh as **Kadogo Ninja** *leads the boys away.*

Boy 1   Kadogo Action.

Kadogo Action   Yes, Teacher Man.

Boy 1   The shirts.

Kadogo Action *brings several shirts and drops them on the floor.* **Boy 1** *looks at the girls one by one and picks the youngest of them, bringing her to stand by his side.*

Boy 1   Girls, walk to the front one at a time and pick a shirt. Clear?

Girls (*faintly*)   Clear.

Boy 1   I can't hear you.

Girls (*loudly*)   Yes Sir!

Boy 1   What did I say you should call me?

Girls   Teacher Man.

Boy 1   Eh? Again?

Girls (*loudly*)   Yes Teacher Man!

Boy 1   Good. Now, move and pick.

The girls come one by one and pick a shirt.

Boy 1   Good. Very good. Now, line up in one file holding your shirts up.

The girls respond immediately.

Boy 1   Good. Very good.

The boys who were led by **Kadogo Ninja** *return acting as commanders of the war, the* **Kadogos** *join them too as commanders. They exchange pleasantries with* **Commander Man**, *shaking his hand one by one as he acknowledges them with their nicknames – Shooter, Danger Hatari, AK 47 and Long Range.*

Boy 1 (*points to the girls*)   There they are. Just grab your shirts.

The commanders each go and pick the girl with their shirt and form two lines, the commanders' line and the wives' line each next to their commander husband, both facing **Boy 1** *with their back to the audience. In military style, he commands them to turn facing the audience, which they do in unison.*

Boy 1   From today onwards, each of you belongs to the commander whose shirt you have picked. Treat them with the same respect and discipline with which you have been treating me. In fact, treat them with more respect than you have given me because they are your husbands.

The girls look at the men in horror.

Boy 1   The boys will be joining different groups. You will all undergo military trainings alike, boys or girls. That will be all. Dismissed.

They exit, each commander walking away side by side with his girl. **Boy 1** *and his bride exit last.*

Hut

Boy 3, *known as Commander Danger Hatari,* **Girl 3**'s *husband re-enters with* **Girl 2**.

Boy 3   Atuku. Tuk. Tuk.

A young but ragged looking woman rushes in.

Girl 3   Yes, Husband.

Boy 3   This is Achan. She is here like you are here.

Girl 3   Yes, Husband.

Boy 3 (*to* **Girl 2**)   Atuku here is my senior wife. Accord her the respect of a senior wife. Whatever she says is final. Clear?

Girl 2   Yes, Teacher Danger Hatari.

Boy 3   It's yes, Husband.

Girl 2 (*resistant*)   Yes, Husband.

Boy 3   Good. I will see you later.

He exits.

Girl 3 (*reaches for her hand*)   So, what is your name?

Girl 2 *pulls away sneering at* **Girl 3**. *She doesn't answer.*

Girl 3   Are you dumb or you don't have a name?

Girl 2   Didn't you hear your husband introducing me?

Girl 3   Our husband.

Girl 2   I am not anyone's wife.

Girl 3 (*stares hard at her*)   Listen, don't think you are too good for some of us. Here you will need friends. May be sooner than you know.

Girl 3 *takes* **Girl 2**'s *hand and they turn to* **Margaret** *who is still offstage.*

Girl 2/3   This is where we stopped.

Margaret *claps passionately entering stage.*

Margaret   Good job. (*To the children.*) Everyone come back.

The children enter excitedly.

Margaret   Can we give a round of applause to Aciro and Abur.

The children clap and cheer.

Omony (*calls out from the door*)   I was told I would find you here.

Margaret *smiles.*

Omony   Can I come in?

Margaret   Sure, it's okay. We are finished for now.

Omony *enters.*

Margaret   Just a minute. (*To the children.*) Let's take a break. We will talk about what we have just seen after the break.

The children disperse excitedly.

Margaret   So, what brings you here?

Omony   I thought we could talk.

Margaret   Talk? About what?

Omony   Listen, about yesterday, I wanted to apologize for my mother's behaviour. She can sometimes be so . . . so . . . you know. Anyway, forgive her.

Margaret   There is nothing to forgive. No parent gives her child away without a fight.

Omony   I am glad you understand. So, are you up for some fun tonight?

Margaret   Depends on what you mean by fun.

Omony   Why don't we explore the concept and see where it leads us.

Margaret   Hey, not anything weird before my children.

Omony   Weird? From who? Me? No way.

Margaret   Do you have time for a quick cup of tea before we resume our session?

Omony   Sure. Who says no to tea with a beautiful woman?

Margaret *giggles as they exit side by side.*

Man's Ancestral Homestead-Compound

Fiona *and two of her cousins,* **Scovia** *about 7 and* **Brenda** *about 10, enter the stage playing jump rope. On stage* **Brenda** *and* **Scovia** *holds one end of the rope for* **Fiona.**

In the nearby neighbourhood, we hear the voice of the **News Anchor** *from a radio, as the children freeze.*

News Anchor (*voice*)   . . . and to end our afternoon edition, the police have not made any breakthrough in the new phenomenon of the disappearance of children that hit Atiak village about six months ago. The police in Atiak, are puzzled by the disappearance of young children between the ages of eight to ten. Since the first case six months ago, three more children have gone missing and still without a trace. This now brings the total to four missing children. Police investigations remain fruitless. There is looming fear that another rebel group targeting children recruits might be responsible for these kidnappings. And with all the four missing children being from the home of the late former rebel lord, Man, police are wary that another rebel group could be mobilizing. The incident has however aroused a number of questions in everybody's mind right now. Has the peace in northern Uganda been short lived? And even more importantly, can northern Uganda afford another endless war? We will keep you updated with this story.

The children unfreeze as the news signature tune runs and fades off.
Brenda *jerks the rope sending* **Fiona** *tumbling down with the rope.*
Brenda *and* **Scovia** *laugh in amusement.* **Fiona** *starts to cry. Touched,*
Scovia *goes to help her.*

Fiona   You did it intentionally!

Scovia   No, we didn't! Just get up and we play, Fiona.

Fiona   You did!

Brenda   Let her be Scovia! Just take the rope and let's continue playing, just two of us.

Scovia *reaches for the rope but* **Fiona** *grabs it.*

Brenda   Give us back the rope, you potato head!

Fiona *and* **Brenda** *struggle over the rope.* **Brenda** *loses it and slaps her.* **Fiona** *cries out loudly, rolling on the floor lets go of the rope.* **Brenda** *takes it, calling* **Scovia** *to play.* **Scovia** *hesitates, feeling sorry for* **Fiona.**

Brenda   Come on Scovia leave that fool alone!

Mother *enters from the opposite side of where the kids entered from. She carries a hoe and some food in a basket, obviously retiring from her garden work. She goes to* **Fiona**, *gets her off the floor and consoles her, cuddling her sweetly.*

Mother   Stop crying now. You will get a headache.

Fiona *stops crying but still sniffs.* **Mother** *reaches into her basket, draws out some guavas and hands them to her.*

Mother   Here, have these and keep quiet.

Fiona *takes them.* **Scovia** *notices the guavas and looks at them longingly.*

Brenda   Haven't you ever seen guavas, Scovia?

Scovia *cowers forgetting about the guavas.* **Fiona** *is obviously enjoying her guavas.* **Brenda** *starts teasing her singing the Acholi rhyme,* Lakoko koko Nguna *(crocodile's tears).*

Brenda (*sings*)   Lakoko koko nguna
Kilubo ki ojweye
Lakoko koko odenge
Kilubo ki ojweye.

[English translation:
She who cries deceitfully
Is identified by the footprints she leaves behind

She who cries like a spoilt brat
Is identified by the footprints she leaves behind.]

Mother *approaches* **Brenda**.

Mother   Why do you enjoy bullying young children? Such a big girl like you who shouldn't even be playing that game now. At your age, I was . . . I was . . . (*Quieter.*) At your age I was a hard-working wife and mother.

Mother *takes* **Fiona**'*s hand they exit.*

Mother   Let's go and leave that bully alone.

Hand in hand, they exit the stage. **Brenda** *sticks her tongue after them.*

Scovia   Brenda!

Brenda   What? Let's compete! The one who skips the longest three times wins!

Scovia (*excited*)   Yes! I'm first!

Brenda   The person with the rope goes first, silly head!

Scovia   Fine. You always want to abuse people.

Brenda *starts skipping.*

Brenda   Babilikan. Babilikan. Number 28. I went for a walk and . . . (*she trips but cheats*) and the break!

Scovia   No, you spoiled. It's my turn.

Brenda   I didn't spoil. It was 'and the break.'

Scovia   You spoiled before 'and the break.'

Brenda   No. You didn't see well.

Scovia   Aahaa. Nooo.

They begin to struggle for the skipping rope. **Brenda** *overpowers* **Scovia**.

Scovia   Okay, I don't want to play with you, you cheat. You play alone. I'll go look for Fiona.

Scovia *exits angry following where* **Fiona** *and* **Mother** *exited.* **Brenda** *continues to play alone still singing* 'Babilikan. Babilikan'. *Moments later, a subdued nerve-chilling scream of a child penetrates the stage.* **Brenda** *is bewildered. She rushes off from where they entered.*

Man's Ancestral Homestead

The things in **Husband** *and* **Wife**'*s house are all scattered.* **Husband** *sits calmly on the sofa reading a newspaper.*

Wife *alights from the bedroom carrying a suitcase. She is furious with* **Husband**, *but he is used to her antics, and so only occasionally glances at her.* **Wife** *puts the suitcase down across the floor.*

Wife   I don't understand why you insist on living here when children are disappearing!

Husband   Come on, don't you think you are overreacting just a little bit? Only four children have disappeared and you . . . . /

Wife   Only four! How many do you want gone before you agree to move? (*Spits her tongue.*)

Husband   That's not what I meant!

Wife   What did you mean then?

Husband   You have to be careful what you say. Evil spirits feed on our fears.

Wife   I don't believe you! Can't you see what is happening here? I am not going to continue living under this tension any more.

She exits and returns with a small travel bag, which she places beside the suitcase.

Husband *now gets up and approaches her.*

Husband   I understand. But it's barely been a year since we moved back home and with father gone, I can't just pack and leave home like I used to.

Wife   So?

Husband   What do you mean, so? Even if I wanted to move, there is the issue of job transfer.

Wife   Then ask for one.

Husband   What? I only recently asked for one. They could misunderstand me and just dismiss me. Listen honey, we can't just move like that without any plans! Without any where to go!

Wife   I don't care where we go as long as we leave this cursed place! Even if it means giving the street children some company!

Husband   How about work? Where will I find a job abruptly? This is not just about you! Do you want to bring up Fiona on the streets?

Wife   I would rather have her alive on the streets than dead in a comfortable house!

She heads back to the bedroom. **Husband** *carries the suitcase following her, but taking it to a different nearby room. He returns almost immediately and calls out to her in the bedroom.*

Husband   Why don't we wait a few more days and see what the police come up with?

Wife (*calls from the bedroom*)   Is this still the same police that have come up with nothing in six months that you are talking about?

Husband *takes the small travel bag.* **Wife** *alights with a mattress. They meet halfway across the floor.*

Wife   Will you stop carrying the things back?

She tries to grab the travel bag from him without success, sending them both tumbling down. Amused, **Wife** *laughs and* **Husband** *joins her. They laugh heartedly.*

Beat.

Husband   These things take time.

Wife   We don't have time. Will you just listen to me and let's get out of here before it's too late!

Margaret *enters.*

Husband   You're early today.

Margaret   I thought I should come back early to help with the move . . . unless we are not moving anymore.

Wife (*rises*)   Thank heavens some people still have sense around here.

Husband *rises with the travel bag in hand.*

Suddenly **Scovia** *enters breathless.* **Husband** *rises.*

Scovia   Aunt, Mama Fiona. Fiona . . . Fiona has . . . has fallen in blood.

Wife   What!

Husband   Where?

Scovia *points at the direction from which she came.*

Wife   Take me there now.

Wife *grabs* **Scovia** *by the hand leading the way.* **Husband** *drops the travel bag down in panic and runs after them.* **Margaret** *follows them in a hurry.*

Mother's Ancestral Homestead

Mother *unpacks the basket of food and is organizing the food when* **Scovia, Wife, Husband** *and* **Margaret** *enter.* **Scovia** *points at the spot where she claims she saw the blood in front of* **Mother***. He then steps aside to* **Margaret***.*

Wife *is hysterical as* **Husband** *struggles to restrain her.* **Mother** *turns facing them calmly.*

Wife   Where is my daughter? Where is Fiona?

Mother   I don't know. I only gave her some guavas. Is that a bad thing?

Wife   Scovia said Fiona was bleeding right here with you. Produce my daughter right now if you know what is good for you.

Mother   Are you choosing to believe a child over me? Like I said, I only gave her some guavas. And that was all. (*She checks around.*) Do you see any blood here?

Wife   Murderer! Murderer! Murderer! She killed my daughter. Murderer . . .

Husband *tries to restrain her in vain. The neighbours dash in, each carrying a weapon that depicts the chores they were engaged in and begin to beat up* **Mother***, while* **Husband** *and* **Wife** *step aside overtaken by the crowd.* **Mother** *never cries out at all. She sits there numb as the people beat her.*

Horrified by the sight of what is going on, **Margaret** *quickly sneaks out, leaving* **Scovia** *who cowers scared.*

A **Woman** *with a mingling stick enters with a loud squeal that makes the other stop. She heads straight for* **Mother** *and hits her with the mingling stick. They all resume beating* **Mother***.*

One of the neighbours paces up and down by the door looking out.

Neighbour   Police. Police. Police.

Nobody hears him.

Juma *rushes in firing bullets in the air, closely followed by the* **CID** *and* **Margaret**. *The crowd disperses leaving* **Wife** *and* **Scovia** *cowering and holding tightly to* **Husband**.

CID *looks back and forth from the trio to* **Margaret**. *He signals* **Juma** *to grab* **Mother** *and they exit.* **Husband, Wife** *and* **Scovia** *follow them.* **Wife** *looks questioningly at* **Margaret** *who doesn't follow them, but paces up and down full of anxiety. She hears a bicycle bell and peeps out.*

Omony *enters with a five-litre jerry-can of kerosene.* **Margaret** *approaches him, anxiously.*

Margaret   You can't stay here.

Omony   Why?

Margaret   You will be killed! They are all very furious. If they come back and find you here, they will kill you. You must run for your life. Run!

Omony   What are you talking about? You are not making any sense, Margaret.

Margaret   They say your mother has killed Fiona. They wanted to kill her but the police rescued her. If they come back and find you here, it will end badly. You must get out of here.

Omony (*shocked*)   What? That's insane! My mother wouldn't hurt a fly. She adores children. She finds a thrill in pampering them with food.

Margaret   I know. But there is no reasoning with these people until the police can clear this. Until then you must first save yourself. Ride back into town and hide. Hide where nobody can find you.

Suddenly they hear sounds of angry people approaching yelling, 'Get him! Kill him! Kill the murderer's blood. Blood for blood . . . '

Margaret   Go now!

Omony   I am not going to run away like a criminal for something I am sure my mother didn't do.

Margaret *is at a loss.*

Margaret   Why are you being so stubborn? Just go, now!

Omony *stands still staring at her. The crowd's noise draws closer.* **Margaret** *grabs* **Omony**'s *hand.*

Margaret   Come with me then. I know the safest place for you to hide.

Margaret *drags* **Omony** *out of room. A crowd floods the house but as they see no-one, they exit yelling bloody murder.*

Prison

Mother *sits quietly in her cell room, the guards still in their position. The* **CID** *and* **Juma** *enter. The* **CID** *is on a cell phone.*

CID   She is still not talking . . . yes . . . I am on it, Sir . . . it is not another rebel group . . . I know from our intelligence, which need I remind you is the best in the region . . . what can I say? You know the press enjoys sensation . . . Yes, I am sure . . . Yes, I know we can't afford another rebel activity . . . yes, I know Boss won't like it . . . yes, I know Boss' current vision for this place is peace and development . . . yes, I will.

The **CID** *hangs up the phone with a heavy sigh.*

CID   Orders. Orders. Orders. I wish he would get out of his comfortable seat and try the field for once.

Juma   I know. All he does is appear on TV and make comments.

CID   Here we go.

The **CID** *draws closer as he bounces a bunch of keys in his palm.*
Mother *isn't intimidated one bit.*

Juma *watches from the side, taking notes.*

CID   Do you know how bad you are making me . . . the police look? Twenty years of my clean reputation going down the drain! So, let's play this nicely. Did you kidnap Fiona? And if so did you kill her?

Mother *changes her sitting posture and begins to hum* Bedo I Wilobo Yelo Wiya.

CID   I will ask you again. Did you kidnap the child? And if so, did you kill the child?

Mother *changes position, humming.*

CID (*worked up*)   Answer me now! If you killed the child just say so, case solved. I go back to my usual petty crimes – a little stealing here and a little wife battering there. And you . . . well; I guess we all know what will happen to you.

Mother *continues humming.*

CID (*yells*)   What on earth is wrong with you, woman?

Juma *signals the* **CID** *to step to the side. The* **CID** *considers.* **Juma** *signals him again with urgency.* **Mother** *silently watches them. They step to the side.*

Juma   Maybe she didn't do it.

CID   What!

Juma   I am saying maybe . . . just may be . . ./

CID   I know what you are saying. But then why doesn't she say so instead of just sitting quietly like she's communing with the gods?

Juma   Who knows? Madness! Insanity! Trauma! Anything! Don't you read the papers? Listen to news? They say all these people are traumatized!

CID   Then how do you explain the bloody child that the little girl saw?

Juma   That is if the little girl saw any blood at all. Children have very wild imaginations. Especially now with the radios singing the news about children disappearing.

CID   This is all so strange. In my 20 years of good police work, I have never seen anything like this.

Juma   Me too, comrade. Me too.

The **CID** *looks at* **Mother** *who looks at him straight in the eyes, silent.*

The **Bishop***, who clutches the Bible tightly, enters.*

CID   Bishop, you came at the right time. She's all yours. I hope you carry a miracle in that Bible. We will wait by the door.

Mother *sits quietly as though she isn't even aware of the presence of the* **Bishop***; until the* **CID** *and* **Juma** *step out. Then without looking at him, she addresses* **Bishop***.*

Mother   Bishop, you are here to purge my soul, are you? Hoping that I would pour my soul out to you and your God.

Bishop   That's not why am here.

Mother   I see. I forgot. You're here because you care.

Mother *gives a big smile and reaches to grab his legs. The* **Bishop** *is caught off-guard and quickly draws back.*

Bishop   Jesus Christ!

Bishop   I am here to do the will of a power beyond us. So, your soul may find peace and rest.

Mother (*rises seductively*)   Peace and rest for my soul. Not bad! Not bad at all! It sounds like a very good offer but just one question – Does this mean I have already been pronounced guilty?

The **Bishop** *is taken aback and tries to make amends.* **Mother** *laughs hauntingly making the* **Bishop** *struggle to get his point across.*

Bishop   Mine is not the will of the state. I come bearing revelation of redemption. We shall all face our creator when that time comes.

Mother   I do hope you are ready when that time comes, Bishop?

Bishop   The Holy Book says thou shall not judge. Ours is a call to embrace heaven's paradise, far away from the fires of hell. (**Mother** *freezes.*) But first we must redeem ourselves. Confess our sins.

Mother   My eyes are too misty to . . . I have been lucky, unlucky then lucky again. (*Withdraws from* **Bishop**.) Heaven and hell . . . (*She smiles.*) Once upon a time I felt heaven so close. Once upon time I grasped my heaven. My heaven came to pass. Once upon a time . . .

A loud lady from the wings sings the Acholi dance song 'Larakaraka', 'Lamele Ye Gini Akuru', *as the* **Bishop** *and guards exit to the wings.*

The rest join in the song, drumming, playing the calabashes and other instruments.

Mother *sits, turning her back to the audience and excitedly watches the procession as she moves to the dance beat.*

Past

Mother's Ancestral Homestead

A big marriage procession with dancers leading the bride and groom enter. When they arrive, the bride dances in front as the crowd marvels.

Ponsiano Latigo, **Mother***'s father, who is the chairman of the marriage ceremony, takes the centre with the Acholi male victory motif.*

Latigo (*chants*)   Acut ma ngute ki olang
Piny bedo ni wici wici
Lwani yeee . . .
Aneko nyong, aculo ku.

[English translation:
The vulture that carries a bell around its neck
Chaos everywhere
Long live Lwani clan
I kill with impunity, and pay not for it.]

As the dancers fade out, the singing lowers but the body movement keeps going, every time **Latigo** *speaks.*

Latigo   You can see for yourself that our daughter is a woman and a half. Let's see if the groom can compete with that.

The groom takes to the dance floor and dances to win the bride.

Latigo   It looks like your son also came very ready.

He dances approaching his bride and together they take the arena and dance powerfully as the crowd cheers them on with excitement.

Latigo   It looks like both the bride and groom are in this to win. They are in this to win! Let's cheer for the couple!

Jubilation fills the air amidst ululations and blowing of horns.

Latigo   It is now clear that both the bride and groom are from very respectable families, who can showcase their might in the dance arena. Can we all now join in the celebration of the happiness of this union of two great families?

The crowd takes to the floor with excitement, ululations and epic poetry recitations.

Young **Mother***,* **Girl 2***, runs to her father calling out.*

Girl 2   Dance with me, Father. Dance with me. Dance with me.

Girl 2 *and* **Latigo** *her father dance as they do the 'get stuck' motif of the dance.*

In her mind, the adult **Mother** *sees herself as the little her, rises and joins the dance trying to dance with her father, who obviously doesn't see her. She gets frustrated each time her father enjoys the dance with little* **Mother***,* **Girl 2***.*

The dance culminates into one big happy mass. The procession begins to exit. **Mother** *still tries to dance with her father, but as he moves towards the exit, she sits down in disappointment.*

All the original characters in the prison cell resume their positions.

Present

Prison

Mother (*in a trance*)   Dance with me, Father. Dance with me. Dance with me.

Bishop *looks at her in wonderment.*

Mother (*smiles*)   My heaven came to pass.

Suddenly her face changes. She wears a heavy sad face. She thought she could talk about the past but now realizes she can't. The sadness still weighs heavy in her heart.

Mother   When in tranquility I sit, and ponder. I ask. Did I not take good grasp of my heaven? (*To* **Bishop**.) Where do you keep your heaven safe? I bet I already know the answer to that. (*In great mockery.*) Far away in heaven where no moles can eat them. (*She laughs. It's laughter of subdued pain.*) You come here bearing news of heaven and hell?

What do you know about heaven and hell? Just go and leave me in peace.

The **Bishop** *not knowing what to say, looks away in shame.*

Mother   I said go!

The **Bishop** *doesn't know whether to take* **Mother** *on her word or not.*

Mother *gets hysterical.*

Mother   GO! NOW! I SAID GO!

The **CID** *and* **Juma** *run in meeting the* **Bishop** *half way, leaving.*

CID   Is everything okay?

Bishop   Everything is fine. I was just leaving.

He remembers the Bible in his hand, turns back and puts it before **Mother**, *while the rest look on. He turns back to walk away but is stopped midway by* **Mother**'s *voice.*

Mother   Why do you all look at me so? Yes, I was happily hopeless with my full mist day but the sun sneaked into my mist. The sun sneaked in, sounding all musical. You all saw or heard. It was in the papers and on radio.

Struck by what is going on, the **CID** *accidentally drops the bunch of keys on the floor and its jingle sound triggers a TV news memory in* **Mother**'s *mind.*

Mother   I had no TV set, but a well-to-do relative who was kind enough to share his with me. You remember watching it on TV, don't you?

Juma *becomes, in her mind, a* **News Anchor**. *She addresses him.*

Mother   Well, why do you just stand there? Didn't you read the news that evening?

Juma *transitions into the* **News Anchor** *and starts to read the news. The news runs like a quick rewind in* **Mother**'s *mind.*

News Anchor   Welcome back from that short commercial break. After nearly a quarter of a decade, the government has finally signed the peace deal with the notorious rebel group, the Liberation Front. The long-awaited peace has finally become a reality in Uganda. The peace deal was immediately followed by the long-debated Acholi reconciliation ceremony of 'Mato Oput' that took place in the northern capital of Gulu, attended by hundreds of Ugandans and international dignitaries from across the world. The ceremony that took place at the Acholi 'Ker Kwaro' was presided over by the Acholi paramount chief and the 24 elders representing the 24 major clans of the Acholi people. New Africa TV talked to some of the Acholi opinion leaders and this is what they had to say.

The **CID**, *who in* **Mother**'s *mind becomes the* **LC 5**, *transitions into the role of the* **LC 5**.

LC 5   As the LC 5 of the northern district, I say . . ./

The **LC 5** *freezes. Loud irritating lack of TV signal beep sound and grains projected on a multi-media.*

News Anchor   We apologize for the minor technical problem, which should be resolved soon.

The **LC 5** *unfreezes and continues. Voices of the different leaders flood* **Mother**'s *mind. The voices overlap. The people in the room embody the voices. The* **CID** *as the district* **LC 5**, **Juma** *as the* **MP**, **Guard 1** *remains as* **Boss**, **Guard 2** *remains as* **Man** *and the* **Bishop** *as himself.*

LC 5   As the LC5 of the northern district, I say this peace deal has been long overdue . . .

MP   Now with partial peace in place, it's now our task as the MPs of the area to see the way forward in the restoration of the region so we can have peace in the full sense of the word.

Bishop   The religious leaders are very happy about this.

LC 5   The people of Acholi are finally resettling back into their own communities. The challenge now is the lack of social services.

MP   Contrary to popular belief, absence of war is not necessarily peace. It's only a great opportunity.

LC 5   But I believe with the Peace, Recovery and Development Program for Northern Uganda, these challenges shall be minimized.

Bishop   In fact, the entire Christian community has been uplifted by this great news.

LC 5   Like the Chinese adage says, 'A journey of a thousand miles starts with a step'.

Bishop   As you know, it has been a long struggle but God has finally answered that prayer.

The leaders reverse to the back as **Man** *and* **Boss** *make their way to the front in simultaneous dialogues.*

Man   I think I speak for all ex-rebels when I say, we are very pleased that the peace deal has gone better than we expected. The community has received us well and I can confidently say we are adjusting well to community life.

Boss   Indeed, the government is very pleased at the success of the Juba peace talks. The northern Uganda conflict has been a priority in our programs and this is another milestone in our democracy. By this we have shown the world that Uganda is a true democracy. Now we have to embark on the recovery and development program for the region.

Mother *turns to* **Juma** *as the* **News Anchor** *again in her mind.*

Mother   You did wrap up the news nicely too, didn't you?

Juma *transitions into the* **News Anchor**.

News Anchor   All that is well ends well, as all the leaders seem to say. We leave you with pictures from the peace signing ceremony that took place at Sparkles Hotel. Keep watching New Africa TV.

In **Mother***'s mind,* **Boss** *and* **Man** *are joined by their peace talk team of dignitaries, as celebratory guitar plays.* **Bishop** *on* **Man***'s team.*

The **CID** *plays his role as the* **Mediator**, *between* **Boss** *and* **Man**, *he encourages them to shake hands, and they exchange plastic smiles. The* **Mediator** *watches, smiling, satisfied with himself.*

Unable to bear it, **Mother** *turns away, enraged. She stares into the audience. As* **Mother** *addresses the audience,* **Boss, Man** *and the* **Mediator** *pose for pictures taken by* **Juma,** *as the* **Journalist.** *The* **Mediator** *later beckons the rest of the dignitaries to join in posing for the pictures.*

Mother   Did you see him? He was there. Did you even recognize him? It took me quite a bit of time but after a while I recognized him. He was with them. Did you see his smile? His laughter? It was no different from theirs. Where was that white robe? That 'God-given' white robe that was supposed to be my liberation? Did you all see him clutching crumbs of his dreams and hopes? Dreams and hopes of power disguised in liberation fights. What about me? What do I do with myself? What about my dreams and hopes? Simply subdued, crashed and robbed without any mercy. Without any regrets or apologies . . .

The characters return to their original characters and positions as **CID** *and* **Juma** *watch the* **Bishop** *exit.*

Mother   What about me? What do I do with myself now? (*Pause.*) Well, at least it was a beautiful function you would say, wasn't it?

CID (*draws closer to* **Mother**)   Listen woman, you better come out of this madness.

Mother *only stares into space.*

CID   Tell me woman, what is it that you want?

Mother   A deal.

The **CID** *is caught off-guard by this.*

CID   What kind of deal? Twenty years of building my reputation, woman. Twenty years! Do you think you can bribe me?

Mother   I have no reason to bribe you, or anyone. I even have no reason to want to leave this place.

CID   You are a strange woman!

Mother   We say that everyday about things we don't understand. Do you want the deal or not?

CID   Let's hear it!

Mother (*hands him the Bible*)   Here take this. I hear it opens the heaven's gates.

The **CID** *takes the Bible feeling awkward and puts it aside.*

Mother   I am willing to talk on one condition.

CID   I don't think you are in any position to make conditions.

Mother   Neither are you in any position to put on airs. Your policing methods are clearly lacking in skills if you don't mind my observation.

*The **CID** swallows hard.*

CID   What's the condition?

Mother   I will tell you everything. And I mean everything. (*Imitates the* **CID**.) 'Case solved'. Isn't that what you want?

Juma   Sure, we could use one solved case.

*The **CID** cuts **Juma** with a sharp look. **Juma** withdraws.*

Mother   But first you must grant me my ritual. You must grant me my complete ritual.

CID   Ritual! What ritual?

Mother   I just said my ritual.

CID   So, you are admitting that you kidnapped the girl?

Mother   I am admitting no such thing and neither am I denying any such thing.

CID   Oh, this is pointless. What is the ritual?

Mother   You wouldn't understand, Afande.

CID   A man only has so much patience, Cecilia. And you have tried that to the limits.

Mother   It's not a good thing for a man of the law to lose his temper, Afande. That's what I learned in my twenty years of life in captivity. Twenty years!

*The **CID** makes to hit her but restrains himself. Instead he turns in frustration and walks away followed by **Juma**.*

Man's Ancestral Homestead

*The things in **Husband** and **Wife**'s house remain as disorganized as the last time. It's literally as though the clock stopped for this family. They both sit down on the mattress; **Wife** holds tenderly onto **Fiona**'s framed photo, which should be projected for the audience.*

They hear a knock at the door. **Husband** *turns and looks at the door.*
Wife *remains staring hard at the photo.*

The knocking continues. **Wife** *gives the door a glance and falls back to
staring at* **Fiona***'s picture.* **Husband** *gets up to go and open but* **Wife**
holds him down.

Wife   I want some peace and quiet. Just by ourselves.

Husband   The people who come, just come to give their support.

Wife   Don't say that! People only give their support if someone is dead.
I refuse to think my Fiona is dead. She can't be.

The knocking persists.

Husband   Whoever it is, I will get rid of them.

Husband *goes and opens the door.*

Margaret *enters dragging* **Omony** *in.* **Husband** *steps aside looking at
them in shock.* **Wife** *rises hysterical.*

Wife   What is he doing here?

Margaret   The angry crowd is after him, Aunt.

Wife   So?

Margaret   I thought he would be safer here.

Wife *is beyond shocked.*

Wife   Are you crazy? You want us to protect the son of Fiona's murderer.

Margaret   Aunt we don't know for sure if she did it until the police
investigates.

Wife   It seems working with murderers has made you immune to them.

Margaret   That is cold even for you, Aunt. Maybe you should come do
my job for a day to get a heart.

Wife   I don't care. Just take him out of here. If you want to continue
sleeping around with murderers go ahead, just don't do it here.

Margaret   What?

Wife   Don't you dare stand there and what me young lady.

Omony (*heads towards the exit*)   It's okay Margaret, I will go. I don't
want to cause trouble.

Wife   Yes. Go. (*She pushes* **Margaret** *towards him.*) And take her along with you and kill her for all I care. That's what she seems to be looking for.

Husband *reaches out to* **Wife** *to calm the situation.*

Husband   That's enough now, Mama Fiona.

They hear a loud knock on the door. **Husband** *goes and opens the door to* **CID**, *which distracts* **Wife's** *attention from* **Margaret** *and* **Omony**, *who exit. The* **CID** *is distracted by* **Fiona**'s *framed photo staring straight at him, smiling; and startled by* **Wife**'s *question.*

Wife   Do you have any good news for us?

CID   What? Right, I am not sure.

Wife   What do you mean you are not sure? Do you at least know if she is still alive out there somewhere?

CID   At this point it's difficult to tell. She could still be alive or . . . anything is possible. She is willing to confess I think.

Everyone is startled by the word 'confess'.

Wife   You think! What kind of CID are you?

CID   We don't know if this woman is sane or insane at this point. All these things she is saying could just be the symptoms of a twisted mind. Like I said, my hunch is that she is willing to confess. But she has a condition.

Furious, **Wife** *approaches the* **CID**, *who distances himself from her.*

Wife   I don't believe this! Since when are criminals in position to give the arms of the law conditions?

The **CID** *says nothing. Only an awkward silence fills the room.*

Husband   What condition?

CID   She will do that only on condition that we allow her to first complete her ritual.

Wife   Her ritual?

Wife *breaks down on her knees, trying not to cry but her pain is no doubt consuming her.*

Wife   Ritual? My daughter is dead. My Fiona is lost to me. She is gone.

Husband   We can't think like that, honey.

Wife *pushes him away rising.*

Wife Don't tell me how to think. She wants to complete her ritual. And you are telling me . . . My sweet, sweet little Fiona.

Husband (*to* **CID**) Did you ask her what kind of ritual she is talking about?

CID You wouldn't understand.

Husband Why don't you tell me and let me be the judge of that?

CID That's what she told me when I asked her.

Wife *goes for the* **CID** *in a fury.*

Wife See what you police have done! We had her right in our hands. If you hadn't interfered she would be dead and gone and we wouldn't have to deal with her.

CID Then you would never know how to find Fiona.

Beat.

Husband He is right, Honey.

Wife Whose side are you on? Mine or the police?

Husband Fiona's side. This is about her. Not you or the police.

Wife Fiona's side? It's your fault she is missing in the first place!

Husband What?

Wife Don't stand there and what me looking so surprised. How many times did I beg you to leave this cursed place? (*Mimics.*) Honey, we can't bring up our daughter on the street. Now we have no daughter to bring up.

Husband I don't believe you.

CID Can we not lose focus of the real problem at hand here.

Husband *takes a heavy breath.*

Husband You are right. So, have you granted her, her condition?

CID We haven't granted her anything. That's why I am here. To see how you the parents would feel about it. If you say yes, then . . .

Wife Every new day brings forth more horrors. I can't go on like this. The not knowing is killing me quietly. So, can we just get this over with?

CID We have to leave right away then. I will fill you in on the details from the police station.

The **CID** *leads the way to the exit.* **Husband** *reaches out for* **Wife** *but she pulls away from him in anger. He shrugs it off and follows the* **CID**. **Wife** *follows them.*

JuaKali Former Child Soldiers Rehabilitation Centre

Margaret *enters dragging* **Omony** *along and pushes him into the room. She stands by the door.*

Omony   You have brought me to the children centre?

Margaret   This is the only place you can be safe. No one will look for you here.

Omony   Will you stop talking like that. No one is looking for me.

Margaret   Not while you are hiding out here, no.

Omony *quickly looks around the place with discomfort.*

Omony   That's not what I meant. I have to go.

He heads towards her for the exit, she signals him to stop.

Margaret   Will you stop being so stubborn, didn't you hear the angry mob out there?

Omony   They are angry at my mother not me.

Margaret   You don't know that. Angry people are without reason.

Omony   Then I will try to reason with them.

Margaret   Why don't you try staying here first?

Omony   I can't stay here!

Margaret   Why not? Do you have a much safer place?

Omony   I mean my mother needs me and I need to be by her side.

Margaret   No, you need to protect yourself first.

Omony   So, what do you want me to do? Just sit here while they kill her.

Margaret   The police already have her, nobody is going to hurt or kill her.

Omony *looks around again, looks at* **Margaret** *then sighs heavily.*

Omony   I just . . . I really have to go.

He approaches her again, aiming for the exit door but **Margaret** *grabs his hand. He halts.*

Margaret (*begs*)   Omony, please don't go. Don't get out there. Do it for me.

Omony *turns to look at her. He is at a loss for words.*

Margaret (*calmly*)   Stay please, until this is all over. I need you.

Omony (*calmly*)   It's not that simple, Margaret.

Margaret   Losing you won't be simple.

Omony   You won't lose me. But I can't stay here, Margaret.

Margaret   Why not? What's wrong with this place?

Omony *surveys the place with a dull absent-minded stare.* **Margaret** *waits.*

Omony   It's a children rehabilitation centre.

Margaret   I know, that's why it's the perfect hideout.

Omony   You don't understand.

Margaret   What don't I understand?

Omony   It's like a camp. When Mother and I were rescued by the army, I thought that was it. But that wasn't it. Mother and I ended up spending weeks at the army camp.

Two soldiers, one male and one female, enter, one from either side. The male soldier drags **Mother** *along. The female grabs* **Omony** *by the arms.* **Margaret** *sits and watches. She turns her back to the audience like* **Mother** *in her flashback moments.*

Past

Army Camp

Each soldier hurls **Omony** *and* **Mother** *upstage, on the floor of different adjacent interrogation rooms represented by* **Omony** *and* **Mother** *sitting back to back as each faces their interrogator.*

Soldier 1 *and* **Soldier 2** *say their first lines together.*

Soldier 1   Are you telling me that a whole son of Commander Danger Hatari would not know what the next destination of your battalion was right before we attacked?

Soldier 2   Are you telling me that a whole wife of Commander Danger Hatari would not know what the next destination of your battalion was right before we attacked?

Omony *and* **Mother** *say their first lines together.*

Omony   A son, I found myself born into. And I was only son number 6 out of how many sons? Twelve sons and 22 daughters.

Mother   A wife I was abducted into. And I was only wife number 25 out of how many wives? Sixty wives.

The sessions overlap.

Soldier 1   I tell you what the problem is with what you have told us, Omony. The problem is you have told us nothing new.

Mother   I swear I have told you everything I know.

Soldier 2   But that is not what your son told us.

Omony   I don't know what my mother told you but that's all I know.

Soldier 2   How about the weapons your son says you returned with?

Omony   Why would my mother say that we returned with weapons?

Soldier 1   You tell me.

Mother   Maybe you scared him.

Both soldiers say their lines together and both **Omony** *and* **Mother** *answer together.*

Soldier 2   Your son says you were the favourite wife.

Soldier 1   Your mother says you were the favourite son.

Mother   A favourite wife, eh? My son would never use that word.

Omony   It bears such horrible memories, the word 'favourite'. You don't know what you are talking about, Afande.

Both soldiers swallow hard, ashamed, quickly check themselves and say the last lines together.

Soldier 2   Your husband Commander Danger Hatari is already dead and gone. So, I hope you know where your loyalty should lie. Because if we find out that you lied to us one bit, mark my words, one bit . . .

Soldier 1   Why such loyalty to a dead father. I hope you are not lying to us. If it turns out so, and believe me, we will find out, and if it turns out that you lied to us . . .

The soldiers simultaneously make the sign of cutting their heads off.

Soldier 2 *grabs* **Mother** *and exits with her, while* **Soldier 1** *exits, leaving* **Omony** *sitting alone.*

Present

JuaKali Former Child Soldiers Rehabilitation Centre

Omony   When I got out of there, I swore I will never stay in a confined place again. We both swore. And that's why we escaped from the rehabilitation centre.

Margaret *goes to him and embraces him tightly with love.*

Margaret   This will only take a short while. Just until the situation cools down.

Omony *nods in affirmative.*

Margaret   The boys won't reveal where you are. They will treat you well.

Margaret *rises to her feet and takes his hand.*

Margaret   Come on, let's go.

They exit entering the back rooms of the rehabilitation centre.

Bush

Live 'Nanga' plays an Acholi last funeral rites song. The actions unfold in slow motion.

Five men enter carrying a pentagram with a cross attached to each of the five sides and a large light burning inside the pentagram, emitting smoke. The inscription, 'Pius for you Papa', 'Lillian for you Mama', 'George for you Odokonyero Richard', 'Daniel for you Omara Paul' and 'Fiona for you Aber Flavia' marks a cross. Each man holds one side of a pentagram, they wear white robes with purple sashes.

The Guards follow as they lead **Mother***, each holding one hand. Four women, two per line follow carrying small covered pots that contain the chopped bodies of the murdered children. Centre is a fifth woman carrying the pot that holds* **Fiona**'s *body. Last in the procession is the* **CID***.*

The men put the pentagram downstage centre and retreat in two lines upstage, then exit from both sides of the stage.

The guards let go of **Mother** *who takes centre position with the pentagram in front of her. The guards step aside, still guarding her.*

Each of the women give her a pot, one at a time; and then follow the men, keeping the two-line formation. **Mother** *takes each pot and puts it next to the cross on the pentagram invoking the name of each of her deceased family members starting with; 'Pius for you Papa, Lillian for you Mama, George for you Odokonyero'. She breaks down, picks herself up, and continues, 'Daniel for you Paul'.*

Happy that she is about to complete her ritual, **Mother** *smiles and in real time says:*

Mother   I killed them all! All the missing children!

As she turns in slow motion, reaching for **Fiona**'s *pot, the* **CID** *signals the guards, who hold* **Mother** *under gunpoint as the last woman withdraws the pot she is holding.*

All actions change into real time.

CID   Leave everything and step aside, hands up!

Mother   What!

CID   I said leave everything and step aside!

The guards each grab her arm. **Mother** *turns to the* **CID.**

Mother   You promised!

CID   Do as I say!

Mother   But you promised! I must complete my ritual! You can't break the promise again. So many promises have been broken.

The guards lead her away as she continues to shout, 'You promised! You promised! You promised!'

Wife *and* **Husband** *enter breathless. They meet half-way.*

Beat.

Mother *halts looking at the couple.* **Wife** *gives her a slap.* **Husband** *restrains her.*

Wife   Why? Why did you do this to us? What did we ever do to you? We lived as good neighbours.

The guards lead **Mother** *away.*

Wife *sees the 'graves' spread before them. She draws closer to the fifth cross with no pot next to it and reads the inscription 'Fiona for you Aber Flavia'. She drops down on her knees and wails in pain calling out* **Fiona***'s name.*

Husband *tries hard to hold his tears but it's difficult. This is also too much for the* **CID** *who watches, finding it hard to control his emotions. Unable to bear the pain,* **Husband** *reaches out for* **Wife** *and leads her away, consoling her. The* **CID** *follows them.*

Jungle

Kadogo NoJoke *leads* **Girl 2**, **Boy 5**, **Boy 4** *and* **Girl 4** *directing each where to sit, forming a circle. He checks the circle. Happy with it, he exits.*

Girl 2, **Boy 4**, **Boy 5** *and* **Girl 4** *have a suppressed argument.*

Girl 2 I told you people, it was too risky, I told you.

Boy 5 Ssshh.

Girl 4 Maybe she wanted us to end up in Southern Sudan.

Girl 2 Well, now we are going to end up dead.

Boy 5 Don't say that, sis.

Girl 4 But she speaks the truth.

Boy 4 I would rather end up dead then than in Southern Sudan. I hear when you cross over there, you never return.

Beat.

Boy 5 It was just too soon to try something like an escape.

Girl 4 And it's too soon to die now too.

Kadogo NoJoke *returns holding two machetes followed by* **Boy 3** *and* **Kadogo Smiles**, *who also holds two machetes and a bible, followed by the crowd.*

Boy 3 So, you four think you are smarter than all of us, no?

They don't respond but cringe in fear.

Boy 3 I asked you a question, you dogs!

All No.

Kadogo NoJoke *and* **Smiles** *stand guard each on either side of the four children in a circle raising their machetes over their heads. The rest form a line across facing the four children in the circle.*

Boy 3 (*quieter*)   Traitors. (*Loudly.*) Traitors! These are the haters of their identity. The very animals that run away from their kind to join the enemy. SU-PRE-MA-CY! That is what we always talk about – our supremacy! But these four, these hypocrites do not want that! They do not want to see Acholi land rise to its rightful place. They would rather lick the boots of slaves!

He pauses and looks around for approval, which prompts the crowd to nod in approval.

Boy 3   Kadogo No Joke and Kadogo Smiles, the tools.

The **Kadogos** *run out and return with machetes.* **Boy 3** *takes one machete at a time giving it to the people in the line while addressing them, keeping one machete for himself.* **Kadogo** *remains with his two original machetes.*

Boy 3   We cannot be deterred in our fight for liberation, for freedom, for supremacy! This is our destiny as it was our father's father's father's destiny. But tell me, how can we achieve our supremacy with traitors amidst us? Whosoever is not for us is . . .?

All   Against us!

Boy 3 *stares hard at the culprits.*

Boy 3   In order to win, we must be united and committed to the liberation. We are here to win!

He bursts into a song.

Boy 3   Lu-holi ocoro i bar yo dano uru aura

The culprits jump to their feet dancing the 'Aguma' dance within the circle in an accustomed way.

Kadogo Smiles *picks up leading the song and the group joins in immediately.*

Kadogo Smiles   Lu-holi ocoro i bar yo dano uru aura

Group   Lu-holi ocoro i bar yo dano uru aura

Kadogo Smiles   Wan uturo gamente

Group   Nginyi nginyi nginyi nginyi ya

Kadogo Smiles Wan uturo gamente

Group Nginyi nginyi nginyi nginyi ya

[English Translation:
Boy 3 The holy ones have occupied the field people are just marveling.

Kadogo Smiles The holy ones have occupied the field the people are just marveling.

Group The holy ones have occupied the field the people are just marveling.

Kadogo Smiles We shall take over the government.

Group Completely, completely, completely, completely, yes.

Kadogo Smiles We shall take over the government.

Group Completely, completely, completely, completely, yes.]

They sing twice or thrice and he waves them to stop. They stop and sit.

He signals **Kadogo NoJoke**, *who gives him the Bible, in an accustomed way.*

Boy 3 (*raises the Bible up*) You see this great book of our Lord? It is a book full of the greatest wisdom ever from the Lord our God himself. It gives wisdom about everything from life to death.

He pauses and looks around.

Boy 3 Kadogos, tell us what this great book tells us about traitors.

Kadogo NoJoke *and* **Kadogo Smiles** *turn in unison facing the audience. The rest give praise and thanks as appropriate.*

Kadogo NoJoke Isaiah 24: 16. I waste away, I waste away! Woe to me! The treacherous betray! With treachery, the treacherous betray!

Kadogo Smiles Isaiah 48: 8. You have neither heard nor understood; from of old your ear has not been open. Well do I know how treacherous you are; you were called a rebel from birth.

Kadogo NoJoke 2 Timothy 3: 4. Traitors, headstrong, conceited, lovers of pleasure rather than lovers of God

Kadogo Smiles Mathew 7: 2. Woe to you, O traitor, you who have not been betrayed! When you stop destroying, you will be destroyed; when you stop betraying, you will be betrayed.

Kadogo NoJoke   Revelation 21: 8. But cowards, traitors, perverts, murderers, the immoral, those who practise magic, those who worship idols, and all liars – the place for them is the lake burning with fire and sulphur, which is the second death.

Kadogo Smiles   Revelation 20: 12. And I saw the dead, great and small, standing before the throne, and books were opened. Then another book was opened, which is the book of life. And the dead were judged by what was written in the books, according to what they had done.

Boy 3 *waves stopping them. They stop and turn back to their original positions in unison.*

Boy 3   The Bible gives us endless wisdom about traitors and in all, there is only one way to deal with traitors. Imagine if Jesus Christ our Lord had dealt with Judas Iscariot. Would he have been betrayed and killed?

Not sure of what to answer, the children murmur inaudible answers except for **Kadogo NoJoke** *and* **Kadogo Smiles**.

Kadogo NoJoke *and* **Kadogo Smiles** (*loudly*)   NO.

Boy 3   I asked, would he have been betrayed and killed?

All (*confident*)   Nooo!

Boy 3   We must not make the mistake Jesus made. We must annihilate all our enemies and anything that stands in the way of our goal, our liberation, our freedom, our supremacy. We must annihilate these four.

Just then **Girl 3** *enters.*

Girl 3 (*entering*)   Who are these that tried to escape?

Boy 3   These traitors, but we are about to deal with them.

Girl 3 *is surprised to see* **Girl 2**, *who looks down in shame.*

Girl 3   There must be some kind of mistake, Husband.

Boy 3   What do you mean?

Girl 3   Achan couldn't have tried to escape. I asked her to come find me at the rocks. I think when they found her they must have assumed she was trying to escape.

Girl 2, *4 and* **Boy 4**, *5 exchange a look of surprise.*

Boy 3 *gives* **Girl 3** *a critical look.*

Girl 3   I wanted to cleanse her at the rocks. Today is her fourth day here and I must cleanse her as your new bride.

Boy 3 (*to* **Girl 2**)   Is this true?

Girl 3 *stares hard at* **Girl 2**, *who hesitates not sure if* **Girl 3** *is setting her up.*

Girl 3   So, you doubt me now, Husband? How long have I been by your side?

Boy 3 *looks at her hard, then at* **Girl 2**. *He looks around as though to ascertain that nobody doubts or questions his judgment and then smiles broadly at* **Girl 3**. *He signals* **Girl 2** *to get up and join the crowd, who he watches to makes sure that no one is questioning him.*

Girl 2 *gets up and reaches out for* **Boy 5**'s *hand.* **Boy 5** *pulls his hand away.*

Girl 2 (*whispers*)   I don't want to live if you are not living.

Boy 5 (*whispers*)   My day is up. It's not your day yet.

Girl 2 (*emotional and slightly louder*)   But I can't survive without you, brother.

Boy 3 *quickly turns at hearing the word brother. He approaches and takes* **Girl 2** *by the hand.*

Boy 3   Sister wants to die with brother. How sweet?

Boy 5 *cringes.*

Boy 3 (*to* **Boy 5**)   Don't worry. I am not such a heartless person to kill a brother and sister on the same day. She will live.

Boy 5 *sighs, relieved.*

Boy 3   Sadly, that's not what I can say about you.

He puts his machete firmly in **Girl 2**'s *hand. She takes it fearfully.*

Boy 3   Now, join the rest and show these hypocrites what we do to traitors.

Boy 5   Please do it.

Girl 2 *looks at* **Girl 3**, *her eyes pleading to say save my brother but* **Girl 3** *can't do anything.*

Boy 5   Do it and save your life.

Girl 2 *joins the line of the crowd.* **Kadogo Smiles** *gives one of his machetes to* **Boy 3** *while* **Kadogo NoJoke** *gives one of his to* **Girl 3**.

Boy 3   Let's send them all home Noooooow!

Drum beats as the group dances forming a circle around the culprits making heavy dark moaning sounds. They dance around the culprits then all stab them at once. The culprits scream in pain dropping dead to the ground, bloody. **Boy 3** *pulls his machete out of the body of his victim and leads the way exiting. Each of them pulls out their machete and follows him in one line.*

The bodies lay on stage in total silence for a few seconds then begin to roll offstage in symbolism of being blown away by the wind.

Lights fade out.

Hut

The lights flare back on a secluded room. **Girl 3** *enters carrying a stool, clay bowl, wooden stirring spoon, a tin-made oil lamp, matchbox and a white sheet hangs on her shoulder.* **Girl 2** *follows her crying.*

Girl 3 (*putting stuff down*)   Will you stop crying now or else you will follow your brother six feet under.

Girl 2 (*emotional*)   In the grave? He is out there in the cold being eaten by vultures.

Girl 3 (*slaps her hard*)   And that's exactly where you will be, you idiot, if they hear you crying for him.

Beat.

Girl 3   There is no place for tears here.

She gives **Girl 2** *the white sheet.*

Girl 3   Wrap this.

Girl 2   What for?

Girl 3   You will do well not asking questions here.

Girl 2 *takes the sheet and wraps.*

Girl 2   Why did you save me?

Girl 3   I thought I just told you, you will do well here not asking questions.

Girl 2 *looks at* **Girl 3** *for a moment, puzzled.*

Girl 3 (*shows her the stool*) Sit.

Girl 2 *sits.* **Girl 3** *kneels, picks up the clay bowl and stirs its content with the wooden spoon. She rises and waves the bowl over* **Girl 2**'s *head four times.*

Girl 3 We call upon you . . .

Girl 2 (*jumps up*) What is that?

Girl 3 *only stares hard at her.* **Girl 2** *sits quietly.*

Girl 3 This is supposed to protect you.

Girl 2 Protect me from what?

Girl 3 Bullets, bombs, pregnancy . . . at least until your body is ready.

Girl 2 *says nothing.*

Girl 3 (*continues*) We call upon you spirit of our ancestors, to purify your daughter, Achan Cecilia.

She puts the bowl down, dips her hand in it and smears **Girl 2**'s *arms.*

Girl 3 Yes, spirit of our ancestors, we call upon you. This shear butter gift from your very own hands to cleanse all evils that our daughter has come with, mixed with our ancestral herbs, provided by your giving hearts, to protect her against all dangers. Protect her from the enemy's bullets. And may their own bullets hit them right back in the chest. And may you keep her womanly well dry until such a time when the rains are needed.

She ends by dipping her finger in the bowl and making the sign of the cross on **Girl 2**'s *forehead.*

Girl 3 You're almost ready.

Girl 2 Does that really work?

Girl 3 Like our Messiah, God's messenger Man, says, the Bible says, whosoever has faith, even as small as this mustard seed, shall move heaven.

Girl 2 And what do you say?

Girl 3 I say, if you don't get pregnant and you escape the bullets of our enemy, your faith has worked. But if you get pregnant or get killed by the bullets of our enemy, then you had no faith.

Girl 2 I don't understand.

Girl 3   You would do yourself a favor not trying to understand.

Girl 2   Why did you help me?

Girl 3   Because you must live and tell your family's story.

Girl 2   I don't understand.

Girl 3   You don't understand a lot of things.

Girl 3 *takes the matchbox and lights up the tin-made oil lamp and walks around* **Girl 2** *holding it four times.*

Girl 3   I know what happened to your family on the way here, your brother and little sister, Flavia. And then Paul. You must live to tell your parents what happened.

Girl 2   My parents are gone too.

Beat.

Girl 3   The more reason you must fight to survive. Forget about escaping. Live.

Girl 2   You call this living?

Girl 3   Survive then.

Girl 2   Is that what you are trying to do? Survive?

Girl 3 *hands* **Girl 2** *the tin-made oil lamp.*

Girl 3   Blow it off.

Girl 2   What am I blowing off? My life?

Girl 3 *ignores the question.* **Girl 2** *blows off the oil lamp.*

Girl 2   Why have you never left?

Girl 3 *looks at her sharply.*

Girl 2   I mean you wield so much power here and yet you do not leave.

Girl 3   What is there to return to? I returned once, only to end back here.

Before **Girl 2** *can say anything, they hear* **Boy 3** *approaching.*

Boy 3   May I come in now?

Girl 3   Just one moment, Husband.

She takes the tin-made oil lamp from **Girl 2** *and puts it down.*

Girl 2   Are you leaving me here?

Girl 3 *looks at her a bit sympathetic.*

Girl 3   Today is your day.

Girl 2 (*confused*)   My day for what?

Girl 3   You are a commander's wife, aren't you?

Girl 2 *looks at her in horror.*

Girl 3   Make him happy. It helps around here. And remember, you must live. (*Calls out.*) We are ready.

Boy 3 *enters.* **Girl 3** *bows in respect.*

Girl 3   Husband.

Boy 3 *takes her hand and looks her straight in the eyes.*

Boy 3   You are a good senior wife, Atuku.

Girl 3 *smiles.* **Boy 3** *leads her upstage. He dances a quick sex dance with her.* **Girl 2** *looks away. Two or three other girls enter one at a time dancing the same quick sex dance with him as* **Girl 3** *grabs all the ritual materials and exits. Each girl exits following* **Girl 3** *after the quick sex dance.*

Boy 3 *approaches* **Girl 2** *in her seat. He takes her hands and initiatives a sex dance.*

Horror music plays to their sex dance.

The sex dance between **Boy 3** *and* **Girl 2** *should be portrayed in a dance that depicts opposite states of mind,* **Boy 3** *excited and having fun in compensation for the alienating, harsh rebel life.* **Girl 2** *is sad and subdued, but pretends otherwise as she 'must survive.' As the dance goes on, every time they pull closer to each other,* **Boy 3** *celebrates while* **Girl 2** *laments as the two key words of* **Girl 3** *echoes on her mind – survive, live – and every time they pull apart,* **Girl 2** *takes a breath of relief, while* **Boy 3** *laments about being away.*

Their celebration versus lament dialogues must over-lap.

Boy 3   This is paradise.

Girl 2   This is hell.

Boy 3   At such moments, I forget the harsh part of this life.

Girl 2   At such moments, I regret having been brought into this life.

Boy 3   Thank heavens I was born a man.

Girl 2   I wish I were born a boy.

Boy 3   Please don't slip away from my arms.

Girl 2   Please give me the space to breath.

Boy 3   I need this paradise . . .

Girl 2   I wish this hell . . .

Boy 3   . . . to last forever.

Girl 2   . . . could go forever.

Suddenly they hear bomb blasts with numerous gunfire interludes. **Boy 3** *dives for cover.*

Boy 3   The gods are so jealous.

Girl 2   God is so merciful.

Girl 2 *runs about, confused.*

Boy 3 (*from his cover*)   Take cover!

Some group members find cover, some run into each other, some drop dead.

Bomb smoke fills up the air.

Boy 3 *notices* **Girl 2** *running about confused.*

Boy 3   God protect my new-found paradise.

He rushes and grabs her taking quick cover. He commands from where he has taken cover.

Boy 3   Take cover! Take cover! Take cover everyone! We cannot fight the fighter planes so take cover. If you see an escape route, then save yourself. Find your way to the rocks. Next destination is Southern Sudan! Do you all hear me? Next destination is Southern Sudan!

Just then, **Omony** *enters shouting above the noise.*

Omony   I can't continue hiding here anymore.

Margaret (*above the noise*)   What?

Omony (*shouts back*)   You said I would only be here for a while.

Margaret (*to the children*)   Okay, everyone stop. Let's stop there for a moment.

The children halt.

Omony   I cannot continue to hide here any longer. I must go and find out what is happening.

Margaret   But that's too risky.

Omony   I can't hide here forever.

Margaret   I am not asking you to hide here forever. Just for a while. Until things cool down.

Omony (*exiting*)   How long is a while?

Margaret (*stutters*)   I don't know. Just a little bit while.

Omony   I am sorry, Margaret. I must go.

Margaret   Omony, wait!

Margaret *drops the work stuff in her hands.*

Margaret (*running after* **Omony**)   I will be back soon.

Girl 3 (*calls after her*)   Teacher Margaret, what should we do in the meantime?

Margaret (*calls back*)   You are in charge for now, Abur. You continue.

Margaret *exits.*

Girl 3   Okay, boys and girls. I am Teacher Margaret for today.

The children boo at her.

Margaret (*runs back in*)   No, take a break. Play football or any game.

The children scream in excitement, some booing **Girl 3** *as they exit.*

The Road

Omony *enters on the opposite side from where he exited.* **Margaret** *enters running to catch up with him. She calls after him, but* **Omony** *doesn't stop.*

Margaret   Will you stop running around putting your life in danger?

Omony   Go away!

Margaret   Will you at least listen to me for a moment?

Omony *halts as* **Margaret** *catches up with him.*

Omony   I have got to see her. Talk to her.

Margaret   I know. But it's risky, you going about town like that when you know there are some people after your life.

Omony   She couldn't have, could she?

Margaret   I don't know. What do you think? You know her better.

Omony   I don't know Margaret, but it's all this ritual talk I heard that is scaring me.

Margaret   Do you think . . ./

Omony   That's the problem. I can't think anymore. I need to talk to her. Get some answers.

Margaret   But how are you going to get through to the prisons without the villagers trying something?

Omony   I can't just go into hiding. I have to know the truth.

Margaret   Okay then. I will come with you.

Omony   No way! I don't want to put you at risk too.

Margaret   You are not putting me at risk. I am volunteering.

Omony   This is my problem, Margaret, so will you let me deal with it my way?

Margaret   You are my boyfriend, Omony. So, your problem is our problem.

Omony   Come on, Margaret. Don't you go complicating things now.

Margaret   I am not complicating things.

Omony   Yes, you are. Imagine if the villagers attacked us. It would be two lives at risk.

Margaret   Well you worry about your life and leave me to worry about mine.

Omony *realizes this is not taking them anywhere and takes another approach.*

Omony   Listen Margaret, this is not a joke.

Margaret   I know, Omony. And I have never taken it as a joke.

Omony   Maybe your Aunt was right. You are risking your life being with me.

Margaret   And what are you trying to say exactly?

Omony   I think maybe . . . maybe it's better if you stayed away from me.

Margaret   Are you breaking up with me now?

Omony   Am only trying to save your life.

Margaret   Don't you love me anymore?

Omony   What has love got to do with anything anymore, Margaret?

Margaret   But I still love you.

Omony *looks away.*

Omony   It's useless, Margaret.

Margaret   Will you at least look at me when you talk to me?

Omony   Go back home. Find someone else and marry.

Margaret   But it's not that simple, Omony.

Omony   That's why it's life.

Margaret   I mean, I am pregnant. I'm carrying our baby.

Omony *is shocked.*

Omony   This can't be. How did this happen?

Margaret   How did this happen?!

Omony   I know how it happened! I meant how could this happen?

Margaret   How could this happen? That is worse! Don't you want to have a child with me? Start a family? Our own family?

Omony   Start a family?! What family? How can we bring up a child in this hostility! This animosity! This cannibalism!

Margaret   I don't know. But we can try.

Omony   Try what, Margaret? (*As though to himself.*) Oh this is just a vicious circle of endless grudges.

Margaret   But it doesn't have to be. We can't look at our unborn as a vicious circle of murder. What if this is the hope? A sign that we should fight for our love? A chance for healing old scars?

Omony   There are scars that stay with us forever.

Margaret   So, you are just giving up on us? Are you not willing to try? To fight for us?

She draws closer to him trying to appeal to him.

Margaret   Come on, Omony. He's here now. We can't run away from this. All we have to do is try. Just try.

Omony   That's why it is important for me to do this alone now. I have to find out the truth about Mother's ritual. That's our only hope, Margaret.

Margaret   And what if she did it? What if she tells you she did it?

Omony *takes a moment to ponder and then talks to her with a weird calm over him.*

Omony   Go back to your work, Margaret. I must do this alone.

And with that he walks away.

Margaret *calls after him.*

Margaret   Will I see you later?

Omony *exits without responding.* **Margaret** *ponders for a moment and exits, disappointed.*

Prison Corridor

Juma *walks out the* **Bishop** *as they chat about* **Mother***'s case. In the background music plays on the radio.*

Juma   I am sorry there was a miscommunication. You were supposed to join the CID and his team with Mother.

Bishop   It's okay. I will come back.

Juma   I still think it would be better now if you waited for them here. They are coming back with her here.

The **Bishop** *contemplates.*

Bishop   Do you think she could be suffering from some kind of insanity?

Juma   To be honest, I don't know. But I suppose she will be taken through some tests before the trial.

Bishop   Some insanities are not medical.

Omony *enters panting. Both* **Juma** *and the* **Bishop** *are surprised to see him.*

Bishop   Young man, are you okay?

Omony   I am here to see my mother.

The **Bishop** *looks at* **Juma**.

Juma   It's not visiting hours yet, young man.

Omony   Could I just have a minute with her? Just ask one question.

Juma   Why don't you come back during visiting hours? Then you can ask as many questions as you want.

Omony   I just have one question. Please.

Bishop   Who is your mother?

Omony   Cecilia Achan.

Juma   Are you the son of. . .?

Bishop   She has a son?

Juma   Why would a mother com. . ./

He looks at **Omony** *and stops.*

Bishop   There are evil acts that are hard to understand and even harder to explain.

Omony   My mother isn't evil. Can I talk to her please?

Juma   Unfortunately, she is not in.

Omony   What do you mean she is not in? Where have you people taken my mother?

Omony *grabs* **Juma**, *who in a trained police way roughs up and pushes him over. The* **News Anchor** *voice on the radio cuts in. They all stop and listen.*

News Anchor Voice   In breaking news, today, the police have finally got a breakthrough after weeks of investigation into the disappearance of the six-year-old girl, Fiona.

The three look at each other.

News Anchor Voice   Fiona was one among the five children who had gone missing. In a shocking turn of events, the suspect, Mother, who was unyielding to the police at the beginning, yesterday confessed to the kidnap and murder of all these children. Now thousands of concerned citizens gather in front of the Gulu High court building ahead of the trial demanding the woman's head.

Sound bites of the rioters yelling all sorts of angry words – 'kill her, she is a murderer, she must die too . . . ' The sound bites fade out.

Without a word, **Omony** *turns to leave but comes face to face with* **Mother** *being led in by the guards, closely followed by* **CID**. *For the first-time* **Mother** *reveals endearing emotions, grappling for* **Omony**.

Mother   My son, you came to see me.

The guards pull her away. **Omony** *halts and turns around, keeping his position.*

Mother   Please just give me one minute with my son, I beg you.

The guards look to the **CID** *for approval, which he gives them. They let go of her but keep a close watch. She draws a little closer to* **Omony**.

Omony   No mother, I did not come to see you. I had come to ask you if you did it but I can't ask you that now, can I?

Mother *struggles to find the words.*

Mother   I am sorry, Son.

Omony   For what, Mother? For all the innocent lives, you took? For messing up my life? Or for both?

Mother   Oh, my son. You are too young. And too hopeful.

Omony   I just want to understand, Mother. Why? Why Mother?

Mother *says nothing, head bowed. For a moment, she feels her son's pain.*

Omony   Please say something, Mother!

Mother *still says nothing. Heavy silence and tension fills the room.*

Disturbed by the uneasy silence the guards reach out for **Mother**.

Omony (*to the guards*)   Please, just a moment. (*To* **Mother**.) Please say something Mother! Tell me something. Tell me you didn't know what you were doing. Tell me you were possessed by an evil spirit or something.

Mother   You wouldn't understand.

Omony   Is that all you can say?

Mother   This was never meant to hurt you, Son.

Omony   Never meant to hurt me? Never meant to . . .? What will I tell people when they point fingers at me saying, 'Look there goes the son of the murderer?' Never meant to hurt me! How do I walk head high ever again in the community? Never meant to hurt me! What will I tell your grandchildren when they come back from school telling me their peers call them names and won't play with them? Asking me why everyone says their grandmother was a murderer. What do I tell them? Don't tell me it was never meant to hurt me! Give me a reason. Tell me what to say. Tell me something else. Tell me anything but that.

Mother   I don't know! I can't tell you what to tell them. But I can tell you they started it. They started it all. I have nothing.

Omony   You have me.

Mother   You are too young to understand.

Omony   I am a man now, Mother.

Mother   Forgive me, Son. My eyes are too misty for you. Pray. Pray for yourself. Pray that God looks down upon you more kindly than he did me.

Omony   You are right, Mother. I will pray to God. But not for me. I will pray that God grant your soul the peace you have yearned for but never found here on earth. (*To the guards.*) Thank you. You can take her away now.

The guards approach Mother to take her but **Margaret** *enters breathless. They halt.*

Omony *turns to leave and comes face to face with* **Margaret**.

Omony (*to* **Margaret**)   I told you to stay away from this.

Margaret   I told you I am in. I couldn't stay away, not especially after what I heard on the news.

She looks at **Mother**, *overwhelmed.* **Wife** *and* **Husband** *enter.*

Wife (*to* **Margaret**)   You said she was innocent, now what do you have to say.

Margaret   I said she could be innocent.

Wife   Well, she is not. You see the kind of people you are sleeping with? Murderers!

Mother (*to* **Wife**)   You don't have any right to call anyone a murderer. You are all born of murderers.

Wife   Just because you are a murderer don't try to make everyone one.

Husband (*tries to control his wife*)   Please this is no time for name calling.

Mother   Wise man. She doesn't know, does she?

Wife   What is she talking about?

Mother   Tell her. Tell her how many your father, Man, 'sent home'. Tell her now. More than the numbers I sent home. She must know.

Wife *looks at* **Mother** *confused.*

Margaret *swallows hard knowing exactly what* **Mother** *means.*

Wife   Will you stop pretending to be mad? You must pay for what you did to Fiona and all the other children.

Margaret   She is not pretending to be mad, Aunt.

Wife   Don't tell me you are still on her side. She is a murderer.

Margaret   I know that. But she has her reasons.

Wife   Are you saying it is okay that she killed all those children because she has her reasons?

Margaret   No. Of course not. I am just saying I understand where she is coming from.

Wife   You understand where she is coming from? What is going on here?

Husband   You will never understand.

Wife   What won't I ever understand? Why isn't anyone telling me anything?

Margaret   Man is my grandfather . . . and Fiona's. He is the grandfather of all the children she killed.

Wife   I don't understand.

Husband   No, you don't.

Wife (*to* **Margaret**)   Your grandfather is dead and gone.

Margaret   But we are still here. The past always haunts the future.

Wife   Is that why my Fiona is dead?

Margaret   It's complicated.

Wife   But my child didn't do anything to her. (*To* **Mother**.) How could you? How could you take out your twisted revenge on my little girl?

Margaret   Aunt.

Wife   Margaret, stay away from this.

Mother *looks at them all, halting on* **Wife***. They all watch her critically afraid of what she might do.*

Mother (*to* **Wife**)   Please don't you stand there and judge me. You don't understand a thing. What do you know?

The guards grab **Mother** *by the arm, lead her downstage centre, sit her down and exit each on either side of the wings.*

The stage swiftly changes into a court room and **Mother***'s trial going on in her mind, and the characters change into court characters. The props and costumes are brought on stage by the dancers.* **CID** *becomes the* **Judge***, who sits on a kingly chair upstage centre, brought in by one of the dancers, along with his robe. Jumaia the* **Court Clerk** *stands next to the* **Judge***.* **Bishop** *becomes* **Mother***'s* **Lawyer***, and moves down stage left by a dancer, where* **Mother***'s family and all who support her sit.* **Wife** *becomes the* **Prosecutor** *and moves downstage right, where* **Man***'s family and all those against* **Mother** *sit.*

Court Room

Court Clerk   The Honourable Judge Galdino Ochan presiding. Case number 1313. The state of the Republic of Uganda versus the accused, Madam Cecila Achan, charged with five counts of murder in the first degree.

Judge   Does the prosecution have an opening statement?

Prosecutor   Yes, Your Honour.

The **Prosecutor** *takes the floor.*

Prosecutor   Today we are gathered here to bear witness to a very sad case – indeed, the murder of five innocent children by none other than a mother. Someone who is supposed to be the protector of children. And those of you who are mothers like me will attest to this fact. So, as we sit and listen, I would like, no, I want to call on all mothers, fathers, grandmothers, grandfathers, aunts, uncles, future mothers and fathers. I want to call on all of you to think. Think about 5 lives. Not 1, not 2, not 3, not 4 but 5 young innocent lives taken away prematurely. Think of the dreams and hopes shattered and buried six feet under. Think of future presidents, ministers, ambassadors, mothers and fathers brutally killed. THINK! That is all I want you to do. The defence might try to lead you to believe that it is an act of insanity. And you might just be tempted to believe them. But let's ask ourselves. What is insanity? Insanity is merely an act that seems different from the ordinary but which comes naturally to cold blooded murderers like the suspect. Actions that manifest themselves in seemingly insane behaviours are actions of long sane harboured intentions. The prosecution will show you that the suspect acted in a calculated meticulous way. This was a simple calculated act of revenge. And we all know that 'an eye for an eye makes the world blind'.

Judge   Does the defence have an opening statement?

Lawyer   Yes, Your Honour.

Judge   Make it quick!

Lawyer   Twenty years ago, we all jubilated because the peace agreement had been reached. Papers were signed. 'Mato Oput' was done. Everything seemed fine. In fact, great! Our leaders were all joy, proclaiming forgiveness on behalf of victims they never consulted. We all lacked the eyes to see that no amount of signatures on paper could make right the wrongs that had been done! That no amount of signatures on paper could take away the pain! And that no amount of 'Mato Oput' could wash away the bitterness! It's this blindness that makes the world blind. It's this blindness that makes the world dark. One thing however cures the world. Just one thing to give the victims closure-justice! Such blindness breeds insanity. So, I say, yes insanity is as real as Butabika mental hospital! And my client suffers such insanity. Insanity I know you will all prove beyond any doubt by the end of this court hearing.

Judge   So, for the case of five counts of murder, how does the defence plead?

Lawyer   The defence pleads insanity!

Mother *jumps to her feet.*

Mother   I am not insane, Your Worship!

Judge   It's Your Honour!

Mother   I am half guilty, Your Honour! I must complete my ritual, Your Honour! I must gain full guilt!

Judge   Counsel, get your client in order!

The **Lawyer** *asks* **Mother** *to sit down.* **Mother** *remains standing, smiling.*

Mother   I must get my heaven . . . oh once upon a time I lived my heaven . . . once upon a time . . .

The smile on her lips grows even bigger as she begins to hear the voices of happiness from the Acholi Larakaraka dance.

She sits down and becomes her 'Little self' swaying to the beats of dance and calls out to her father.

Mother   Dance with me, Father. Dance with me. Dance with me, Father . . .

She continues to sway to the beat only she can hear, and then suddenly her demeanour changes and becomes melancholic.

Mother   And then my heaven was penetrated. First it was them. They came in large numbers and they came with a vengeance.

She turns around with her back to the audience and watches the past upstage.

Past

Mother's Ancestral Homestead

Mother*'s* **Mother, Amal** *and* **Mother***'s Father,* **Latigo** *cower centre stage.* **Amal** *is pregnant.* **Soldier 1, 2** *and* **3** *follow closely by their feet.* **Soldier 1** *and* **2** *roughs them up, dropping them on their butts.*

Soldier 1   Where are the rebels?

Latigo/Amal   We don't know.

Soldier 2   Why are you protecting them?

Amal   Afande, we are not pro . . ./

Soldier 5 *kicks her hard in the belly.*

Soldier 3   Anyanya. Shut up. Do you think you are still in control?

None answer.

Soldier 2   He is asking you, you dogs.

Latigo/Amal   No Afande. No.

Soldier 3   Who is in control now?

Latigo/Amal   You, Afande.

Latigo *sees Little* **Mother** *approaching, that is,* **Girl 2**. *He tries to signal her to turn back. Little* **Mother** *stops and hesitates.* **Soldier 1** *notices.*

Soldier 1   Who is that?

Latigo   No one, Afande.

Soldier 1 (*looks at* **Girl 2**)   No one Afande gani. (*Kicks him hard.*) Tumbafu ya mama yako.

Soldier 1   Is she your rebel daughter?

Amal   She is just my daughter, Afande.

Soldier 1 *heads for* **Girl 2**.

Soldier 1 (*to* **Girl 2**)   Wewe kuja. Come here quick.

Solider 1 *grabs her tight by the arm and drags her in.*

Amal   Please don't hurt her, Afande.

Soldier 1   Don't worry, we have no intention of hurting her.

Soldier 3   Our intention is to only make her happy. To make all of you happy wives.

Mother   And what happened next was never to have been expected. EVER. Not even our elders in the years they have spent on the face of the earth could have . . .

Soldier 2 (*to* **Latigo**)   Wewe.

He beckons **Latigo**, *who gets up and moves to the front.*

Soldier 2   Shusha suruwali kisha uiname.

Latigo *hesitates.*

Soldier 2   Nimesema, pants down and bend over.

Latigo *makes to remove his pants.* **Amal** *and* **Girl 2** *look away.*

Soldier 3   Why are you looking away? Watch.

He forcefully turns their heads to watch. In a rape dance, **Latigo** *is raped in turn by* **Soldiers 2** *and* **1** *respectively as* **Soldier 3** *make sure the wife and daughter watch.*

Soldier 1 (*to* **Amal**)   Now, your turn.

Amal *gets up, shaking.* **Soldier 3** *gets excited.*

Soldier 3 (*to his colleagues*)   I love them pregnant. So, comrades, may I have the honour?

Soldier 3 *grabs* **Amal**, *who resists. He slaps her hard on the face. She falls.* **Soldier 2** *raises her legs up.* **Soldier 3** *unzips and gets on top of her while* **Soldier 1** *holds* **Girl 2** *at gunpoint to ensure that she watches; and all except adult* **Mother** *freeze.*

Present

Court Room

Mother   And like that we were all, fathers, mothers, sons and daughters, raped in turn while the rest watched the spectacle. (*To the audience.*) Why do you all stare at me quietly? It happened to you too. You think silence will save you the shame, the humiliation, take away the dehumanization? Say something. Give your testimony. Tell your story, and let the world be the judge.

Silence.

Then suddenly a victim stands up from the audience. House light fades on.

Man 1   Your Honour, they came to my home, called me father of rebels. They asked for cattle and I showed them the kraal. They accused me of feeding the rebels with my cattle. A big number of them went ahead to the kraal where the boys were and led away the cattle. A few of the soldiers remained behind, gathered all of us in the homestead, a true extended African family. They tortured us, beat us, tore off our clothes and in the darkness, they threw us down, pinned us hard to the ground and group raped us. Fathers, mother, sons and daughters, it didn't bother them one bit. They said they wanted to show us that we are all women, we are not men like them . . . and with their cock in my anus, in our ears and mouths and anuses, I . . . we had all been made women!

Another victim rises. **Man 1** *remains standing.*

Woman   They surrounded our homestead and gathered us at a
nearby primary school. They gathered the whole village. At the school,
we were all gathered in one large classroom. They took us one by one
and did with us what they wanted. When they were done with us, they
brought us back to the same room. It was as if to humiliate us further,
all sitting in that classroom knowing what just happened to us . . .
knowing that it also happened to the other person, who was taken and
brought back. When we were released that evening, we all walked
away quietly to our homes, heads bowed down, swearing inwardly,
never to speak of these happenings ever. As though the desecration of
our bodies weren't enough, our homes were desecrated too. They
defecated in our water pots, maize flour and all food stuff they laid their
eyes on.

Another victim rises. **Woman** *remains standing too.*

Man 2   It had become my life style. I decided to get used to it. For what
could a man brought down to ashes ever do? Mine was a lone homestead,
your honour. I had lost all my family members, not to war. To all kind of
illness. And here I was, a childless widower waiting for my day to return
to dust. They came to my home too. Like three or so of them. They raped
me and then grabbed a couple of my chickens and goats. I had no cattle.
And then they came back again, raped me and grab a couple of chickens
and goats. And then again and again and again, nine times, maybe twelve
times, I'm too old to have kept count. The next time I woke up, it was in
a hospital ward, Lacor Hospital. I don't know who took me there. A
Good Samaritan, I supposed.

Man 1   How could I ever be a respectable father and husband again
after this? How does a father ever be a father after not only failing to
protect his family, but submitting as a wife to 'real' men?

Woman   And how could I ever be a respectable Mama and tell off other
men to keep their hands off, for I belonged to only one man? How?

Man 2   What elderly wisdom could I ever give again if I, like the kids,
had been . . .

Man 2 *is unable to complete his thought.*

Man 1   Tell me, how does one forgive these things?

Woman   Forgive the desecration of the womb . . . the womb of motherhood?

Man 2   Forgive the feel of fellow men's cock in . . . (*hesitates, then strongly*) in the ass of an old man?

House lights black out and the victims sit.

Mother *rises.*

Mother   My justice. Where is my justice? They said FORGIVE! Who are they to say that? What did they lose? Who did they lose? Did they bury their mother? Their father? Their sister? Their two loving brothers? Who did they bury? Did they have their lips chopped off? Their teeth all out at the same time? Their hands maimed? Their ears? Their noses? Their legs? FORGIVE they said! Who asked me whether I wanted to forgive? Forgive they said! Forgive! Forgive! Forgive!

The **Judge***'s and* **Lawyer***'s dialogues overlap* **Mother***'s repeated 'forgive'.*

Judge   Counsel will you do something about your client?

Lawyer   Your Honour, the defence calls for your indulgence.

Mother   I was happily hopeless with my full mist day. But the sun sneaked in with promises and disappeared almost immediately.

Lawyer   As the defence has already mentioned earlier, my client suffers insanity.

Mother   My pot of hell overflowed. My heaven became hell and my hell my heaven. I was rich in hell. I am still rich in hell.

Judge   Will you be quiet now?

Mother   Where is my heaven? Why am I surrounded by nothing but hell? I had a bit of heaven too. A bit of heaven, a bit hell. Heaven, hell. Heaven, hell. My heaven was here . . .

The **Judge** *bangs the gavel on the table calling* **Mother** *to order, which instead triggers another memory which she turns to watch, her back turned to the audience.*

Past

Mother's Ancestral Homestead

The Larakaraka *dance at the marriage ceremony picks up from the point when the crowd has joined the bride and groom. They sing the 'Ajolina' song now totally enjoying themselves.*

Mother   And then my heaven was gone. Nothing but hell surrounded me. The second hell. The hell that was meant to be my liberation.

The dance culminates in a climax when the bride notices **Man***, the rebel leader and starts to scream out loud in fear, holding tightly to her groom.* **Man** *and his men enter with threats and the dancing villagers cower together as some of* **Man***'s soldiers set houses on fire.*

Man *grabs the bride from the groom and gives her a slap on the cheek that sends her tumbling down hard in front of the crowd. The groom overwhelmed with fear runs and hides amidst the crowd.*

Man   Everyone stay where you are quietly. How can you celebrate at a time like this? You are enjoying while we suffer on your behalf. While we suffer to bring you liberation. What reason do you have to celebrate when our people are reduced to slaves by those who used to be ourselves?

He moves and stands over the bride.

Man   The Bible says, if any of your body parts brings you trouble then it is better that you cut that body part off. (*Pauses.*) Kadogo Action, help her cut off her lips. They seem to bring her trouble making loud alarms.

The **Kadogos** *lead the shaking bride off-stage. A loud scream of the bride's pain emits from the wings bringing a chill to the villagers on stage.*

Man   Let that serve as a reminder to the people of this land never to make an alarm, reporting us.

Man *pulls the children out from amid the villagers, one at a time giving them to the* **Kadogos***, who lead them off-stage.*

Man   And now to teach the people of this village to stop unnecessary partying and join the liberation. (*To the* **Kadogos***.*) Open fire!

The **Kadogos** *fire randomly at the villagers. Live 'Nanga' plays as sounds of bullets fill the air and bodies drop dead.*

Man   Enough! Let's go! Let's go! Quick!

They exit, **Man***'s voice fading off as he yells, 'Let's go. Let's go.' 'Let's go quick!'*

Present

Court Room

Mother *crawls on the floor in mourning as if she still sees the bodies in a pool of blood in the compound. She touches the bodies as she says her lines and each body she touches rolls off-stage.*

Mother   Nothing but hell surrounds us. We are pursued in all corners. We have no escape. We are like punch bags, like the grass that suffers when two elephants fight. We are like little balls. Tossed left and right. Back and forth. Centre. No matter how far we run we get picked up and back and tossed again. We have no voices of our own. No directions of our own. We don't know who to trust. Who to be loyal to. Either way we always lose. We are but a bunch of miserable losers. We have nothing of our own. No heaven. No hell. We get cheated. Cheated even out of our hell. (*In a trance.*) Yes. I was happily hopeless with my full mist day. But the sun sneaked in with promises and disappeared almost immediately.

The **Lawyer** *approaches and shakes* **Mother** *to bring her back to her 'senses'.*

Lawyer   Stop it! Get out of this insanity!

Mother *just continues like a zombie.*

Mother   All I need is my ritual! I was denied my ritual! Promises were made and not kept! And now I am half guilty and half free! Denied my full guilt and freedom! You must grant me my ritual, Your Honour! That is all I ask of you, Your Honour!

She gets hysterical and starts to head towards the **Judge**.

Mother   Don't be afraid, Your Worship! Your King! Your Everything! Just grant me my ritual. Grant me my full guilt and freedom! Grant me my ritual. Grant me my full guilt and freedom! Grant me my ritual. Grant me my full guilt and freedom!

There is commotion in the courtroom as the scared **Judge** *calls for security.*

The guards rush in, grab **Mother** *and lead her away.*

Mother'*s scream of 'Grant me my ritual. Grant me my full guilt and freedom!' fades off in a distance.*

The **Judge** *bangs the gavel adjourning the proceeding and exits.*

The court crowd rise in commotion marveling at what just happened with everything unfolding in slow motion.

Only **Omony** *and* **Margaret** *remain sitting.*

A court attendant reaches for **Margaret**'s *hand to exit together but she turns him down.*

Some of the crowd are happy, excited or surprised to see friends or people they know. They wave, shake hands, and hug. Others argue over one thing or another and others leave together side by side discussing the incident.

When the last of the people are exiting, **Margaret** *rises and approaches* **Omony***, who rises, and action resumes in real time.*

Margaret *reaches for* **Omony**'s *hand and places it on her belly.* **Omony** *is hesitant as first but then begins to caress it, enjoying it. He checks himself and withdraws his hand, taking a step or two back.*

Omony   It's hopeless, Margaret. The battle was lost long before you and I were even born.

Margaret   What! What are you saying?

Omony *says nothing. He looks at her hard and long then quietly exits.*

Margaret *goes down on her knees centre stage, alone with her thoughts. She looks around at the bare world around her. She gently caresses her belly, torn between the horror of becoming a single mother and of the thrill of the baby in her womb. She smiles to herself talking to her unborn baby.*

Margaret   Well my baby, looks like it's just me and you (*As though to herself.*) So who may hear my case? Who shall be my judge? Is there a court of love? Who shall fight for love? (*To her unborn baby again.*) Listen to me my baby. Listen to your mama; you can't join the vicious circle. This vicious circle of man's destructive nature. You must not be a part of the problem. You must be a part of the change. You and I must not give up.

She gathers herself up, hand on belly and exits.

Epilogue

Prison

Darkness reigns.

The guards enter leading **Mother***, her legs heavily chained. She sits quietly as the guards go to their guarding position.*

A very small ray of light from a small prison ventilation sneaks in.

Mother*'s eyes fall on the little dirty old plastic bucket that stands close by. She stares hard at it, in deep thought, then stares hard into the audience vacantly.*

Mother   Why do you all look at me so? If my abduction, my captivity was my liberation, freedom and restoration to supremacy then how did I end up subdued, caged and lowly?

Pauses.

Mother   It's so quiet in here. It's so quiet like my home. It's home. Is your home quiet and bleak like mine? Of course not. I can hear them. Your children and grandchildren fill your compound buzzing with delight like bees. Running around in glee. Laughing at my empty compound.

Wife *and* **Husband** *enter holding hands.*

Mother *continues to stare straight at the audience almost as if she doesn't recognize the entry of* **Wife** *and* **Husband**. **Husband** *lets go of* **Wife***'s hand.* **Wife** *draws closer to* **Mother** *while* **Husband** *looks on.*

Wife   We just came to say two things: Firstly, that we are sorry for everything that happened to you. And secondly, that our daughter, our Fiona . . . our innocent Fiona didn't have to pay for other people's mistakes. (**Mother** *doesn't stir.*)

Mother *still just stares straight at the audience like a zombie.*

Husband   We forgive you. But we hope you can forgive yourself.

Husband *reaches out for* **Wife**.

Husband   Come, let's go Honey. It's useless.

Wife *takes* **Husband***'s hand and they turn to leave.*

Mother   Wait!

Wife *and* **Husband** *halt, thinking* **Mother** *is talking to them, but* **Mother** *continues without acknowledging them.*

Mother   I can hear them. Do you hear that?

Both **Wife** *and* **Husband** *hear nothing. Neither do we.*

Mother *(singing)*   I can hear them. They're coming. I can hear them.

Voices of the ghosts of victims start to whisper off-stage, 'What about us?' 'What about me?'

Mother (*singing*)   I can hear them. I can hear them again. They're coming. They're here. They're all here now.

All make their way to the stage.

Live 'nanga' and any other appropriate musical instruments play as they all march to the musical beats of the instruments. Once the cast are on stage, there is a transition in the music beat and they all sing the theme song, 'What about us?'

All   What about us? What about us? What about us we ask? (×4)

1. Ghost of **Mother**'*s family*
We come weary from the dead
Mourning for a world lost to us
Forgotten souls cry out, we cry.

All   Wuuu waaa wuuu
Awiya haya awiya hayaya
What about our lives, our dreams and hope?
Buried in the ground, cast away
Forgotten souls cry out, we cry.

All   Wuuu waaa wuuu
Awiya haya awiyahayaya

2. **Mother**
I am an empty soul, devoid of life
Robbed of my family, humanity, sanity
Broken haunted voices cry out.

All   Wuuu waaawuuu
Awiya haya awiya hayaya

3. Ghost of the children killed by **Mother**
What about the right to innocence?
To be a child
To be untainted, undamaged, undestroyed
Don't let innocence die
Killed by endless adult wars.

All   Wuuu waaa wuuu
Awiya haya awiya hayaya

4. **Wife** *and* **Husband**
What of the dreams in our children's eyes?
Killed before the crack of dawn?
What of justice?

What of the law we ask?

All   Wuuu waaa wuuu
Awiya haya awiya hayaya

5. **Margaret** *and* **Omony**
Margaret   What about love, hope? What about the future?

Omony   What about the things to make the world a better place?

Both   What is the world without love and no freedom?

All   Wuuu waaa wuuu
Awiya ha awiya hayaya Bridge.

Margaret   Let's save love

Omony   Save love

Margaret   Save the future

Omony   Save the future

Margaret   For all we've lost

All   Ahhh, haaah

Both   Let us save all we can

All   We stand joined as one
Let our voices reach far out
We call out and shout
Let our justice now resound
We cry . . .

Child 1   What about us?

All   We cry . . .

Child 2   What about me?

Child 3   What about us?

Child 2   What about us?

All   We cry . . .

Child 2   What about me?

Child 3   What about us?

Child 1   What about us?

Margaret   We cry, we cry . . .

Child 2   What about me?

Child 3   What about us?

All   We cry . . .

All   What about now?

Margaret   We're tired of waiting.

All   What about now?

Omony   We're here to say

All   What about now?

Mother   What about the future

All   What about now?

Husband   What about the peace?

All   What about now?

Wife   We're tired of waiting

All   What about now?

Margaret   We call on you

All   What about now?

Omony   To lend a hand

All   What about now?

Margaret   For a new day

All   What about now?
We ask, we ask . . . (×4)
What about now?!

All freeze.

The End

Unsettled

JC Niala is a Kenyan poet, screen and playwright currently resident in UK. Her radio play *The Strong Room* was shortlisted by Wole Soyinka in BBC Africa Performance 2010 and went on to be produced for the stage both in Nairobi and London. Her 2015 film *Wazi? FM* won several awards including an EU Award for promoting peace and cultural understanding. She has an MSt in Creative Writing from Kellogg College, University of Oxford. Her historical research on women in Oxford and African soldiers in the First World War is featured on the University of Oxford's iTunes educational channel. She received a Community Engagement and Academic Merit Award for this work. She was the V-LED Writer-in-Residence from 2016–2018 using verbatim theatre to stimulate local climate action in Kenya, South Africa, the Philippines and Cambodia.

Production history

The first rehearsed reading of *Unsettled* took place in October 2017 at the University of Oxford.

Critical introduction

Plus ça change, plus c'est la même chose

In writing *Unsettled* I was interested in examining what has changed in Kenya since independence, especially when it came to issues at the intersection of gender, race and social class. It can be easy to despair. Land (a key resource) remains contentious but yet alongside it, there are also positive changes in many parts of the country. I therefore set *Unsettled* in a place where there is still a population of Kenyans who are descendants of (largely) English settlers and at the same time is growing and changing the town rapidly.

Often, Kenyan plays feature communities within their own particular cultural or social context and so it is common to see on the stage a play featuring only Kenyan African, Kenyan White or Kenyan Asian stories. While this does reflect some of the social separation that still exists, it is not the full picture. Kenyans of all races and cultural backgrounds also interact with each other and it is often in towns like the one in which *Unsettled* is set, that the relationships are nuanced and complex.

It can be easy to 'take sides' and quickly categorize people as 'good' or 'bad' particularly against a backdrop of historical injustice. My interest is in the liminal spaces where things are not so clear. Another area explored in *Unsettled* is the idea of complicity within a society. The ways in which eyes can be wide shut to what is going on in order to maintain a delicate fabric of existence, particularly when it is felt to be under threat. Under these circumstances, there is sometimes no obvious 'winner' to moral dilemmas, and I wanted my characters to wrestle with the choices that they make, that will impact not only their lives, but the lives of those around them. I was interested in the question of what it feels like to sit with the weight of a choice, not in isolation, but in full view of your community who know, but yet might not understand or choose to understand. Finally, I had a concern with the thorny question of is it better to potentially change many lives at the expense of one? Democracy which encompasses the utilitarian principle of the majority is something that is regularly sold to African countries as a basis of salvation from current political maladies. However, in the day to day existence of individual lives, what does it feel like to sacrifice that one for the many? Is it clearly and easily recognizable as the right and good thing to do?

Just as in the tangle of our own lives, I did not expect the characters to sit easily with what it was they decided to do. They are each bound by certain limitations of who they find themselves to be in a particular time and place.

What I hoped for was a small space of hope that even within the complexities of an ever-changing world, there is a possibility for at least some things to have a different outcome – even while the process leaves us unsettled.

Characters

John Spencer, *a Kenyan White man, second-generation 'settler' (also called Kenya Cowboys – he has a typical KC accent which has hints of its British origins but is slower and with an African lilt and peppered with Kiswahili words spoken with a British sounding accent), late fifties/early sixties.*

Stephen, *a Kenyan African man, late twenties, speaks excellent English with an easy to understand Kenyan accent.*

Mimi, *a Kenyan White woman, third-generation 'settler', KC accent, early forties.*

Cikú, *a Kenyan African diaspora woman, British accent, early forties.*

Young White Woman, *indeterminable European accent, twenties.*

Linda, *a Kenyan White woman, second-generation 'settler', KC accent, late fifties/early sixties.*

Martha, *a British White woman, lived in Kenya for the last 40 years, British accent, early sixties.*

Setting

Just after the short rains before the full heat of the hot dry season. The entire play takes place in the Cypress Café, which is decked out with an odd assortment of hand crafted wooden tables and chairs. The Cypress Café is in Nanyuki, which was once a small town on the edge of a wildlife conservancy at the foot of Mount Kenya, but the town is growing fast and is also close to a British Army base.

The play takes place in the present day but the second- and third-generation settlers still live as though from a previous age. Their accents were once British but British accents have changed since, and theirs have not.

Notes on staging

/ denotes where dialogue starts to overlap

Act One

Scene One

Early morning at the Cypress Café.

John *is reading the newspaper at one of the tables and when* **Stephen** *brings in his breakfast he barely lifts the paper so that* **Stephen** *has to contort to place it squarely in front of* **John**.

Stephen   Sir.

John *slightly nods his head and* **Stephen** *retreats to a safe distance from which to watch* **John**, *ready to be called on again.* **Stephen** *consciously does not turn his back on* **John**.

John *carefully folds his paper before placing it down. He unrolls his napkin and re-lays the table to his own personal specification before he starts to eat.*

John *takes his first bite.*

Stephen *is about to leave when* **John** *startles him.*

John (*gruff*)   My bacon?

Stephen   Yes.

Beat.

John *glares at* **Stephen**.

Stephen   Sir.

John   Tastes off.

Stephen   I can change . . .

Mimi *breezes in. She is dressed casually with clothes that were once smart, but that are now just this side of falling apart. Corduroy slacks, a man's shirt with the sleeves rolled up and a pullover jumper over her shoulders with the sleeves loosely knotted over her chest.*

When she sees **John**, *she braces herself a little and then forcefully engages in conversation.*

Mimi   Didn't expect to see you here today.

John   Needed breakfast.

Stephen *takes the opportunity to exit.*

Mimi   I always stick my foot it in.

John   It's OK. It still doesn't seem real.

Mimi   We'll miss her at the next committee meeting. She was the only one who ever got anything done.

John   Bacon's off.

Mimi   It's yours.

John   Doesn't taste right.

Mimi   I don't expect anything will taste right for quite some time, have a coffee.

John   I haven't been sleeping.

Mimi   I could stick a whisky in it.

John *shakes his head and makes another attempt at the food.*

Mimi (*trying*)   At least you *are* trying to eat something.

John   Got to try keep going haven't I?

Mimi   I'll go get myself a coffee, I'll be back in a minute.

Mimi *starts to leave but* **John** *shouts.*

John   Stephen!

Mimi *has to stay.*

Mimi   She was such a . . .

John *raises his hand to silence* **Mimi** *and she changes the subject.*

Mimi   How is the farm?

John   How do you think?

Stephen!

Stephen *appears.*

John   *Leta mama kahawa.*

Mimi   It's alright, I'll get it.

John   What do you pay him for?

Stephen *looks from* **John** *to* **Mimi** *who nods and* **Stephen** *rushes off.*

Mimi   At least we've had good rain.

John   Road's a mess.

Mimi   Don't know whether to bother getting the road to here tarmacked again. Put millions into it over the years.

John   Going to the dogs, this country.

Mimi   All for a few hundred yards. Guess you'll be coming to the meeting then?

John   Humph!

Mimi   Maybe the British Army will see to it.

John   The British Army get off their fat arses? They spend most of their time sitting in here don't they?

Mimi   Not since one of the wives opened a place in town.

John   They'll come back.

Mimi   Went off well yesterday (*beat*) at least.

John   You always know how to put on a good spread.

Mimi   Got to keep on top of things.

John   Humph.

John *finally gives up on his breakfast.*

John   Sorry.

Mimi   It's on the house, I'll go check my freezer. The *stima* has been on and off since the rains and I'm not sure that the *watu* put the generator on when I am out. Bacon's sensitive.

John (*smirking*)   Bacon's sensitive?

Mimi   Delicate, you know what I mean – I haven't had my coffee yet.

Mimi *starts to clear* **John**'s *plate away.* **John** *grabs hold of* **Mimi**'s *arm, which makes her flinch.* **John** *pretends not to notice.*

John   Thank you.

Mimi   It's nothing.

John   For yesterday.

Stephen *appears with* **Mimi**'s *coffee so* **John** *lets go of* **Mimi**'s *arm and gets up to leave.*

John   I'd better clear off, death's bad for business.

Mimi   It's bad full stop.

John *leaves and both* **Mimi** *and* **Stephen** *exhale.* **Stephen** *places* **Mimi**'*s mug on the table and touches her arm lightly where* **John** *was holding it.*

Stephen   *Uko sawa?*

Mimi (*curtly*)   Fine.

Leaving her coffee, **Mimi** *heads out to the back.* **Stephen** *starts to clear up and begins to set the tables for lunch.*

Lights fade.

Scene Two

Lunchtime at the Cypress Café.

Stephen *is bustling between busy tables at the café. Nearly all of the customers are white, there is a table of British Army soldiers in uniform one of whom is black. There is only one empty table.* **Cikú** *walks in and makes a beeline for the table.* **Stephen** *blocks her path.*

Stephen   *No ucoke guku twarie riria gutari na mundu?*

Cikú   What?

Stephen (*looking around and realizing that* **Mimi** *is hovering closer, louder*)   Fine, thank you. Have you got a reservation?

Cikú   No.

Stephen   We're full.

A **Young White Woman** *on a neighbouring table has been listening to the conversation and packs up her laptop.*

Young White Woman   I'm leaving, you can have my table.

Cikú   Thank you.

Stephen   I'll need to clean it first, you'll be waiting for a long time.

Mimi *appears behind* **Stephen**.

Mimi   Not like you to turn down business.

Stephen   The regulars will be here any minute.

Mimi (*clearing the table and ignoring* **Stephen**)   Sit down, I'll just go get a cloth to give the table a wipe.

Mimi *and the young woman leave while* **Stephen** *busies himself.* **Cikú** *carefully sits down at the table observing* **Stephen** *quizzically.*

Mimi *returns.*

Mimi   We had a wake here last night, Steve's tired.

Cikú   *Poleni sana.*

Mimi   Life.

Beat.

Have I seen you here before?

Cikú (*offering her hand*)   I'm Cikú.

Mimi (*not taking it*)   You remind me of someone, are you South African?

Cikú   Cikú is not a South African name.

Mimi   You certainly sound it, or something like it. Strange accent you have.

Cikú   I lived in the UK for over 25 years.

Mimi   Well, you don't *sound* English.

Stephen *arrives awkwardly carrying a huge chalkboard menu.* **Mimi** *slopes off.*

Cikú   Thank you, I'll have the butternut soup.

Stephen (*through gritted teeth*)   *Nikii urarega gucoka?*

Cikú (*slowly, with emphasis*)   I'll have the butternut soup.

Stephen   *Uretua nikii ati ndungiaria ruthiomi ruitu.*

Cikú   I'm not pretending. I can understand if you speak slowly, but I can't speak it.

Stephen (*slowly*)   *Wimenyerere.*

Cikú   What? Why?

Stephen   *Utuku ucio ungi.*

Cikú *startles but* **Mimi** *returns with the place setting, which is* **Stephen's** *cue to leave.*

Cikú   I-I-It's a nice place that you have here.

Mimi   Thanks.

Mimi *is not really looking at* **Cikú** *but already trying to see who else is coming in.* **Cikú** *gives up trying to make conversation and takes out her mobile phone.*

Cikú (*on the phone*)   Michael, it's me. Do call back soon, I have my UK number on today.

Stephen *brings the soup over and serves* **Cikú.** *Smiling so as not to draw attention, he speaks softly.*

Stephen   We can't talk now, please come back later when there is no one around.

Cikú   Why?

Mimi *starts to hover again so* **Stephen** *realizes he has to be quick.*

Stephen   I know what you saw. I can help. Come around three.

Cikú *nods though it is not clear whether she has understood or agreed.*

Lights fade.

Scene Three

Empty Cypress Café. **Cikú** *approaches with caution.*

Cikú   Hodi!

Stephen *appears quickly.*

Cikú   Nimefika.

Stephen   But you still speak Kiswahili?

Cikú   Nilisoma schuleni, inasaida.

Stephen   I need your help.

Cikú   Oh.

Stephen   I need you to go and tell the police that you made a mistake. It was dark, you were scared, confused, anything. I need you to change your statement.

Cikú   Huh?

Stephen   You need to withdraw your statement.

Cikú   How do you know I went to the police?

Stephen   Everyone knows everything around here.

Cikú *starts to get nervous and looks around wondering whether she did the right thing by coming.*

Stephen   It's not what you think.

Cikú *shakily reaches into her bag.*

Cikú   I have the OCS's number here on speed dial, if you try anything funny.

Stephen   Don't be stupid; if I was going to try anything I wouldn't do it here, where I work.

Cikú   How should I know?

Stephen   Why do you think I was trying to warn you earlier?

Cikú   Warning? I thought it was *ubaguzi*.

Stephen   How exactly am I supposed to discriminate against you?

Cikú   It happens all the time in Kenya. Trying to gain favour with the *wazungu*. Do you think that in their country they would do the same for you?

Stephen   Ha! I'm not a fool.

Cikú   Then what's this all about?

Stephen   Witnessing a murder is one thing, but being responsible for another is something else.

Cikú   There's nothing I could have done to stop it.

Stephen   I don't mean her, I mean/

Cikú   /are you suggesting that by making the statement now they are going to blame me?

Stephen   Not you.

Cikú   Who then? What other murder are you talking about?

Stephen   They'll kill him, if he gets out.

Cikú   Serve him right too.

Stephen   Not him! John was here this morning.

Cikú   Bullshit.

Cikú *starts to walk off,* **Stephen** *grabs her to stop her, when she starts to wrestle away he pulls back apologetically.*

Stephen   *Pole. (Beat.) Pole sana.* I'm scared too. It's dangerous for me to even talk to you about this.

Cikú *is backing away.*

Stephen   I promise you, he was here. This morning, eating his breakfast/

Cikú   /I'm going straight to the OCS to tell him what you have asked me to do.

Stephen   *Ninaomba/*

Cikú   /you

Stephen   Whose wake do you think it was here yesterday?

Cikú *stops and looks queasy.*

Cikú   You're lying.

Stephen   Go on, call the OCS then. Ask him.

Cikú   About the wake?

Stephen   Just call him!

Cikú *looks at her phone and hits speed dial. She watches* **Stephen** *carefully as she speaks slowly in fits and starts, her face changing.*

Cikú   Hello Sir. . . . Sorry to disturb you . . . yes, it's Cikú. . . . Oh, no, I didn't see your missed call. *Pole.* Yes, I am Ok, thank you for asking. . . . . . Oh, I see. . . . Yes . . .

Stephen *pulls up two chairs. He places one next to* **Cikú** *who flops down into it.*

Stephen   I told you.

Cikú   They have made some arrests.

Stephen   Some, exactly.

Cikú   It was an armed robbery.

Stephen   Thugs.

Cikú   They didn't mention/

Stephen   /him.

Cikú   How did you know?

Stephen   Because one of the alleged thugs is my brother.

Cikú *is clearly shocked and gets up a little unsteadily. She walks away and* **Stephen** *does not try to stop her. Instead he checks his watch and begins to lay the tables for afternoon tea.*

Lights fade.

Scene Four

Mimi *is sitting with* **Linda** *and* **Martha** *in the Cypress Café. They are having colonial style tea and biscuits.* **Martha** *is making appreciative noises as she eats her biscuits. The conversation is ongoing.*

Mimi   This American woman makes them. She's a great baker.

Linda   So many foreigners here these days.

Mimi   Everyone wants to get out of Nairobi.

Martha   Can't say I blame them.

Linda   Wish they all wouldn't wash up here though.

Mimi   It's been good for business.

Linda   Everything is business with you.

Mimi   One has got to live.

Linda   Looks like the new development is going to go ahead.

Martha   Well, with everything that has gone on, John can hardly fight it anymore.

Linda   Poor sod, right next to his farm, low cost housing!

Martha   There used to be such a nice view when we went there for sundowners.

Linda   Well that will be going now.

Martha   Should be protected somehow.

Linda   In our day, everyone knew their place.

Mimi *checks the teapot and finding it cold calls for* **Stephen** *to bring a fresh one.*

Stephen   Very good.

Mimi *waves him away.*

Martha   He's a good one isn't he?

Mimi   I'm lucky, one has to be careful these days/

Martha   /What with all the robberies. Wouldn't be surprised if killing the poor woman turned out to be some sort of intimidation.

Mimi   We all know who did the intimidating in that house.

Linda *and* **Martha** *pretend not to have heard* **Mimi**.

Linda   And there was the Canning-Smiths. You heard what happened, they pressed the button but nobody came.

Mimi   They're tight. I wouldn't have been surprised if they hadn't paid their bills.

Linda   Minerva!

Martha   You think everyone is tight who doesn't spend a small fortune in here.

Mimi *shrugs*.

Mimi   Talking of bills, whose slate is this going on today?

Both women suddenly start to busy themselves as though they had not heard **Mimi**.

Linda   Has he said whether he'll come to the meeting?

Martha   I hope you didn't ask him Mimi, given everything.

Linda   It's unfortunate but there's a question of time too. If he doesn't oppose that development double quick, he'll be stuck with it and where will we all be? It'll be the beginning of the end.

Martha   It's always the beginning of the end with you/

Mimi   /I did ask him.

Martha *and* **Linda**   And?

Mimi   Non-committal.

Linda *looks at* **Mimi** *expectantly.*

Mimi   And no Linda, I did not push it.

Linda   If you want a lift Martha, I have to pick up some things in town on the way.

Martha *glances at* **Mimi** *apologetically.*

Martha   I better had, my car is still at the *fundis*.

Mimi   Clear off, both of you. It's a wonder I have two shillings to rub together with all my charity.

Linda *and* **Martha** *leave surprisingly quickly.*

Lights fade.

Scene Five

John *is drinking whisky chasers at the Cypress Café. It is later on the same day. People (all white) are leaving around him and the odd person either nods to him, says goodbye or whispers something about him to someone else. He motions to* **Mimi** *that he would like another and* **Mimi** *intervenes.*

Mimi   Steady John.

John   What for?

Mimi   I suppose you are right. Steve!

Stephen *brings* **John** *another whisky and beer opening the beer bottle in front of him. He places a white wine in front of* **Mimi**.

Mimi *sips from her white wine but does not sit at the table with* **John**.

Stephen   Very good, sir.

John   Aren't you going to sit down?

Mimi   In a minute, still got some things to do.

John   You work too hard.

Mimi (*testily*)   It's not like I have some *bwana* at home to share this work with.

John   None of your siblings interested?

Mimi   Hospitality is not for everyone.

John   Family business is hard, none of my kids want the farm.

Mimi   William?

John   Least likely. Can you believe he actually likes London?

Mimi *shudders.*

Mimi   Can't stand the place myself.

John   It's miserable. Katie might. It depends on the husband. She'd like to turn everything organic – big market for it apparently.

Mimi   You can charge a lot more.

John   I'm done.

Mimi (*checking her watch*)   I thought William would be joining you.

John   Yup, he's got the *gari*. . . . Running around catching up with everyone.

Beat.

Whoever is left in this Godforsaken place anyway.

Mimi   Oh, there's been a steady trickle back. They get their British passports and then come home. The life there is not a life for anyone.

John *swiftly downs the whisky.*

John   I never bothered with it myself, we're the lot who handed our passports in at independence.

Mimi   I know.

John   The husband is one of those *maji* engineers.

Mimi   I remember him, very polite.

John   To the point of saying naught, couldn't survive a day in the bush.

Mimi   Still, he brought her back.

John   Just about. Who knows how long they will stick around.

Mimi   Give them a bit of time. A few tuskers and William won't want to back to go that real ale nonsense.

John *and* **Mimi** *laugh a little.*

John   I miss her.

Mimi   You will.

John   It's not supposed to be like this, men usually go first.

Mimi   It *is* more dignified being a widow.

Stephen *approaches* **Mimi** *cautiously and whispers to her.* **Mimi** *pulls back with* **Stephen** *out of earshot to hear what* **Stephen** *has to say.*

Mimi   Tell him to come in.

Stephen *gives a slight nod towards* **John**. **Mimi** *gets it and walks back towards* **John**.

Mimi   William's here.

John   Well, why isn't he coming in?

Mimi   Something about a delivery/

John   /What delivery?

Mimi *looks at* **John** *blankly.*

John *(getting up, swaying slightly)*   I suppose I had better find out.

John *takes a big gulp of beer straight from the bottle and heads off.*

Stephen   Very good.

Mimi *watches* **John** *until she is sure that he is out of earshot.*

Mimi   Don't forget to add that to his tab, we can take it off the next delivery.

Stephen *doesn't move.*

Mimi   What's up with you?

Stephen   I think you need to find someone else.

Mimi   What?

Stephen   I can't do this anymore.

Mimi *reaches for* **Stephen** *but he steps back so she can't touch him.*

Mimi   I know it's difficult.

Stephen   It's too much.

Mimi   What would I do/

Stephen   /There's hundreds out there like me, you've said so yourself.

Mimi   Only when I've been pissed off with you.

Stephen   I'll find you someone.

Mimi   Steve, please. I'm sorry.

Stephen *starts clearing up slowly.*

Mimi   Would you at least give me a little time?

Stephen   Why should I?

Mimi   You have a point, but don't leave, not just now. I couldn't handle it.

Stephen   It looks like you are handling it just fine.

Mimi   Am I, Stephen? Look at me.

Mimi *reaches her hands out at looks at* **Stephen**. *Her hands are shaking.* **Stephen** *puts down the tray and takes her hands for a moment. They look at each other.*

Stephen   Go home, I'll take care of everything here.

Mimi   *Asante*, Steve.

Stephen *gently lets* **Mimi**'*s hands down.*

Mimi   Will you?

Stephen *shakes his head.*

Mimi   I can't be alone/

Stephen (*resigned*)   /how many times have I heard that one before?

Mimi   /not now Stephen. With all this going on.

Stephen   Just go home Mimi.

Mimi   You've moved on – haven't you?

Stephen   What?

Mimi   Her – earlier.

Stephen   That's why you were my shadow today?

Mimi   What am I supposed to think?

Stephen   Whatever you like – evidently.

Mimi   Stephen, please.

Stephen   Mimi, stop it. Not here, not now.

Mimi *pulls herself together and heads off pulling a brave face. She calls over her shoulder.*

Mimi   *Na wachana na pombe yangu!*

Stephen (*shouting back half heartedly*)   Very good.

Stephen *stops for a moment, takes out his mobile phone and returns it to his pocket. He looks around the café and immerses himself in the cleaning up.*

Scene Six

Cikú *creeps in to the Cypress Café startling* **Stephen**. *She is still a little shaken.*

Cikú   *Ulisema ukweli.*

Stephen (*composes himself quickly and carries on clearing up*)   *Sasa unaiamini?*

Cikú   I guess I had to see for myself.

Stephen   So you withdrew your statement?

Cikú *shakes her head.*

Stephen   What? Why not?

Cikú   You're asking me to lie about a murder.

Stephen   I'm asking you to prevent a real murder.

Cikú   You're going to have make yourself clear.

Stephen   Anyway, I am not asking you to lie, just don't talk about what you saw.

Cikú   I know what I saw.

Stephen   And it wasn't murder.

Cikú   How do you know, it's not like you were there?

Stephen   She used to come here, always quick to talk about her 'accidents.'

Cikú   I can't believe none of this bothers you. A woman dies, is killed by her husband and you expect me to do nothing about it?

Stephen   Not nothing.

He takes his time to choose his words carefully.

But can I ask you something?

Cikú *shrugs.*

Stephen   Did you actually see her die?

Cikú   Not exactly, I saw her fall down.

Stephen   So how do you know she was dead?

Cikú   What is this?

Stephen   I'm only asking you what you are going to be asked over and over again.

Cikú   He was holding a gun/

Stephen   /they probably thought that you were an intruder/

Cikú   /it was covered in blood.

Stephen   Security isn't what it used to be.

Cikú   I don't have to do this, I'm going.

Stephen   They will want to know you know, what you were doing going over there that night.

Cikú   I wanted to talk to them both, I thought with Mrs. Spencer there that it might be easier . . .

Cikú *trails off as if she has remembered that she should not be saying what she was about to say next.*

Stephen   You can talk to me, I am the only one here.

Cikú   You?

Stephen   I don't see you rushing off back to the police station?

Cikú *shakes her head.*

Stephen   Let me get you a drink and I'll try to explain.

Cikú   There is nothing to explain.

Stephen   *Tafadhali?*

Cikú   OK, a cup of tea.

Stephen   What?

Cikú   I don't really drink.

Stephen   You won't fit in around here then.

Cikú   Drink ruins lives.

Stephen   You really don't drink? Not even wine?

Cikú   The odd glass, but I've got to drive back/

Stephen   /never stops anyone else here.

Cikú   One of the many problems in this place. The roads are terrifying.

Stephen *laughs.*

Cikú   It's not funny.

Stephen   How long has it been since you were home? Only someone with no problems could find it 'terrifying', the rest of us are busy just trying to get somewhere.

Cikú   I like to arrive in one piece.

Stephen   What are you doing driving at night on your own anyway? Like that night, going to his farm? Don't you have a driver?

Cikú   We were neighbours, when I was a child.

Stephen   Really?

Cikú   This is home.

Stephen *looks surprised.*

Cikú   I refused to call it home at the time, hated coming here to 'Geshagi'. I used to wish my parents were from the coast or somewhere much more exciting.

Stephen   I grew up here.

Cikú   *Pole*, that's not what I meant. I was a spoiled young child, didn't appreciate this place.

Stephen   You appreciate it now?

Cikú   The traffic coming up was impossible. Not like when I was a child, I've been coming here for a while now but it feels so lonely – not knowing anyone. I got here much later than I expected. After dark. I was alone and I wanted to see a familiar face. Mrs. Spencer was always kind to me.

Stephen   She was a kind woman.

Cikú   And now she is dead.

Stephen   It comes to us all.

Cikú   How can you say that when/

Stephen   /I knew her?

Cikú *nods. Beat.*

Stephen   That man's free and my brother was arrested?

Beat.

Stephen   There are only two things that matter in this country: power and money. I have neither. I learned a long time ago that for someone in my position its best not to take on the system.

Cikú   But what about your brother? The injustice?

Stephen   That London you live in, is there justice?

Cikú   Generally speaking – yes.

Stephen   Even if you are *Mafrika*?

Beat while **Stephen** *looks incredulous.*

Cikú   They have systems that work.

Stephen   And the system that brought *Mr. Spencer's* father here, was that justice?

Cikú *shakes her head.*

Cikú   What are you doing working here?

Stephen   It's a job.

Cikú   But you seem so/

Stephen (*smirking*)   /educated?

Cikú   I meant/

Stephen   /I know what you meant. You're no different to them, even if they will never accept you.

Cikú   *Pole.*

Stephen   I hear in Hollywood many actors wait tables while they are waiting for their big break.

Cikú   You've made your point.

Stephen   But here you know that I am unlikely to be moving on to something better, *ama*?

Cikú   It's different here.

Stephen   Exactly. I am stuck.

Cikú   Not necessarily – did you go to school?

Stephen   Ha! A minus form four.

Cikú   A minus?

Stephen   Don't believe me?

Cikú   You could get a scholarship with that.

Stephen   It wouldn't cover my siblings' costs and we are orphans.

Cikú   I'm sorry. An office job?

Stephen   I do the book keeping here.

Cikú   Nairobi has more opportunities.

Stephen   And end up living in a slum. I have three days off a month here and I know a secret valley where I like to fish.

Cikú *motions around.*

Cikú   But you could do so much better than this.

Stephen   Could I?

Cikú   I think you could.

Stephen   Ok, let's imagine I make it to Nairobi. I pull together a suit, if I walked into your office, a guy fresh from the slopes of Mount Kenya, no city references, would you give me a job?

Cikú *and* **Stephen** *take each other in for a moment.*

Stephen   I thought so.

Cikú   That's not a fair example, what about starting a business?

Stephen   Imagine that you're the bank manager.

Cikú   You have thought about this, haven't you?

Stephen   Which is why I don't notice the terror on our roads.

Cikú *and* **Stephen** *take each other in for a moment.*

Cikú   You still haven't explained why you want me to withdraw my statement.

Stephen   Because if you don't, my brother will be released and someone will have to pay for her death. It is not going to be John. Out here, there can be another type of justice. . .

Cikú   Eh?

Stephen   I can see that this is going to take some time. I'm getting a drink, do you want one?

Cikú   More than tea, you mean?

Stephen   I know a decent taxi driver, you can pick your car up from here in the morning.

Cikú   OK, I'll have a white wine.

Stephen *heads off.*

Cikú (*despite herself mimicking* **Mimi**)   *Na wachana na pombe yangu!*

While **Stephen** *is away* **Cikú** *checks her phone and then sits down.*

Stephen *returns with a tray carrying the drinks, coasters, a small vase with flowers and a bowl of crisps. He lays everything out carefully.*

Cikú   Wow, thank you.

Stephen   Make no mistake you are paying for the drinks.

Cikú, *embarrassed, catches herself and reaches into her purse pulling out a one thousand shilling note. When it looks like* **Stephen** *is going to go for change she shakes her head.*

Cikú   Keep it.

Stephen (*mimicking* **Cikú**)   Wow, thank you.

Cikú (*to herself*)   Touché.

Stephen   I know that this place is not much to look at but it has its appeal. If there is one thing that I have learned working here, it is about the small details.

Cikú (*doubtfully*)   You could say it has a certain charm.

Stephen   All of these odd bits of furniture, its actually to make you feel at home. Cosy.

Ciku *is not yet convinced.*

Stephen   OK, take the food. You get these people who come in from Nairobi and ask why are there only a few items on the menu. It's because every single thing is cooked to perfection and is fairly priced.

Cikú   The soup was excellent.

Stephen   And anyway, too much choice confuses most people.

Cikú   You made it sound as though people here do not have enough choice.

Stephen   Tito, my brother did – he went to university.

Cikú   All the more reason not to let him rot.

Stephen   But you would let me rot?

Cikú   I didn't mean it like that.

Stephen   I know, but you should listen to yourself.

Cikú   How come/

Stephen   /he did and I didn't? I gave him my place.

Cikú   Why? How?

Stephen   He got a B but he was restless. I had a sponsor and he could only afford to send one person and anyway someone had to look after the younger kids/

Cikú   /What did he study?

Stephen   I don't know.

Cikú   Huh?

Stephen   He went to campus in Nairobi and came back with money. He said he was into a lot of things and the story changed every time. He paid the others' school fees and I was too scared to ask. The plan was once he was done, he'd pay for me too.

Cikú   Didn't your sponsor want to see his papers?

Stephen   He asked all the time.

Cikú   So, what did you tell him?

Stephen   Nothing, I dodged and avoided him. Our relationship broke down.

Cikú   Oh.

Stephen   He's left Kenya now, I'll never see him again.

Cikú   Couldn't you try and explain?

Stephen   I'm too ashamed.

Cikú (*changing tack*)   When did your brother come back?

Stephen   I don't know, he didn't tell me, I was told.

Cikú   Who told you?

Stephen   Your friend the OCS. I got a call from the police one day. My brother was inside in connection with a robbery.

Cikú   No!

Stephen   My brother was being stubborn about sharing money and so the paperwork wasn't going to disappear. The OCS thought I might help my brother come to a practical decision.

Cikú   What did you do?

Stephen   I wasn't going to leave my brother in prison.

Cikú   You didn't want to find out the truth?

Stephen   Truth?

Cikú   Oh, so now this is some sort of delayed punishment?

Stephen   It's not like that.

Cikú   You don't even know, he may not have been involved with the robbery. Didn't you want to ask him?

Stephen   Oh, so how would that go? 'Hello bro, longtime! You are a thug these days?'

Cikú   But didn't you want to reconnect with him?

Stephen   Let me tell you what it was like after we lost our parents. Two teenagers, three younger kids, alone in a house surrounded by a plot of land.

Cikú   Social services?

Stephen (*laughs bitterly*)   You have been away too long – relatives.

Cikú   I see.

Stephen I'm not sure that you do. We thought they were there to help, Tito being older than me faced the worst of it. They stole everything.

Cikú Wasn't there anything you could do about it?

Stephen We were kids.

Cikú *Poleni.*

Stephen We had a dog, Lucy. She had puppies but by this point we were barely being fed ourselves. My uncle and aunt did just enough to maintain the appearance that all was well. We knew there was no way we could keep the puppies.

Cikú So what did you do?

Stephen I had this idea that we could try to sell them to some *wazungu* – get some money and the puppies a home.

Cikú Did your plan work?

Stephen *shakes his head.*

Stephen Never got to try. Tito made us each take a puppy and carry them to the pit latrine.

Cikú *covers her open mouth, aghast.*

Stephen One by one he forced us, I tried to fight him but he held me down. He made the kids throw them in – and mine/

Cikú /I am not sure I can hear this/

Stephen He crushed his head in front of me.

Cikú *takes a gulp of her wine.*

Stephen He said we were like those puppies. We needed to learn what happened to defenceless creatures in a world like this. Since then, we have all been a little scared of him.

Cikú Look, I get it, I'll withdraw my statement.

Stephen No, you don't. You are just reacting to a terrible story that I have told you. If you withdraw your statement, know I'm doing it to try and save his life.

Cikú You keep saying that.

Stephen People liked Mrs. Spencer. There is no confession like that of a dead *Mafrika* man and right now Tito is safer inside where it looks like justice is being served.

Cikú I can't believe it.

Stephen Think about it, one of the *Kaburus* shoots not one, but two *Wafrika* and do you know what they say when they are talking about the case, 'He was such a nice guy, always kind to me.'

Cikú I know, they covered it in the papers in the UK.

Beat.

Stephen What did they say about it there?

Cikú They tended to stick to the facts, I guess they thought it was complicated.

Stephen Facts? I wonder if they would have thought it was so complicated if it was the other way around? You should have seen the sympathy he had around here, poor him – for killing a couple of *watu*.

Beat.

Tito may be sick, he may even be a bad man, I don't know for sure but with the puppies that day, he was trying to teach us something.

Cikú What? Exactly.

Stephen About life. Later I realized those puppies would have died anyway. What *mzungu* would have bought puppies from a bunch of scruffy *Wafrika*? I was living in a fantasy world.

Cikú But why did he have to make you do it? He could have just quietly gotten rid of them himself.

Stephen I asked myself that many times. I still don't know. Maybe it was a kind of weird initiation. Maybe he was scared too. There are so many things I want to find out about him and I can't do that if he doesn't survive this.

Cikú OK, so how do you know my statement is true? The police say that not a single farm worker will come forward to say that they saw me at the farm that night.

Stephen What would you have to gain from making up a story like that?

Cikú I could have my reasons.

Stephen True, but I do know one thing. Tito was nowhere near the farm that night.

Cikú   How can you be so sure?

Stephen   Because he was with me.

They hear a car pull up which shocks them back into the moment.

Stephen *jumps up and starts clearing up the table to make it look like there was only one person,* **Cikú** *is digesting the conversation.* **Stephen** *exits.*

Mimi *looking more composed walks in just after* **Stephen** *has left.*

Mimi   Oh.

Cikú   Sundowners.

Mimi *looks at her watch.*

Cikú   Stephen was helpful.

Mimi   I'm sure he was, but it's getting late.

Cikú   He said he was going to call me a taxi.

Cikú *motions at her drink.*

Stephen   I'll just go and check for you.

Mimi *finishes clearing the table even though* **Cikú** *hasn't finished her wine.*

Mimi   Thank you Stephen.

Mimi *waits until* **Stephen** *is out of earshot.*

Mimi   Plans for the development moving well Rachel?

Cikú *looks shocked.*

Mimi   It is you Rachel, isn't it?

Cikú   No one calls me that anymore.

Mimi   I have heard that there is a fashion for people to use their African names.

Cikú   But earlier/

Mimi   /it took me awhile but then I remembered. Next door to the Spencers. Used to come up for the holidays.

Cikú *nods.*

Mimi   Good luck getting it through, they're going to fight you, you know.

Cikú   I would have thought that John would have other things to deal with right now.

Mimi   Dreadful business, isn't it?

Stephen *walks back in.*

Stephen   The taxi's here.

Mimi   Do walk her out Stephen, make sure that she is safe.

Stephen *and* **Cikú** *walk out.*

Blackout.

Act Two

Scene One

Mimi *and* **Stephen** *are clearing up at the Cypress Café. It is midafternoon. It looks like there has been a meeting. The chairs are arranged in a semi-circle and the chalkboard menu has scribbling on it pertaining to legal matters.*

Linda *and* **Martha** *are sitting at their regular table and are a little restless. They want* **Mimi** *to join them.*

Linda   Why bother paying him if you are going to do it all by yourself?

Stephen *hears and ignores* **Linda**.

Mimi   If you recall I got left in the lurch by Sospeter. I may have been a bit quiet recently but it is still a job for two.

Linda   Never did like him, always felt like he was up to no good.

Mimi   It seems that you were right then, he didn't turn up one day and then sent round a *boda boda* driver with a note asking for his gratuity, the cheek!

Martha (*under her breath*)   Linda is always right.

Louder.

You've been on your feet all afternoon, come and sit for a moment.

Mimi   I suppose you're right. I'll get us a sherry.

Linda (*firmly*)   Sit down!

Linda *shouts in broken Kiswahili as though she were saying Yoo Hoo.*

Linda   Stephen! *Leta Sherry sasa hapa! Na glasi muruzi!*

Martha   It went well though, didn't it?

Linda   Depends what you mean by well, everyone is in agreement to stop this housing development but what can we actually do about it?

Martha   You heard the lawyer, as long as we can get John on board we can get an injunction and hold things up.

Mimi   And every day they cannot do anything costs the developers. We all know how slow the courts can be. If they overrun too long/

Linda   /honestly you two, I was there, you don't have to spell it out again.

Stephen *arrives with the sherry and three sherry glasses. He carefully arranges everything on the table around the women who do not move a whisker to accommodate him.* **Linda** *inspects the sherry glasses carefully before nodding approval.*

Stephen   Very good.

Stephen *starts to turn away but* **Linda***'s voice stops him.*

Linda *speaks in a loud voice as though* **Stephen** *cannot understand her. Broken Kiswahili.*

Linda   *Saa hii ni sundowners, wapi bitings?*

Stephen *takes* **Linda** *in, bows slightly and goes off to get the bitings.*

Stephen   Very good.

Linda   I mean really, he may have been a funny one but Sospeter was always on top of the bitings.

Martha *shoots an exasperated look at* **Mimi***.*

Martha   I suppose it is inevitable one day though. The population is growing and people need somewhere to live.

Linda   Not on my *shamba*!

Martha   Hardly!

Linda   It's not my fault if the *watu* refuse to practise birth control. What is it now? An average of 9 per family? At independence, we had a population of 4 million – its grown tenfold in 50 years – it's not sustainable.

Mimi (*laughs a little*)   Well I'm glad you find it funny.

As **Linda** *has been delivering her speech and the women continue to chat,* **Stephen** *delivers the bitings, refreshes their drinks and carries on clearing up. They do not notice him at all.* **Stephen** *takes his moment to head off to the kitchen.*

Mimi   Sustainable? I've never heard you use that word before.

Linda   I'm quite up-to-date, I'll have you know. There's too much pressure on the land.

Martha   Then maybe this type of housing will provide a solution to a problem that already exists.

Linda   Not bloody likely! You know what will really happen don't you?

Mimi   Go on, enlighten us.

Linda   It's all the mob from Nairobi who will snap it up. The *watu* that the housing is supposedly intended for will never get to live in it. Anyone really looking for low cost housing will not be able to buy it and anyone who buys it will push the prices up. The town will be swamped with God-awful weekenders and it'll be the beginning of the end. I'll have to pack up and move down to Bissel.

Mimi   Might be good for my business.

Linda   You really want that lot in here?

Mimi   I guess not, but I'm not going anywhere.

Martha   Me either. I gave up my British passport when I came here. I like my life here.

Linda   You could always get it back, not like me, I'm second generation Kenyan. Our way of life should continue. We left Nairobi to them and look what has become of it – endless subdivisions, even Karen now. It used to be that you couldn't subdivide a plot in Karen to less than five acres, now it's an acre and you know – they are building what they call these ambassadorial residences on the whole damn plot with barely a postage stamp as a garden. Have you been to Mtwapa recently? Den of inequities – they are ruining the coast too! All these old men with young girls barely out of nappies wearing hardly anything at all. We can't leave anything to them – to think it used to be such a great country.

Mimi   You're just saying that because you don't have a look in with any of those old men.

Linda   You're as disgusting as they are!

Martha   That was a bit much Mimi.

Mimi   Fair enough, I'm not excusing it but what by the way of work have they got down there anyway – tourism is sighing out its last breath.

Linda   Minerva! Sometimes I worry about you. You hardly said anything in the meeting and here I was thinking you would take charge.

Mimi   How exactly?

Linda   You know what these meetings are like – everything goes around in circles unless someone holds it all together. We need someone who speaks as plainly as you do to lay it out – we want this place to stay as it is – God knows they are squeezing us out of the rest of the damn country!

Mimi   I suppose there are rather a lot of them.

Linda   Breeding can be a form of resistance you know.

Mimi (*under her breath*)   I think you'll find it's more about a lack of education and access to health care services.

Linda   What was that?

Mimi   I do have a business to run you know.

Linda   It's always about money with you.

Mimi   I have to feed you two at any rate.

Linda   What are you worried about? It's not like you have children to leave it to.

Martha (*shocked*)   Linda/

Mimi   /It's OK Martha, this thing has got us all on edge. We all want what's best/

Linda (*unbowed*)   /and that would not be a bunch of *watu* settling next to John's farm.

The women are quiet for a moment sipping their sherries.

Martha   I miss her.

Mimi   She didn't have a mean bone in her body.

Linda   Foolish though, how she put up with John all these years.

Martha *stands to leave.*

Martha   I've had enough for today.

Linda *also stands and ignores* **Martha**'s *huff.*

Linda   So, have I, I want to drive home while it is still light.

She digs into her handbag and, pulling out a purse, puts a few thousand shillings on the table before starting to walk off.

Don't want you saying I don't honour my bills.

Linda *strides off and over her shoulder says loudly to* **Martha**.

Linda   Do you still want that lift or not?

Linda *exits.*

Martha *starts to rummage through her bag but* **Mimi** *stops her touching her lightly on the arm.*

Mimi   I'm sure she has it covered.

Martha   Thank you.

Mimi   Don't know why you put up with her though.

Martha   Probably for the same reason as you do.

Martha *leaves and* **Mimi** *gets up and starts clearing up. She has her head down as* **John** *enters the café quietly. He is just behind her as she lifts her head, startling and sending the sherry glasses flying – they shatter on the floor.*

Mimi   Jesus John!

John (*with a wry smile*)   You almost sounded religious there.

Mimi   That's not funny, you scared me.

John   And here I was thinking you were made of sterner stuff.

John *picks up the sherry bottle and inspects it.*

John   The coven were here for the meeting then?

Mimi   And where were you?

John   These things always run late, I can't believe it's finished already.

Mimi (*having composed herself*)   Couldn't face it you mean.

John   What?

Mimi   Look, I had better get this cleared up.

Mimi *starts to walk away,* **John** *grabs her arm and leans in.*

John   What were you saying?

Mimi *tries to pull her arm away but* **John** *has a firm grip.*

Mimi (*trying to soften*)   Look John I know it is difficult.

John (*hard*)   You have no idea.

Mimi   Steve!

Then to **John** *as she hears* **Stephen** *start to come running.*

Mimi   Unlike you, I clean up after my messes.

John *quickly lets go of* **Mimi***'s arm and her demeanour changes.*

Mimi   *Pole* Steve, could you clean up here? I'll just go get John a drink.

John   No need, now that I have missed the meeting, I might as well just go home.

Mimi   As you like.

Stephen   Very good.

John *walks off, barely containing his anger.*

Stephen   *Uko sawa?*

Mimi   *Kabisa.*

They both pause for a moment taking in the scene. **Mimi** *is rooted to the spot so* **Stephen** *takes charge.*

Stephen   Please go home, I can take care of things here.

Mimi   You've been doing a lot of that lately.

Stephen   It's not like I have anyone to go home to.

Mimi   You know you could always . . .

She catches herself and changes tack.

You're right. You deal with this. I'll be in early tomorrow and we can go over the books. Anyone else who was going to come here today has already left.

Mimi *starts to head off when* **Stephen** *calls after her.*

Stephen   Your car keys!

Mimi *tuts at herself and then heads back in the direction of the office to get her keys. She emerges quickly with the keys and nods at* **Stephen** *who looks* *at her with feeling as she walks out.* **Stephen** *examines the sherry bottle and then shrugging to himself he opens it and takes a swig. He grimaces, as he does not like the taste. Wiping his mouth with the back of his hand he then screws the top back on the bottle and continues to clear up.*

Scene Two

Stephen *goes into the back to get a dustpan and brush and while he is away,* **Cikú** *arrives and looks around the scene puzzled.*

Stephen *returns and is unsurprised to see* **Cikú**, *he carries on with the job at hand as they talk.*

Cikú   *Nini kilitokea hapa?*

Stephen   *Na habari ya jioni.*

Cikú   *Habari.*

Stephen   What is it with you diaspora? You come back with no manners.

Cikú   *Pole.*

Stephen   We're closed.

Cikú   I went to remand.

Stephen (*uneasy*)   How is Tito?

Cikú   You would know wouldn't you – if you had been to see him.

Stephen   It's been hard to get away, my job.

Cikú   All that talk about how much you care about him.

Stephen   What did he say? Has he been getting the food I send him?

Cikú   Not that he would eat it.

Stephen   He's not – physically hurt, is he?

Cikú   Physically, he is OK. He says he is used to it and that you know that.

Stephen *winces.*

Stephen   As you yourself know, sometimes people are not always who they seem to be.

Cikú   What do you mean by that?

Stephen   Some people might say that it's a useful coincidence that the one person who could stop your clever development is/

Cikú   /I didn't kill her.

Stephen   It was helpful timing though.

Cikú   You're sick.

Stephen   You're the one with the problems, we don't need your project you know.

Cikú   Maybe not you, but there are many who will benefit from the houses – this town is growing, you want to end up with slums like Nairobi, you said yourself there is so little choice. People need somewhere decent to live – somewhere they can afford.

Stephen   So you think that by coming here and upsetting everyone you are helping?

Cikú   Not so long ago, you were asking for my help.

Stephen   That was before I knew who you were. You want them to accept you, that's why you are hiding, isn't it?

Cikú   I am not the only one here with something to hide Stephen.

Stephen   What do you mean?

Cikú   Remind me again why you gave up your university place for Tito?

Stephen   I told you about that – my sponsor could only afford one place.

Cikú   It's a very big thing to do for the person who killed your precious puppy.

Stephen   What has Tito been telling you?

Cikú   There was something about that story that bothered me. It's possible that Tito was, is a terrible person, and he could be a good liar except why would he go to the trouble of making up criminal records?

Stephen   I don't know what you are talking about.

Cikú   Except I think that you do.

Stephen   You know what – your statement is not worth what you think it is anyway, not unless I can also prove that Tito was with me that night. No one else will speak up for him.

Cikú   And you know how he is used to that.

Stephen   That was different, I was just a kid.

Cikú   What are your real reasons for wanting Tito to stay inside?

Stephen   I know you may not believe me, I don't know what Tito has told you. But I really am trying to protect him, this time.

Cikú   He told me that the thing with the puppies happened after he came out of approved school. That he took the blame for something you know you did/

Stephen   /it's true. Tito went to that children's jail because of me. When he came back, he was changed. I thought if I could give him my opportunity/

Cikú   /Do you even know what he went through?

Stephen *shakes his head.*

Stephen   I can't talk about this/

Cikú   /what too painful for you/

Stephen   /I meant here. Let me cash up, get organized and then we can go somewhere in town.

Cikú *looks at him scornfully.*

Stephen   Please, it'll only take me ten minutes. Not for my sake – for Tito.

Cikú *nods her head slowly.*

Cikú   *Sawa*, I'll wait.

Cikú *sits down, takes out her phone and starts to look at a few messages.* **John** *storms in making a beeline for* **Cikú** *who, thinking that it is* **Stephen***, stands up abruptly.*

Cikú   That was quick.

Cikú *freezes as* **John** *has command of the situation.*

John   I was surprised to see you heading here.

Cikú   What?

John   You cut it fine, you might have caught the end of the meeting.

Cikú (*trying to regain some control*)   Why were you following me?

John   I can help you.

Cikú   You?

John   I had been wondering why it was you were coming to see us that night.

Cikú   I liked Mrs. Spencer, I/

John   /it was about the development, wasn't it?

John *moves which startles* **Cikú**.

Cikú   Stephen will be back any minute.

John   Your man is he?

Cikú   I'm just letting you know that I'm not alone here.

John (*mimicking* **Cikú**)   I'm just letting you know that I am not alone here.

John *bears down on* **Cikú**.

John   You've been trying to keep your identity as the developer secret haven't you? They don't know, do they?

Cikú   I could say the same to you and we both seem to be doing a particularly bad job of it.

John   Why weren't you at the meeting then?

Cikú   I was actually coming to talk to Mimi about it.

John   Ha! Very convenient.

Cikú   You know nothing about my intentions.

John   I do know that they could have you run out of town if they found out who you are.

Cikú   I have a life in the UK.

John   Do you? You want to save the world, that's why you are back. It would be such a disappointment not to see the fruits of your labour.

Cikú   So why weren't you at the meeting?

John   I think we know that in the end, it comes down to me and you.

Cikú   What do you mean?

John   They can't get their injunction without me.

Cikú   So you are going to try and hold them to ransom?

John   I don't care what they think.

Cikú *and* **John** *hear* **Stephen** *in the background and he calls out to her that he will just be a few more minutes.*

John *(softly)*   Answer him.

Cikú *(forced shouting)*   Sawa!

John   Right now, you are the only person between me and a quiet life.

Cikú   How?

John   I will have to pay for years to keep that statement at bay.

Cikú   Oh?

John   Don't play dumb – you withdraw your statement and I will not stop your development.

Cikú   But/

John   /but nothing. You came back didn't you, to save the *watu*? To change lives. This is your chance, but you had better decide fast.

Stephen *comes through to the front of the café where* **Cikú** *is just as* **John** *makes a sharp exit so that* **Stephen** *doesn't really see who it is.*

Cikú *is clearly shaken.*

Stephen   Uko sawa?

Cikú *nods.*

Stephen   Who was that anyway?

Cikú   Just some *Kaburu* looking for Mimi. Come on, let's go.

Stephen   Are you sure you are OK?

Cikú *doesn't answer but is already leading the way out of the café with* **Stephen** *following quickly behind.*

The café looks as though no one has been there.

Lights fade.

Scene Three

Early morning in the Cypress Café.
Stephen *and* **Mimi** *are going through the books.*

They are mid conversation.

Mimi   I don't know why I bother with this. Everything is always in order. If you are fiddling, it is either so minor it's not worth bothering about, or so clever you probably deserve it.

Stephen   More coffee?

Mimi   A small one.

Stephen   It's been a bit better the last couple of weeks.

Mimi   That's because of the rubberneckers.

Stephen   What?

Mimi   People who are hoping to catch a glimpse of John, see if they can read guilt on his face, if the rumours are true. Between that and the meetings about the development. It'll die down again.

Stephen   We could get a pool table.

Mimi   Leave that to the bars in town. This place is on its last legs. I am on my last legs.

Stephen   You're not that old.

Mimi   Steve, you don't have to be kind. I won't be thinking of you when I shut up shop, just my quiet life ahead.

Stephen *hands* **Mimi** *her coffee and starts to gather the books.*

Mimi   What will you do?

Stephen   I'm not going anywhere.

Mimi   Steve, I get it, you need to move on.

Stephen   Everything I need/

Mimi   /have I ever told you why this place is even called the Cypress Café?

Stephen   You like the trees?

Mimi   This whole area was covered in them. Beautiful cypress trees. All gone now of course. That was the time when things really seemed possible. Those trees ended up all over the world. My father's was the only place for miles where people could come and get a decent meal. Those were the real adventurers then. Just the explorers, the animals and the plains.

Stephen (*sarcastically*)   I can't imagine.

Mimi   Steve, my point is, times have changed and so have you – you can't hold yourself responsible for Tito for the rest of your life.

Stephen   But if he had not gone to the approved school – then maybe/

Mimi   /and you would have survived it? He was right – you are too soft.

Stephen   I was hard enough to steal the exam papers.

Mimi   Desperate more like. That was all a long time ago – you tried to make amends and anything he did after that was his own undoing. You were a child.

Stephen   So was he. I ruined his life.

Mimi   And you are doing everything that you can now. You both have to sit tight until this thing blows over.

Stephen   And what if it doesn't?

Mimi   It will come right in the end Steve. I'll put these books away – you better head off and make sure you've sent Tito enough food for the rest of the week.

Stephen   Mimi.

Mimi   Just go.

Stephen *gets up and walks off leaving* **Mimi** *behind sipping her coffee thoughtfully.*

Lights fade.

Scene Four

Cikú *arrives at the Café.* **Stephen** *is sitting at one of the tables, lost in thought.*

Cikú   *Nikwega.*

Stephen   *Nikwega muno.*

Cikú *smiles tentatively.*

Stephen   So you still remember how to greet in our language.

Cikú   I've thought about it all.

Stephen   Eh heh?

Cikú   You really don't care what I have to say anymore, do you?

Stephen   No, not really.

Cikú   Well, at the very least don't you want to hear what I have decided/

Stephen   /your decision, my decisions. What difference do they really make?

Cikú   You seemed to think a big one.

Stephen   Because I am a coward.

Cikú   What?

Stephen   Did I really need you or was I only scared for myself?

Cikú   We can all feel powerless sometimes.

Stephen   Or refuse to take the power we do have.

Cikú   I didn't fully understand your position.

Stephen   And you think you do now?

Beat.

Cikú   I'm not sure, but I do know that it wasn't as clear as I first thought it was.

Stephen   Maybe there's something about it not being clear that suits all of us.

Beat.

Even though we'd never admit it.

Stephen *gets up and storms off.* **Cikú** *does not try to stop him. Lights fade.*

Scene Five

It's mid-afternoon at the Cypress Café. **John** *is lazily poring over a newspaper when* **Mimi** *approaches with a sheaf of paper in her hands.*

John   What's this?

Mimi   A deed for one of the houses.

John   What would I want this for? I'm going to be living next to the blasted thing as it is.

Mimi   I thought you were off to Bissel, or maybe Kilifi is more your style?

John   Why? I have a perfectly good farm here.

Mimi   Ha!

John   Besides who would supply you with such great pig if I didn't?

Mimi   Aren't you going to look at them?

John   Why should I?

Mimi   Because you owe him?

John   Who – exactly?

Mimi (*quietly*)   Steve.

John   You can't be serious.

Mimi   Never more, John.

John   I always knew he must have been screwing you, you buy him the damn thing yourself.

Mimi   That's not the point.

John   So you are not denying it then?

Mimi   No, I am not dignifying your aspersions with a response.

John   Why should I even consider this ludicrous idea of yours?

Mimi   It might be the one thing that you get right in your life.

John   You're a fine one to talk.

Mimi   Whatever you say John but we are not cut from the same cloth.

John   I think you'll find that we are.

Mimi   Burnished by the same sun, maybe, but I have made peace with the fact that things have changed. It's a different world than I grew up in.

John   A bloody sorry one at that.

Mimi   You really don't give a damn do you? Have you ever looked around and seen that anyone who has ever had anything to do with you has fucked off?

John   You are hardly Miss popular.

Mimi   Do you even miss her?

John   How can you ask that after everything I have been through?

Mimi   You've been through?

John   You're hardly the one destined to share your *shamba* with a bunch of *watu* in your golden years.

Mimi   You could have done us all a favour and cleared off.

John   This conversation is going nowhere – I'm off.

John *is about to stand up but* **Mimi** *puts her hand firmly on his shoulder.*

Mimi   You're not going anywhere until you've signed.

John *easily shrugs her off and stands over her menacingly.*

John   Oh yes, what are you going to do?

Mimi   Who do you think will even look at you when they find out all of the truth?

John   What?

John *has his hand around* **Mimi**'s *throat and begins to choke her.*

Mimi (*gasping*)   Go on John, are you going to kill me too?

Her words get through to **John** *who crumples.*

Mimi *spits the words at him as she rubs her throat.*

Mimi   You're a coward.

John   I didn't mean to/

Mimi   /you never did. Where do you think she stayed all those nights eh?

John *shakes his head.*

Mimi   I wish I could get away from this place. I'm sick of all of this pretence like nothing is going on.

John   I didn't/

Mimi   You *broke* her, do you know that?

John   She wasn't the easiest of people/

Mimi   Christ John, you're pathetic!

John *catches an escaping tear.*

Mimi   And to think that at the beginning I was jealous you chose her.

John   It could have been different.

Mimi   I wouldn't have taken your shit.

John   There wouldn't have been any to take – with you.

Mimi   I should've known better than to try and make you see sense. You're past it.

John   What's that supposed to mean?

Mimi   You and half the people that come here. Stuck in your own private hells.

John   We keep you in brass tacks.

Mimi   I wasn't excluding myself.

John   Then what are you still doing here?

Mimi   I'm a fool – same as you.

Beat.

Can't you see this as a sort of redemption?

John   How?

Mimi   At least Tito will have a roof over his head if he ever gets out.

John   What's that got to do with me?

Mimi   He's doing your time.

John   I'd have been better off inside.

Mimi   Don't be ridiculous.

John   Others have survived it.

Mimi   At what cost?

John   Why don't you want me inside?

Mimi   Look we are both being stupid, those housing developments are going to happen anyway. It doesn't matter if we go to Bisssel, Kilifi – have you been to Mtwapa recently? We can't out breed them. Wherever we go, there they are.

John   Except you want me to help one of them?

Mimi   You know this is different.

John   Is it?

They look into the distance for a moment, taking it all in.

John   *Pole*, Mimi.

Mimi   What?

John   Did I hurt you just now?

Mimi *shrugs it off.*

John   I really am sorry.

Mimi   Never heard you utter those words before – what's brought on the sudden change of heart?

John   I didn't realize how much you despise me.

Mimi   Until just now, neither did I.

John   I can see it in everyone's eyes you know.

Mimi   What?

John   What they think of me, what they think I have done.

Mimi   The world doesn't revolve around you, you know.

John *is not really listening to* **Mimi.**

John   I feel like a person that's been run over. Lying there on the road with a wide space around me that no one dares step into.

Mimi   Poor you!

John   The kids won't be back.

Mimi   Can't say I blame them.

John   When did you get so hard, Mimi?

Mimi   When did you?

John   I hadn't touched her in a really long time you know.

Mimi   She'd certainly not stayed at mine for a while.

John   Then out of the blue she said she was going to leave.

Mimi   She should have done.

John   Katie had sent her a ticket.

Mimi   I pleaded with her so many times not to go back to you.

John   After all these years, just walk out.

Mimi *changes tack.*

Mimi   She would want you to do this you know.

John *looks at* **Mimi** *as though he has nothing left to say.*
Lights fade.

Scene Six

Stephen *is sat at a table in the Cypress Café looking through the papers that* **Mimi** *had tried to give* **John**. *It is in the evening and the café is closed.*

Stephen   *Siwezi.*

Mimi   *Kwa nini?*

Stephen   There's got to be a catch.

Mimi   There isn't one.

Stephen   You haven't got the cash for this, you can't afford it.

Mimi   There's an expression Steve: it's called looking a gift horse in the mouth.

Stephen   So it's really mine?

Mimi   Well, they haven't built it yet, but when they have.

Stephen   No, I can't.

Mimi   Why not?

Stephen   It doesn't *feel* right.

Mimi   Then sell it, I don't care. Buy a *shamba*. I would wait a few years if I were you, those houses are going to double in value once the word spreads.

Stephen   It's not about the money.

Mimi   Stephen, you are the only Kenyan I know who would not jump at the chance to own a piece of land, what's wrong with you?

Stephen   Nothing.

Mimi   I know it's been hard – Tito and/

Stephen   /but you still deal with John like nothing happened, after everything.

Mimi   That's not fair.

Stephen   You could have banned him from here.

Mimi   You said it yourself, there's not much I can afford. You know how tight things are with the business, banning people isn't going to help.

Stephen   Then you keep this.

He thrusts the papers at **Mimi**.

Mimi   To do what with? I have no one to leave it to.

Stephen   I thought you might leave me the business – I was going to approach you with a plan.

Mimi *laughs until she realizes* **Stephen** *is serious.*

Mimi   What would you want with this place?

Stephen   Run it, like I do now, except we would be partners.

Mimi   Stephen, this place is finished, can't you see that?

Stephen   You've just run out of ideas.

Mimi (*with feeling*)   This place. (*Almost whispering.*) I, it's not your future.

Stephen   Why not?

Mimi   Who do you think will come here if we were partners? The *Wazungu* would move on and the *Wafrika* have their places in town. Don't make me spell it out for you. Together we're neither fish nor fowl.

Mimi *looks at* **Stephen** *warmly.*

Mimi   I've been selfish and this is your chance.

Beat.

Would it make you feel any better if I told you John paid for it?

Stephen   I knew there was a catch – blood money.

Mimi   You and I both know that John would have found a way out. With or without Tito.

Stephen   But Tito stops the hangman's noose from swaying above his head.

Mimi   I thought you were cleverer than this. Can't you see this for what it is?

Stephen   This whole thing makes me sick.

Mimi   You know me Steve, I've never sweetened anything. Life doesn't throw up too many chances.

Stephen   Couldn't it be different somehow?

Mimi   Listen to me Steve, I'm going to die here. I'm not going anywhere but you still can. You still have a future. Wife, kids, the lot. You don't have to do anything different for a while but at least take it. The thing isn't even built yet. It's the best I can do for you. There are some things we just can't change.

Stephen *doesn't respond but takes the papers and looks at them slowly. He nods his head in agreement.* **Mimi** *starts to get ready to leave.*

Stephen   Yet.

Mimi *doesn't try to say anything else to convince* **Stephen** *and instead makes it clear that she is leaving. They nod goodnight to each other.*

Stephen *has a sombre expression on his face.*

Scene Seven

Cikú *walks in to the Cypress Café as* **Stephen** *is still looking at the papers. He barely acknowledges her and starts to talk as if to himself but is actually asking her questions.*

Stephen   It's happening then?

Cikú   Off plan sales like that.

She points at **Stephen** *'s papers.*

Cikú   Look like they will be good.

Stephen   You must be feeling proud of yourself.

Cikú   Huh?

Stephen   Well, you've got what you wanted – when are you going to break ground?

Cikú   You got what you wanted too.

Stephen   It never feels quite like you imagined, does it?

Cikú   No, it doesn't. Before . . . I thought I might stay here myself, you know come home.

Stephen   So now *geshagi* is home?

Cikú *shakes her head.*

Cikú   I'm not sure there is anywhere that is, but I can see this through/

Stephen   /from Nairobi, most likely?

Cikú (*resigned*)   I'll still be up at the site a lot.

Stephen   I see.

Cikú   Will you take it?

Stephen   What choice do I have? Anyway, if sales go well, I can sell it and move on.

Cikú   Is that what you want?

Stephen   Where would I go? This is home for me, at least soon rent won't be an issue.

Cikú   It's not easy.

Stephen   I guess it could be worse.

Lights fade.

Scene Eight

Early morning at the Cypress Café.

Everything looks exactly the same as always.

John *is reading the newspaper at one of the tables and when* **Stephen** *brings in his breakfast he moves his chair backwards to give* **Stephen** *the room to place his breakfast down.*

Stephen *looks at* **John** *with an air of expectation but does not say anything.*

John *slightly nods his head and* **Stephen** *retreats to a safe distance from which to watch* **John**, *ready to be called on again.*

John *carefully folds his paper before placing it down. He rolls the napkin and re-lays the table into his own personal specification before he starts to eat.*

John *takes his first bite.*

Stephen *visibly relaxes a bit and is about to exit when* **John** *startles him.*

John (*gruff*)   My bacon?

Stephen   Yes

John   Good Stephen, very good.

Curtain

Glossary of terms

In order of appearance in text:

Leta mama kahawa – Bring Madam coffee (commanding, impolite)
Stima – Electricity (Kiswahili)
Watu – 'Settler' term for African people: derogatory (Kiswahili)
No ucoke guku twarie riria gutari na mundu? – Can you come back when
   there is nobody here so we can talk? (Kikuyu)
Poleni sana – Condolences to you all (Kiswahili)
Nikii urarega gucoka? – Why can't you come later (Kikuyu)
Uretua nikii ati ndungiaria ruthiomi ruitu. – Don't pretend you can't
   speak our language (Kikuyu)
Wimenyerere – You have to be careful (Kikuyu)
Utuku ucio ungi – The other night (Kikuyu)
Hodi! – Knock knock! (Kiswahili)
Nimefika – I have arrived (Kiswahili)
Nilisoma shuleni, inasaidia – I studied it at school. That helps (Kiswahili)
Ubaguzi – Discrimination (Kiswahili)
Wazungu – White people (non derogatory) (Kiswahili)
Ninaomba – I beg you (Kiswahili)
Pole – Sorry (Kiswahili)
Fundis – Mechanics (Kiswahili)
Gari – Car (Kiswahili)
Maji – Water (Kiswahili)
Na wachana na pombe yangu – And leave my booze alone! (Kiswahili)
Ulisema ukweli – You told me the truth (Kiswahili)
Sasa unaiamini? – So now you believe me (Kiswahili)
Tafadhali? – Please? (Kiswahili)
Geshagi – Upcountry rural home (Kikuyu)
Mafrika – African (Kiswahili)
Ama – Isn't that so? (Kiswahili)
Poleni – Sorry to all of you (Kiswahili)
Wazungu – White people (non derogatory) (Kiswahili)
Mafrika – African (non derogatory)
Wafrika – Africans (non derogatory) (Kiswahili)
Mzungu – White person (non derogatory) (Kiswahili)
Kaburu – Kenyan white settler (derogatory)
Wafrika – Africans (non derogatory) (Kiswahili)
Boda boda – Motorcycle taxi
Leta sherry sasa hapa! Na glasi muruzi! – Bring sherry now here! And
   nice glass! (Kiswahili)

Bitings – Nibbles

Saa hii ni sundowners, wapi bitings? – This time is sundowners, where snacks? (Kiswahili)

Watu – African (derogatory) (Kiswahili)

Uko sawa – Are you OK (Kiswahili)

Kabisa – Completely/ Absolutely (Kiswahili)

Nini kilitokea hapa? – What happened here? (Kiswahili)

Na habari ya jioni – And a good evening to you (Kiswahili)

Habari – How are you? (Kiswahili)

Sawa – OK (Kiswahili)

Watu – Africans (derogatory) (Kiswahili)

Uko sawa – Are you OK (Kiswahili)

Nikwega – Good morning, how are you (Kikuyu)

Nikwega muno – Good morning, fine (Kikuyu)

Shamba – Garden/farm (Kiswahili)

Watu – Africans (derogatory) (Kiswahili)

Siwezi – I can't (Kiswahili)

Kwa nini – Why (Kiswahili)

Shamba – Garden/ Farm (Kiswahili)

Wazungu – White people (non derogatory) (Kiswahili)

Wafrika – Africans (non derogatory) (Kiswahili)

Mbuzeni

Trans.: The act of asking God or a human being for an answer

Koleka Putuma

Koleka Putuma is an award-winning poet and theatre practitioner who has taken the South African literary scene by storm with her debut collection of poems *Collective Amnesia*, which sold over 3,000 copies in less than 9 months, and has been prescribed for study at tertiary level in South African universities. She is the winner of the 2014 National Poetry Slam Championship, was nominated for the Rosalie van der Gucht Prize for Best New Directors at the annual Fleur Du Cap Theatre Awards (2015), and won the 2016 PEN South Africa Student Writing Prize for her poem: *Water*. She has been named one of Africa's top 10 poets by Badilisha, named one of the young pioneers who took South Africa by storm in 2015 by *The Sunday Times*, one of 12 future shapers by *Marie Claire* SA, one of the 100 young people disrupting the status quo in South Africa by independent media, and recently has been awarded the 2017 Rising Star award at the annual Mbokodo Awards.

Her plays include *UHM* (2014), *Mbuzeni* (2015/2016), *Woza Sarafina* (2016).

Plays for young audiences include *Ekhaya* for 2–7-year-olds, and *SCOOP*, the first South African play for children aged between two weeks and twelve months.

Production history

Mbuzeni was created in 2014 through a process of critical dramaturgy, and structured improvisation based on a pre-determined story outline conceptualised and created by me while I was at the University of Cape Town Drama School. Through several series of improvisations based on the structured outline, the cast and I discovered the textual and physical material that later became the final storyline. The story and text were then deepened in the writing stage. It was later then rewritten and reconstructed in English.

The original play was devised in IsiXhosa, Zulu and English.

Mbuzeni was then read at the ASSITEJ African Youth Theatre and Dance Festival in 2015, after which I further developed the text. The final draft was developed through the New Visions New Voices International Playwright's Intensive held at the University of Maryland and The Kennedy Center, USA. Staged in 2018 at the Edinburgh International Childrens' Festival.

The original cast was Naledi Majola, Noxolo Blandile, Diana Mokokobale Makgopa, Sivenkosi Gubangxa.

Special thanks to Mark Fleishman, UCT Drama Department, Mandla Mbothwe, Artscape Theatre, ASSITEJ South Africa, University of Maryland, Kennedy Center for the Performing Arts, and the current and original cast.

Critical introduction

Mbuzeni, a play targeted at young girls aged 17–25, aims to shift and challenge the stereotypical representations of the contemporary South African black female narrative on stage and in playwriting, a narrative currently embedded in historical and patriarchal oppression. To sculpt and stage stories for and about the contemporary South African black women that a) do not depend on the approval of the male or white gaze, and b) create stories for and about young black girls that do not render them powerless, objectify them or subject them only to the role of maids and slaves in theatre. *Mbuzeni* tells the story of four little girl orphans; their sisterhood, and their fixation with burials. The story takes place in an unnamed village, the time: present or a suggestion of the afterlife.

Throughout my undergraduate programme at the University of Cape Town, the inability to source plays published from 2004 to 2014 by black South African women playwrights (to stage and perform), perturbed me for two main reasons: the first being that black women currently making original work exist, some who also identify as playwrights. The second being that I began to notice that black female narratives were reliant on authorial prejudices in texts that were written by black and white men, as well as by white women playwrights. I was bothered by how these narratives were still detained in stereotypes, and how the black female in these narratives could not exist as an agent of her own identity and destiny.

Currently there aren't enough narratives that counter the plot we often see staged for the black female body. Ultimately, my aim with *Mbuzeni* was and still is to place the 'untold' black female narrative at the forefront of South African theatre. I wanted the audience to allow the black girl child their obsessions and experiences, especially as bodies and lives which are constantly subjected to an imposed narrative from birth.

Characters

Note on the characters below: All the girls *must* be black. They should possess an ability to communicate physically through movement and have adequate singing voices. Throughout the play all the girls, except Tinky, double up as the crow.

Gogo/Narrator, *narrates the prologue. A ghostly figure in human form. Her relationship to the girls is one of watching. She lives with the villagers. This character is doubled by the same actress who plays Tinky.*

Rivo, *orphan, 13 years old. The oldest. She assumes the role of keeper and protector of the pack. Lost her family in a fire that swept through their village.*

Vuvu, *orphan, 12 years old. Impulsive. Mother died during child birth. Father left her while she was still young. She was shuffled around different family members before coming to live with the other girls.*

Lindi, *orphan, 11 years old. Easily persuaded. Family sent her to an orphanage after finding out she was raped by the Uncle who is the sole income of the family.*

Tinky, *orphan, 10 years old. The youngest. The other girls use her as the corpse when they require one at all burials. She has a comb that she does not part with, which was given to her by her Grandma. Her mother disappeared, and her father hanged himself. Later on, her Grandma passed away.*

The Black Crow, *a conduit to the world of the spirit and is associated with dying or bringing a message of warning. The black crow is a totem that the people in the village have used as a mechanism to make sense of the mysteries they encounter with the dead. The myth in this village is that if the black crow follows you, either you or someone near you will pass on, because of mourning the death of a loved one.*

The girls embody the bird in different parts of the play. Sometimes the bird is not a physical presence in the space.

Note on the text

The action is continuous, and the scenes flow into one another. The scene numbers here denote chunks of action rather than separate scenes.

Travelling sequence

The run should be choreographed as a specific travel sequence and marked as the route to and from the graveyard.

Setting

The entire action takes place in an unnamed village; the time could be present time or a suggestion of the afterlife. The village is made up of centuries of myths, a small community, and a forbidden cemetery and the shack where the girls live. In this community, the villagers do not mourn; they only concern themselves with the living. The cemetery separates the villagers and the orphans' dwellings. *Note*: The villagers are unseen, only alluded to.

The village on stage

The aesthetic is constructed of rostrum, fence and reeds. The rostrum is merely to construct a divide. The rostrums demarcate the travelling space, the cemetery and the girls' living space. However, the play could still function without them. *Note*: the above may be discarded or changed.

Preset

An old woman in a dim light.

Prologue

Gogo This.

This is the cemetery of this village.

The villagers who live on this side of cemetery (*she points to the left*) come here to pay their respects and remember those who have passed on to the other side.

On this other side of the cemetery are four girl orphans, who make a mockery of this sacred place. The two sides do not get along very much. The cemetery separates the girls from the villagers. The cemetery also separates the living from those who have died. The girls live in an abandoned shack built by a man we all knew as Tata sticks, who died mysteriously years ago. When the sun sets, I cross the cemetery to watch them play these burials; fascinated by weeping and burying each other. Sometimes they sneak over to our side when we are asleep, to steal our leftovers. They think that we do not see them. But we do. Or at least I do. They saw me once, watching them. Usually I am not one to concern myself with other people's business, *but*, there is something rather strange and unsettling about these children.

The villagers pass around many stories about how these orphans came to live in that hole away from all this life. But I wonder and wonder . . . and I still do not know.

I simply don't.

She leaves.

A crow appears. It speaks of death, and how the dead, here, are never forgotten.

One: The Graveyard

The cemetery.

Rivo, **Tinky**, **Vuvu** *run in with shovels; they are veiled from head to waist.*

They begin to dig in hushed tones.

Lindi   Tinky is digging her own grave.

Tinky   I don't want to be buried again. And why are we playing Gogo's funeral if she is still alive?

Lindi   Because nosey people who spy on other people should die. Hold on, where is Vuvu?

Vuvu *enters.*

Lindi   Where were you?

Vuvu   I am here now. Who are we burying?

Rivo/Lindi   Tinky!

Lindi   We doing that snooping Gogo's funeral.

Tinky   But guys, she's still alive.

Vuvu   But she's going to die now. It's play play, Tinky. Just die.

Tinky   Of what?

Pause.

Rivo   Chickens.

Vuvu   Rotten. Headless. Chickens. In your stomach.

Tinky   I don't want to die of rotten headless chickens in my stomach.

Lindi   But it's not you. It's you dying as the Gogo.

Tinky   But why is it always me being buried? It's not fair.

Lindi   If you don't want to, then you're never going to come play with us again.

Tinky   But, but, you forgot me here the last time. And you just ran away.

Lindi   Just get in *maan*; dead people don't talk as much as you do.

Tinky   Promise you won't leave me here again.

They promise.

Tinky *climbs into the grave.*

Tinky   Wait! I must die first

Rivo   Yes. Yes. Die and make it quick.

Tinky *pretends to die.*

Rivo   Ok that's enough.

Tinky *falls to the ground with her eyes wide open, making chicken noises.*

Lindi   You look funny. Close your eyes.

Rivo   Oh Father, we cannot question your timing. She is gone. This Gogo.

Tinky (*sits up*)   Wait, does she have a name? You have to bury people using their name. Give her a name.

Vuvu   Nosey-Spy-Gogo-died-of-rotten-chickens-whoever-no-one-cares. Shut up and die Tinky.

Rivo   Whoever this Gogo is, she is dead. We bring her spirit before you Lord. May it find rest somewhere, anywhere.

Vuvu *mockingly starts wailing and falls to the ground.*

Lindi   Rivo, Vuvu is starting with her rubbish again. Do you want to cough all your lungs out? Do you want black blood to come out of your ears? Do you want your *nyash nyash* to close? Remember what the villagers say happened to Sisi Dudu.

Vuvu   I don't believe in those rubbish stories these old people tell us. And it's not like Tinky is really dead, or the Gogo. Or whatever.

A dog barks.

They run leaving **Tinky** *behind.*

Tinky   Wait for me!

All   Come Tinky!

Tinky   Wait! My comb.

They run home.

The crow flies past their home as they enter.

The appearance is a warning.

Two: Home

They remove their veils.

Tinky   I am never going to the graveyard with you again. You forgot me . . . again. You promised you wouldn't leave me and you left me behind with dead people.

Lindi   We got caught because of you, how does a dead person talk huh? And it's because of your rubbish crying Vuvu that the crow followed us *maan*. Now you going to die. You know you not allowed to cry for dead people. Yho. You guys make me hungry!

Tinky   I think we should stop going to the graveyard anyway.

Rivo   Why? Are you scared?

Tinky   No . . .

Vuvu   If you are scared, you should not come play with us then.

Tinky   I'm not scared; I just don't want to die of chickens talking inside me, or my boobs to have sour milk, and then they have to cut them off. I don't want those bad things the pastor says will happen to the aunties who cry at the funerals.

Vuvu   But it was nice wasn't it?

Tinky   No! Because I never bury. I'm always buried. I want to be part of the burial for once.

Rivo   Ok, ok. Tomorrow. You will bury.

They bring their pinkies to the centre.

All   On our parents' graves and ours.

We grieve in Spit. (*They spit.*)

May the dead:

Lindi   Never wink at us in their coffins.

Tinky   Or become fish paste on our bread.

All   Or haunt us while we are breathing.

Vuvu   And if the crow follows our footsteps, may death never knock our door.

Rivo   This we ask on our parents' graves and ours.

All   This we ask on our parents' graves and ours.

They fall asleep.

Three: Tinky Dreams of the Crucifixion

Tinky *is mumbling in her sleep,* **Rivo** *mumbles back.*

Rivo   Tinky shut up, and sleep.

A Dream Begins.

Tinky *dreams she is being crucified.*

Tinky *sits at a table with the other girls.*

On the table there is bread, chicken and grape juice.

Lindi *stuffs her face.* **Tinky** *watches. She does not eat.*

Lindi *is mumbling something underneath her breath,* **Vuvu** *keeps denying it.* **Tinky** *cannot hear what is being said.*

The dream changes suddenly: **Tinky** *is being crucified.*

She calls out to the other girls. As they come nearer, they morph into animalistic creatures who torment her with shovels and words she can't make out.

There is white noise playing loudly in the background while **Tinky** *is nailed to the shovel.* **Tinky** *cries out in discomfort.*

The creatures begin to turn on each other.

Vuvu *is now nailed to a shovel.*

Lindi *is now nailed to a shovel.*

Rivo *has disappeared.*

Lindi *tries to free herself from the shovel.*

The heat is getting to **Tinky.**

Tinky   Vuvu why are we here? Where are we? It stinks here. It's so hot. I can't breathe. Vuvu please can we get out of here. I don't want to be here. I'm scared Vuvu.

Lindi *appears as Jesus Christ.*

Jesus   Please stop complaining, you're giving me a headache.

Tinky   Vuvu, who is this? (*She points to* **Jesus/Lindi**.)

Jesus   I am alpha and omega.

I died for your rubbish sins.

People fast and pray for serious things.

And here you are, complaining about little things.

Mimics **Tinky**.

Jesus   'It's hot Vuvu.' 'It stinks Vuvu.' 'I'm scared Vuvu.'

There are those who go up mountains and ask for rain:

'Lord, Lord, please we need rain.'

Is my name Rain-Maker?

There people who pray for distinctions, but they did not study the whole year.

Municipality is also failing.

There are potholes everywhere.

Children playing on the road.

Buses are overtaking taxis.

Taxis are overtaking cars.

There are bicycles and old people on the pedestrian.

The robots aren't working . . .

and all of this is happening at the same time.

Next thing – boom – accident!

Then I must also decide:

who leaves

and

who stays.

Rivo *reappears as the crow.*

Tinky   Vuvu, do you see this bird. Please take the bird away from me.
Please.

The black crow embraces **Tinky.**

The crow suffocates **Tinky** *to stillness.*

The crow disappears.

The dream ends.

Wakes up.

Tinky   Take this bird away from me! Take this Bird Away Please Rivo. Take the –

Rivo   Sshhh. It's okay Tinky, it's us.

Lindi   It's just a dream.

The girls sing a song to comfort **Tinky.**

Four: Joko Dies

Daytime.

The girls play Puca.

Vuvu   I'm first.

Rivo   Second.

Lindi   Third, Tinky you last.

Vuvu   You have to stump on the ground three times. You can't organize the stones. You can't catch with two hands. You have to have five stones in your hand when you are out for you to keep them.

Rivo   We know that Vuvu.

Tinky   Rivo, can I play with my eyes closed?

Rivo   No! Tinky that one takes too long. Here's a stone, play like the rest of us.

The girls play until they are all out, and it's **Tinky**'s *turn. She plays with her eyes closed anyway.*

Tinky   My turn!

Rivo   No man Tinky! Why do you like playing *Puca* with your eyes closed, is it 'cause you spent a lot of time with your mother in the dark.

Tinky *starts to cry.* **Vuvu** *plays and she is out.*

Rivo   You out!

Vuvu (*whispers in* **Tinky***'s ear*)   No! Tinky don't cry. Tell her about her Grandmother.

Tinky   Your Gogo was a witch! We saw her the other day at the grave with her bum in the air.

Rivo   What!? What did you say Tinky? What did you say?

Tinky   I did not say anything . . .

Rivo   My Gogo is a witch? Huh? Was she a witch to you? At least my grandmother died, and she loved me. At least she left me with a birth certificate. She didn't leave me with some stupid comb. Don't make fun of my Grandma when your stupid father hanged himself, but he knew he had a child he was leaving behind. Don't talk about my Grandma.

Lindi   Yho, Rivo why are talking about Tinky's family?

Rivo   Am I talking to you Lindi? Do you want me to talk about what your Uncle did huh?

Vuvu   Your Uncle raped you!

Lindi   Your aunty gave you chicken bones for supper.

Rivo   Why are you talking about Vuvu's chicken bones huh? No wonder your family left you and picked your Uncle over you.

Lindi   They didn't pick him because they wanted to.

Rivo   How do you know that?

Lindi   Because. Because. They said he wasn't going to give money to the family anymore if I told the Soldiers about what he did, and they said I'd be bringing hunger to the family because Uncle is the only one working. So they picked him so they could have food and stuff. Then one day a car came to our house, and took me to an orphanage. It was nice at the orphanage, I learnt how to speak good English there. But after some time, the orphanage people said I eat too much. Then another car came to the orphanage and took me from the orphanage, but I didn't know where it was going. Then I saw that it was bringing me here to this stupid desert . . .

Rivo   Is this a desert Lindi?

Lindi   Yes, it's like where you come from, a fire came and destroyed everything.

Rivo So what? Even if a huge fire came and destroyed everything. At least I'm the last man standing. (*Hears* **Vuvu** *playing in the background.*) Vuvu it's not your turn, why are you playing while I'm talking. You don't listen *maan*. No wonder your mother left you and your aunty gave you chicken bones under the table to punish you.

Vuvu Lies. Lies. My mother did not leave me. I was born in a hospital. My mother didn't make it then my father came one day and kissed me on my forehead and said he was going to work, then he didn't come back then I went to my great Aunt's house there was too much alcohol and music at the shebeen and she gave me chicken bones under the table to protect me from the men in the shebeen then my mother's aunt took me in and then my Aunt's little sister took me in and then my grandfather's little uncle took me in then the neighbour's cousin's cousin took me in then my third cousin's brother took me in then I don't know, next thing I was here.

Lindi Yho. Vuvu's story changes all the time.

Rivo So what if her story changes all the time? At least she doesn't say this is a stupid desert. You Lindi are rude man. I jump fences, I get bitten by dogs and shouted at by the Gogos on the other side, so I can get you clothes and food and you say this is a stupid desert. You don't even know what a desert looks like dummy. Come. Come here. I want a meeting now!

The girls come closer to **Rivo**.

Rivo Who is older here Tinky?

Tinky You are.

Rivo Who is younger?

Tinky I am.

Rivo You, Lindi. Who is older?

Lindi You are Rivo.

Rivo Who is younger?

Lindi I am Rivo.

Rivo You and Tinky are very cheeky and when Vuvu and I hit you, you guys are gonna cry the whole night.

Tinky (*diverting* **Rivo**'*s attention*) Look! Rivo, here is Joko.

Joko, a dog from the village, appears.

Vuvu *throws a stone at Joko.*

Vuvu   Voetsek!!

The dog is run over by a car.

Lindi/Tinky   *Alala dudu.*You killed Joko. You going to die. *Alala dudu!*

Rivo   You two, shut up! Let's just bury it.

Lindi   Where?

Rivo   Here.

Tinky   In our play yard?

Vuvu   No *siesmaan.*

Rivo   Take it back to its owner then.

Tinky   Ok. Rivo, we'll bury it.

Lindi   How do you bury dogs?

Rivo   You dig a hole stupid.

They all dig the hole, **Rivo** *dumps the dog in the hole, they cover it.*
Vuvu *pisses on the grave like a dog would.*

Tinky   No man! Now Joko is going to haunt you. You don't piss on
dead things *maan.*

Vuvu   Rivo, Tinky is swearing.

Tinky   So what? Piss. Piss. Piss. Piss!!

Rivo   Stop it! Come.

They join their pinkies.

All   On our parents' graves and ours.

We grieve in Spit. (*They spit.*)

May the dead,

Never wink at us in their coffins

Or haunt us while we are breathing

If the black crow follows our footsteps, may death never knock on our
door.

Rivo   This we ask on our parents' graves and ours.

All   This we ask on our parents' graves and ours.

The girls bark a traditional funeral hymn.

It starts to rain.

They pick up their umbrellas and head toward the cemetery.

Five: Aunt Gcina's Funeral

At the cemetery.

Rivo (*nudges* **Lindi** *to start*)   Lindi.

Lindi   Oh. Mam'Gcina. The village has put me here to speak on their behalf. To talk about the wonderful woman that you were. But I will speak the truth Mam' Gcina. I am happy that you are dead because we will no longer hear lies about other people's business, you liked talking rubbish rubbish –

Tinky *nudges her to stop.*

Lindi   Er. Mam'Gcina. We will remember you and your beautiful garden. But now at least now we will know that all the gossip we hear around here is true. We won't have to put up with your rubbish lies.

Tinky *nudges her again.*

Lindi   Mam'Gcina we brought you a gift. You must use this gift to nourish your garden in heaven. That's if you going to heaven. But here is your gift Mam'Gcina.

Lindi *grabs* **Tinky**'*s comb, throws it in the grave*

Tinky   No!

Lindi   You will get your comb after the funeral *maan.*

Rivo   Let us close our eyes and pray. Father God, in the mighty name of Jesus. We bring before you Mam' Gcina's spirit. We also bring her family before you mighty God, breathe healing into hurt, father God. Breathe the fire of the holy ghost into their home. I remember (so clearly) in your word Father, when you put Jonah in the dolphin mighty God, and delivered him on the other side. Oh Alpha and Omega. Oh my sweet Jesus. You are Jehovah Jirah, the lord who provides, the lord who sees. Water Walker. Wine Maker. Jehovah nice nice. Jehovah peace. Jehovah the legit Jehovah, Oh Mighty Lor –

Lindi   The pastor then said . . . (*hinting at* **Rivo** *to move on.*)

Rivo   Oh, Yes. Ashes to ashes and dust to dust.

Vuvu   I remember when the coffin went down, Mam'Gcina's daughter was like (*wailing hysterically*) 'Mama . . . Mama . . . Mama!! Mama!!!!!'

Vuvu *pretends to toss herself at the coffin.*

Tinky   And the pastor said, 'Demons out in Jesus name!'

The other girls join in in casting out the spirit in **Vuvu**, *they stop suddenly when* **Vuvu***'s enactment gets more and more wild.*

Vuvu   Mama, Mama, Mama!!!

All   VUVU! VUVU! VUVU! STOP IT *MAAN!*

Vuvu *laughs hysterically.*

Lindi   Vuvu, you play like rubbish.

Tinky   You mustn't do that *maan.*

Lindi   Can we go eat from Sisi Thuli's bin tonight. I could smell chicken coming from her house. Mmmmh Vuvu, those chicken bones.

Vuvu *pounces on* **Lindi**, **Rivo** *breaks them up.*

Rivo   First we must finish the funeral. Let's sing Mam' Gcina's song.

They sing a melody of disjointed funeral hymns.

A dog barks.

The girls run home. Halfway **Tinky** *realizes that she forgot her comb at the cemetery. She wants to go back, but the girls promise that they will go back to the graveyard later that night to get her comb. She reluctantly agrees.*

They crow appears again.

Another warning.

Six: Heaven

At their home.

Rivo   It's the second time the crow follows us, and it's because of your demonic playing Vuvu. Tomorrow we are going to bury you.

Vuvu   I won't be buried if Tinky is here.

Tinky *interrupts.*

Tinky   It's the third time I am seeing the crow.

Rivo   Did you go to the graveyard alone Tinky?

Tinky   No I had a dream about it. We were all in the dream. All I remember is that crow's wings around me. I couldn't move or breathe.

Beat.

Where are we going when we die?

Rivo   Are we dead Tinky? How are we going to know that?

Vuvu   I know we are not going to some Rubbish hell.

Rivo   How do you know that?

Vuvu   Where does some rubbish Satan get so much money to braai a million trillion people with some rubbish fork and throw some rubbish party. Me, I am going to heaven shem.

Lindi   And what kind of heaven is that?

Vuvu   It has lots and lots of fruit. Bananas, peaches. Strawberries. Because I will die of an illness. And I will need lots of fruit when I am dead.

Lindi   Yho! Sana. Me I am going to die from being too pretty, and my heaven has angels in black high heels and velvet lipstick.

Rivo   My heaven has lots and lots of chocolate and sweets. But I won't die of shame. I'll just go there with a lift to visit and come back here on earth whenever I want.

Vuvu   That's not fair. You can't come back. When you go, you go forever.

Rivo   Shut up Vuvu, you are going to die doing the number two. And your brains are going to fall out. And your heaven is going to stink like dry *kaka*.

Tinky   My heaven is quiet.

Lindi   Boring.

Tinky   I don't know how I die yet.

Rivo   Just pick a death *maan*. We all have to die. Of something.

Tinky   Maybe one day I'll just disappear.

Vuvu   Impossible. People don't just disappear.

Tinky   My mother disappeared.

Rivo   Was your mother an albino?

Tinky   No my mother was not uh albino.

Rivo   If. If you say your mother disappeared and she wasn't buried, then it means she was an albino. Only albinos disappear and don't get buried.

Vuvu   That's what they say Tinky! It's true.

Lindi   And if you say it happened to your mother then it means it will happen to you.

Tinky   No! She wasn't. She wasn't one!

Rivo   Okay. Okay. Sorry, she wasn't one. Come let's sleep.

Rivo   This we ask on our parents' graves and ours.

All   This we ask on our parents' graves and ours.

The girls sleep.

Beat.

Tinky *wakes up and realizes her comb is missing. She goes over to* **Lindi***.*

Tinky   You are coming with me. Now.

Lindi   Where?

Tinky   To get my comb.

Lindi   No Tinky! We can't go to the grave so late by ourselves you know that.

Tinky   You promised.

Lindi   But Rivo and Vuvu also promised you.

Tinky   You know Rivo will never allow us to go to the grave this late and Vuvu always calls death for us. And I need to fetch my comb NOW! You know what will happen to me if I don't. You remember how sick I got the last time I lost my comb. Gogo said I must never lose it.

Rivo *shuffles and mumbles something in her sleep. The girls duck down and pretend to be asleep. Beat.*

Tinky   You don't want to?

Lindi   No. I don't. Go Tinky. I want to go sleep.

Tinky   If you don't come with me I'll tell on you. I'll tell Rivo about the day you ate her food when she was not here.

Lindi   I'll also tell on you. The day I saw you here at home rubbing your *nyash nyash*.

Tinky   I wasn't rubbing it, I was itching.

Lindi   Go, you going to wake Rivo up.

Tinky *runs to the graveyard.*

She frantically begins digging where they were playing last.

She finds it.

Tinky   Lord we are here today to celebrate the life of Comb. Comb you will be missed. I will remember our good times and our bad. I am grateful that you always kept my hair neat and clean, rest in peace comb. Wait you have to die first.

At the house. **Rivo** *wakes up.*

Rivo   Lindi, where is Tinky?

Lindi   Huh?

Rivo   You heard me *maan*?

Lindi   She went to wee.

Rivo   Lindi, Lindi (*menacingly*), where is Tinky?

Lindi   Tinky went to the graveyard. She woke me up but I told her we can't go. Because it's dark. But she said –

Rivo   Shut up. Vuvu! Vuvu!! This rubbish let Tinky go to the grave by herself.

Lindi   But I –

Rivo   – Come!

They arrive at the graveyard.

Tinky   Found it!

They go home.

They encounter the black crow.

They lie down. **Lindi**, **Tinky** *and* **Vuvu** *exchange middle fingers,* **Rivo** *shoots them a look and they sleep.*

An *Unmaned* Scene

That night Tinky's spirit leaves her body.
That night Tinky takes her final breath.
That night Tinky joins the other side.

This scene is an enactment done in movement/physical theatre. **Tinky**'s *spirit is leaving her body while the other girls are asleep. In this scene the other girls may assist in creating the atmosphere of* **Tinky** *dying by embodying ancestors/angels that come and transport* **Tinky** *into the spiritual realm.*

Seven: Gone

The girls wake up except **Tinky**.

Beat.

Beat.

Lindi   Yho! Tinky likes to sleep.

Vuvu   What are we doing today?

Silence.

Rivo   Let's go to a funeral.

Vuvu   Let's play Tata Stick's funeral.

Lindi   I don't like playing his funeral. No one even knows how he died. And that family doesn't have any food at their burials.

Rivo   Ok, what about Mam'Gcina's funeral?

Vuvu   Yes! I love her funeral.

Lindi   We always playing funerals, let's take a break now.

Vuvu   Let's wake Tinky up, she will want to go to a funeral – we'll tell her that today we won't bury her.

Vuvu *tries to wake* **Tinky** *up, but she is still. The other girls shake her. She is still.*

Rivo   Tinky stop playing like rubbish.

Lindi *moves her arm, it flops over limply.*

Vuvu   Why is her body like a jelly.

Rivo   Tinky we are going to leave you and you'll stay here by yourself, playing your stupid games.

Lindi   I've taken your comb Tinky. (*Beat.*) Tinky stop it! Wake up.

Rivo   We're playing Mam' Gcina's funeral. Lindi is gonna be the body.

They giggle.

Rivo *goes down to tickle* **Tinky**. *Silence.* **Tinky** *does not move.*

Rivo   Tinky! Get up. We not going to bury you. We promise.

Beat.

Tinky!

Tinky!

Vuvu   Tinky, waaaaaaaaaaaaaaaaaaaaaaaaaakkkkkkeee – uuuuupppp!

Beat.

Lindi   Why is her body cold and floppy?

Rivo   I'm scared, why is Tinky like this. I'm going to other side to get someone to help us.

Lindi   I'm also going.

Vuvu   Me too.

The girls run out of the house calling for help in the village.

The old woman appears.

She takes a step into their dwelling.

She sees **Tinky***'s body.*

She covers **Tinky***'s body.*

The girls stare blankly at her.

She gives them **Tinky***'s shoes and comb.*

The old woman walks out of the house.

Eight: The Final Burial

The three girls make their way to the graveyard. They arrive. Dig a hole in silence. Place the shoes in the middle of the pit. **Rivo** *sings a hymn* **Tinky** *liked. The girls join in.*

The crow appears.

Light fades on the girls looking up.

Lights up on the old woman who enters the graveyard.

Gogo   I still do not know.

I simply don't.

Lights fade on **Gogo**.

Lights fade on **Tinky**'s *shoes and comb.*

The End

Glossary

Alala dudu – A chant/melody sung by children to indicate to each other that one of them is in trouble. Often sung to mock/irritate whoever it is being sung to. Melody/rhythm can be made up.

Gçina – Name of a woman, pronounced: gc – ee-nah. The 'gc' is created by sucking the upper teeth.

Gogo – A grandmother, the title for an older woman that is polite and shows affection. Pronunciation: gho-gho.

Kaka – Crude word for shit or poop. Pronounced: kha-kha

Maan – Has no meaning in particular. Synonyms (depending on geography): 'yo' or 'man'.

Nyash nyash – Term used for vagina.

Puca – A coordination game played mostly by young girls. Ten stones are placed in a circle or a square. Each player then tries to grab the most stones, throw them in the air and catch them in one hand until all the stones are back in the circle or square. Pronounced: poo-ca. The 'ca' sound created by sucking upper teeth.

Sana – Affectionate word commonly used among women. Synonym: 'girl'/'honey'/'sister'. Pronounced: sah-nah.

Shem – Slang word for 'shame'. Pronounced: sheym.

Sies – A South African word used to express disgust/disapproval. Synonym: 'eeeuw'/gross.

Tata – Word used to refer to an elderly man. Synonym: 'papa'/ 'uncle'. Pronounced: tah-tah

Voetsak – Afrikaans word for 'Get lost'. (Not a swear word! But rather crude like the English 'bog off'.) Synonym: shoo/go away. Pronounced: foo-tsek.

Yho – Sound/word for irritation, which also can be used to punctuate. Synonym: 'damn'/'aaagrhh'. Pronounced: y-oo-h.

Bonganyi – A Dance Drama

Sophia Mempuh Kwachuh

Sophia Mempuh Kwachuh is from the north-west region of Cameroon, and works fluently in both English and French. She freelances in translation, communication and marketing, and is Vice Dean of Studies and Manager of the English Campus of Powerbache Education, a professional institute with a record of producing Majors in the National Exams. She studied at the University of Yaounde I, in the Department of Arts and Archeology, Performing Arts (MA). She is a dancer and actress, and theatre and film maker. She trained in film directing (documentary) with MALO Pictures. She is the CEO and founder of I RISE AGAIN (IRA), a non-profit organization that focuses on the promotion of education, especially for girls and women; and SHAMAH Production (audiovisual works). She worked as Vice-President for ASSITEJ (International Association of Theatre for Children and Young People), Cameroon, is Administrative Assistant for FATEJ (Festival Africain du Theatre pour L'Enfance et la Jeunesse), Vice-Secretary General for CID (Conseil International de la Dance Cameroon, Yaounde), and director for Theatre for Children.

Sophia has written and directed several plays: *Divine Providence, Shanine and Shanone* (2006 for FATEJ festival), *My Guavas* (2008), *Boganyi* (2010), and *My Father's Treasure* (for a Playwright Slam in South Africa). *Boganyi* was performed in India in 2014, and has been prescribed at Michigan University, USA. Sophia has also written for screen: *La Belle Affaire, Fadimatou, My Album* (documentaries on kola nut, albinism, FGM), and for Black History Month in 2000, 2001, 2003, 2012, 2014 and 2015.

Production history

The play started off when we wanted to do a TV drama that required two plays and we had just one. So, I came up with this story. The story was rehearsed in fragments, which we assembled, workshop style. The script was brief, as most of the action was expressed through physical performance. I was then asked to read the first five mins of a play for a playwright slam organized by Kim Peter Kovac in Denmark during the ASSITEJ International World Congress in 2011. I had a 24-page script as a starting point, but each time I went back to it, it grew. I was selected for a young leaders' program in the US, the IVLP – International Visitors Leadership Programme – where Ram Mohan Holagundi produced the play in India with his theatre company Nishumbita. It has also been used by Jenny Sawtelle Koppera in the University of Michigan school curriculum.

Critical introduction

Bonganyi is a play that is told from the perspective of a ghost. It is a common belief in Africa generally, and in Cameroon specifically, that people don't completely cease to exist when they die. They transcend from the earth to the world beyond, and can communicate with their loved ones. Ever since precolonial times, it is believed that after a person dies, you could invoke the person's spirit and they would come back and recount the events leading to their death.

The play is set in the precolonial period when people in Africa lived in small communities and not nations. In Cameroon, we had Fondoms, chiefdoms and kingdoms, dependent on the name given to the head of the village or area – chief or king. And when a kingdom went to war with another and subdued them, the subdued nation became the servants of the victor. The treatment of the slaves or servants varied from place to place. In some places, it was mild whereas in others it was really very harsh. Contemporary Cameroon is a country with about 328 villages and 228 different dialects, where we still have villages and paramount chiefs who rule over strong kingdoms that have subdued a good number of small villages or which has a large population and thus has acquired much land. Paramount chiefs sometimes have about 10 different sub-chiefs who owe him tribute and loyalty.

Bonganyi depicts a typical situation of a people who have been subdued into servitude. Today we can liken this to the way so many political leaders in power subdue natives from other clans, making them their subordinates by calling them sub-humans. In Cameroon the ruling tribe subdues all other tribes especially tribes from the opposition.

So Bonganyi stands as a symbol of a nation who has been enslaved for a generation. She decides to take part in the Annual Regional Cultural Extravaganza so that once her victory is ensured, she should be able to fight for the liberation of her people. Unfortunately, a mysterious snake bites her and she dies. It is believed that when our independence leaders were fighting for the freedom of the land, they were subdued, arrested and executed mysteriously. And most often they were betrayed by their close ones. Thus the source, whereabouts and destination of the snake in the play remains a mystery. However, Bonganyi's efforts are not in vain because those who have sympathized with her, like Ntem, are ready to speak out for her cause.

Duration 50 mins.

Age Teens and above.

Set A courtyard with trees, a traditional basket, a hoe, cutlasses (×3).

Characters and original cast

Bonganyi *(Kami Joyce), a young and very beautiful girl. She is a slave and hates being treated as a half human being. Due to her beauty, most of the boys in the village want to court her. And her being a slave makes them want to intimidate her into accepting them. She is very hardworking, and her greatest dream is to be free one day. That is why she wants to be the best dancer.*

Ntem *(Fokumlah Burnley Yaya), a good looking young man who is kind and respectful to Bonganyi. He loves her and would do everything within his power to protect her.*

Atem *(Tinsay Luh Ignatius), a very proud son of a plantation merchant. He doesn't hesitate to indicate the wealth of his father and his absolutely flourishing businesses. He is very protective of his father's businesses.*

Asong *(Suimola Humphrey), the son of a great warrior. He is a robust young man. His father is a legend in the village. And he believes that gives him a VIP entry and accord even to Bonganyi.*

Mofor *(Achilles Kolong), son of a widow. He is also unable to speak and in love with Bonganyi. He is very humble and modest, and grateful to have been accepted as a friend by his peers. He does his best to be a loyal friend.*

A percussionist *(Fokumah Magloire).*

Costumes

Bonganyi wears a short loin skirt, but originally, she would wear a raffia skirt made from the bark of trees, called Bibus or Obom (tissue of the bark of the Aloa tree). She has decorations drawn on her arms and legs, with the head of a tortoise drawn on her right shoulder. She wears anklets made of raffia and locally-made bells made from dried seeds, linked by a raffia rope.

All the boys are dressed in the same manner, in an Obom. They have the design of a leopard on their right chests. Some have designs on their foreheads too.

The setting

Is a courtyard, full of trees planted in the garden: banana trees, sugar cane trees, pear trees and plantain trees. There is dead silence on the stage. Two groups of people come out from either side of the stage singing a dirge. They come together in a synchronized way and stand in two lines, they are carrying an invisible corpse. They are on their way to a grave.

Act One

Dirge song:

Solo   Yondo yondo yondo.

Chorus   Yondo sélélé.

Solo   Mama Yondo yondo yondo.

Chorus   Yondo sélélé.

Solo   Yondo sélélé.

Chorus   Yondo sélélé eh yondo sélélé.

Solo   Yondo eh.

Chorus   Yondo sélélé eh yondo sélélé.

Both lines come to centre stage. They stop, still holding the corpse as if performing a ritual. They stand facing each other, all the while singing. The air is tense. We can hear birds of the night chanting songs of sadness far off. They take the corpse to down stage right and drop on the floor. While bent the second song is tuned by the solo and they start singing.

Chorus   Mama ehe e e
Bato baseh ba tiyana eh mama
Mama ehe e e.
Bato baseh ba tiyana eh mama.

Solo   Mama a ndedi eh o.

Chorus   Mama.

Solo   Bato base ba tiyana eh o.

Chorus   Mama.

They get up slowly, finally stop and stand, still as robots, humming. As if transfigured into another world.

A young girl skips from the group into the circle. She stands in the middle, where the corpse is supposed to be. She sings the dirge aloud and starts speaking while the others are humming the tune.

Bonganyi   Isn't this wonderful.

Beauty is in all its display.

But who can stand as a witness to fineness?

Isn't this great?

What am I talking about?

I breath painfully with words that transcend my body.

I gasp as the last words transposed in my memory flow out to show

Thoughts of my mind kept hidden in the confines of my existence.

This is marvelous

I stand in memory of me, I and myself. . .

Since I have no advocate to my cause. . .

I might as well defend my case.

A case I know not if the judge shall forbear.

For forbearance indeed comes in the presence and assistance of the real.

Am I real?

Are you real?

Unfortunately, I bear no body to proceed with an answer.

I faint to speak . . .

I gasp for my last words.

Words of love

Love of me

Me, confined in the real realism of my truth

A truth only I, you, us, we, can understand.

We who stood firm but whom the earth decided to swallow up to the knees.

And us who spent the rest of our time half human on our knees

But bestowed with beauty untold.

Beautiful.

Marvelous.

I mean interesting.

She laughs out loud, looking meaningfully at the audience.

I stand today in glory.

I stand in freedom.

Freedom that exhales my thoughts,

Thoughts kept and suppressed for years, decades . . .

Thoughts of our fallen heroes.

Thoughts of my father . . . my fatherland.

Thoughts of the earth, the real earth that birthed me.

Thoughts of betrayal of one person of another.

Thoughts that made one die and another sink in the muddy congregation of troubles,

Troubles rising up to the knee.

Thoughts of streams of blood that flowed for me, I, you, us . . .

But thoughts that stand in victory hidden forever.

Who shall believe our report?

Who will tell the story?

The story of a land.

The story of a people . . .

Gone with steps of victory . . .

Stopped in their tracks with defeat from betrayal . . .

Drown to their knees.

Bleeding for me, I, you, we and for us

For the first time in my life everybody is looking at me,

Everybody's attention is focused on me.

She squares her shoulders and stands like a heroine.

I am at the centre of attraction!

Do you see me?

Please see me.

This is my moment.

Tell me you see me, I, you, we and us?

Tell me you look out in the air and think of me as I was . . . as I am

As I am?

What am I? Yes, who am I?

Gone or present?

For the first time, people are around me.

I have never had a birthday celebrated

She shakes her head from side to side.

When a maiden has a day,

That day is a day of decoration,

That day is a day of beauty,

The day is the day of a journey . . .

A journey conveyed from the present to the future.

A day when an approval affirms her breast.

A day of approval that confirms the softness of her thigh . . .

And on this day the 'heiné' drawn on her body carves the curves of her beauty waiting to be consumed in the fire of the passion.

A passion that stands as the witness of who she is . . .

In the middle of the celebration of her coronation as beauty . . .

As the only one deemed for the night.

So, this is my day.

I have never had a day during which everybody's attention is focused on me.

She screams as if taken out of a dream. She looks around and a thought strikes her.

She holds her head as if refusing the truth about something. She shakes her head from side to side, then starts dancing all around, going from end to end of the performance space.

Dancing in between those who carried the corpse.

She dances in a frenzied way now, coming up to centre stage and falls on the ground. Breathing as if struggling to remain alive. She is desperate, her whole body is tensed in anxiety, as if each fibre is telling a story.

Bonganyi   I wish I had made it

I wish my feet suddenly grew from under the earth.

I wish I stood up tall

Looking at you eye to eye, brow to brow.

But I lived a life not mine, but mine still to behold.

I wish I showed you the patterns from my mother's field

I wish I showed you the dexterity of her dynamic beautiful earth, the one that gave peace, the one to whom you ran for wisdom.

I wish I could make you understand that my granny's kitchen fed your sons, daughters and dogs too.

I wish I showed you the dance steps my mother taught me;

The swinging of my hips to the soft and sweet rhythm of my land.

The swinging that takes my feet from within the earth to its surface.

I wish I showed you the dance of victory.

The dance that was given me by my own from afar.

I wish I was there at the gathering, where each maiden's hips catches the glimpse of its owner.

Hips that were a possible prominent source of rejuvenation

An owner who will make the prowess of her hips very popular.

Yes, I had that wish . . .

To take me, I, you, us and we from under the ground to the top, just with the swinging of my hips.

From less than human, to being human,

Just with the smile of my face.

Then you would have known that I had descended from a line of fighters, darers and people ready to defend their own.

I wish I was at the Annual Regional Cultural Extravaganza.

Oh, it would have been a day of glory

She smiles as if picturing an imaginary land full of beautiful things.

It would have been a day of grace

It would have been a day of sunshine

It would have been a day of peace

It would have been a day of Liberty

It would have been a day for me to tell you the tales told in times of old, through my own, my own story.

The story of me, I, us and we,

A story I have nurtured in the bosom of my heart

A story that was ready to be heard, prepared in all earnestness.

The earnestness of the beauty of who I am . . .

And what I want to become . . . free to show you how much I too can love.

Oh, a great day for me.

She shrugs her shoulders as if shaking off the dream from her mind.

Anyway, let me contend myself with the day of today.

At least it's still my day. It is my burial.

Let me show you my car.

The only car that will take me on my last journey to my space of rest.

She beckons to the audience to come and see.

See . . . look at it

Eih!

It is painted in brown,

I love colours.

I dream of colours that tell me, you and us who we are.

I wish for a colour that tells my story.

I long for a colour that tells you where I come from.

I know the colour that could have taken me to where I should go to.

Why brown for Bonganyi?

I know the colour that should have carried me to my final destination:

Ivory, aha!

First class offer for Bonganyi,

A maiden, a princess in a struggle for her hegemony.

She moves round the coffin exclaiming:

Ah ah eh e!

My body lay in rest, awaiting in a nest.

Beauty leaks grief,

As pain spreads with no relief.

I lay my bones, dying in hope for ropes to cut,

Now I know

That life is high

But that death like a knife is higher in esteem and vigour.

I lay in wait for the honours,

But just like the whisper of magic it all remains in my dream

She covers her eyes.

Indeed, the truth, crystal, white, immaculate, is glaring.

In report to the last road, alone by and by, alone to and fro.

On that journey, alone and unclothed.

Clothed only by what was harboured in your heart while in body,

Look at me, slim Bonganyi, ahaha

Is this an insult?

She moves around, ululating.

I dreamt of the day my mum will chant songs of freedom.

Speaking a language that is far from the natural sounds of the cockcrows and birds.

A language only free people could chant and dance.

I longed for the moment I will be arrayed with beautiful ornaments,

The reality hits back,

Hard as a rock, unflinching and painful.

Look at my dress

In a daze of what it shows, I gaze at the waves of pain in display

My stockings with holes, even on this day?

She claps her hands in surprise.

I lift my head

And I see the dignity of those who looked at me from above the ground standing firm in loyal lethal pride and titles

And I tell you I hoped for a day.

The day which I too would stand above the ground and tell my story.

A story to restore my title.

But I console myself with the last and only one I ever would have . . .

BELOVED DAUGHTER

Aha, so simple, yet true;

Beloved daughter.

I think I deserve more don't you think so?

Yes, I deserve it, I worked . . . hard, and harder each day, so that one day I will chant the song of maidens on a trip to the river.

Swinging my most treasured treasures, fully blown, not minding the oppressed earth and air that threatened to choke the little freedom I had.

And each day I got up feeling I was closer to a day, that day.

The day I would shout.

And allow the vibrations of my body to speak of stories forbidden to the ears and eyes of onlookers.

My voice is choked.

My words stuffed down my throat

My emotions left for a soothsayer to guess . . .

A day, that day, the day the bells at my feet will chant a different song.

A song of freedom.

At last at last,

I longed for the day I would stand poised, in a position straight as a soldier and sing a song of freedom from slavery.

Here I lay, no word, no title, no name, no identity, no freedom.

Just a body, beholding beauty so great but lost in coldness

A rose withering into cold rest

Tell me now what could I have done, what, what?

This is what I wanted:

Bonganyi:Winner and the Best Dancer in The Annual Regional Cultural Extravaganza

Ah!

Aha, my worth have protruded like *ndong ne beuh* (sweet yams).[1]

Cooked from the pot of *Yaa* (Granny).

Such would have given meaning to a life without meaning,

Such would have changed the tune of the song, with no tune,

Such would have written a name in the book of life, in the book of rights.

How I wish I danced to tell you where I come from . . .

To tell you a story of my body,

To tell you the story of my head, my feet,

And of the fullness of my womanhood . . . my maidenhood . . . the symbol of our liberation

Because yes, on this day you would have seen my feet for the first time . . .

I faint . . . my voice faints . . . all these are wishes . . . how I wish you could hear me,

I wish you could hear my cry of distress.

---

1 Sweet yams are cooked on very special occasions, also used by some elders to signify that a maiden is beautiful and ripe for marriage.

My cry for motherhood,

My cry to be held as a maiden in glory

As a fighter in victory

As a human equal to you, him, her and they . . .

She stops in her tracks. There is silence. Then she starts singing the dirge again as she wanders from side to side, swinging in light dance steps as if in a daze or in a trance. These movements take her to the position of the corpse. She stops, as her body silently and slowly crumbles to the floor.

Ntem *detaches himself from the group.*

Ntem   I am called Ntem.

I come from Balamba village,

A village noted for producing the best dancers in the annual regional cultural extravaganza.

There is Bonganyi,

Bonganyi . . . I can hear voices . . . her laughter,

Bonganyi so beautiful.

Bonganyi so hardworking.

My choice was set, my vote was cast

I would give her victory because . . . because . . . because . . .

I can hear her laugh.

Bonganyi *laughs, as if each time her name is mentioned it gave her strength to come back on her feet. She laughs lightly as if in a murmur. She moves around in a daze.*

Ntem   I can hear her footsteps.

He moves around as he speaks, dancing and eager to feel her. His dances takes him to her and their hands meet. They both execute dance steps as if they were two blind people, searching each other's heart and soul.

They dance as two hearts who have come together, who can't seem to accept the separation.

They dance as two lovers who have been ordered to part ways. The dance movements take them apart in a separation that is difficult to accept.

Ntem   I feel her presence everywhere!

I can feel her all around me all around me everywhere

If a man abandons his sugar cane . . . on that day he will confirm from ants that unity begets success.

Bonganyi, Bonganyi. She used to be the best dancer

Bonganyi used to dance for me.

She dances from side to side on stage, floating in a mesmerizing way.

I used to call her my dance queen

My world, my breath my all

Ah ah.

But now she is gone

Bonganyi is gone

He shivers.

I am cold.

How am I going to continue without you Bonganyi?

Who is going to represent the village at the Annual Regional Cultural Extravaganza?

He asks the question going towards the audience as if to a particular person or as if to no one.

Who is going to win the first prize, a prize that we have worked so hard for?

Bonganyi used to be a good dancer,

Her body, her arms, her size . . . ah!

The smile on her face would make anyone know love and joy is within reach.

Love and joy, riches so far-fetched in our lives, transported by her unto us.

Bonganyi *comes in and they dance together again.*

Ntem   She dances, she floats like a bird in romance waiting to elope . . .

Her smile each time she dances pierced the hearts

Ah aha so charming.

Bonganyi, Bonganyi, Bonganyi, Bonganyi, Bonganyi!

Bonganyi   My name . . . who is calling my name?

A spotlight on a corner of the stage, **Bonganyi** *is seen as she speaks. The light goes out.*

There is complete darkness on stage.

Can I speak?

I will speak.

I will speeeaaaaaakkkkk!

'Water has gotten into the holes and ratmoles are out in the open.'

There is a scream in the dark and then silence.

Act Two

Bonganyi is seen carrying a basket on her head with a hoe at her shoulder. She skips from the corner of one farm to the other. It's a sugar cane plantation with very healthy sugar canes. The way to her mother's farm is long. She decides to pass through the sugar cane plantation of Pa Atah. As she skips, her legs mistakenly break a sugar cane shoot.

Bonganyi   Wo sugarcane oh!!!!!

Precious sugar cane oh.

She skips from one side of the stage to the other.

I hope nobody has seen me oh!!!

I hope no one has seen me.

She looks left and right again just to make sure. She tries and adjusts it with a stone and goes over to their farm. **Bonganyi** *starts working. She takes her cutlass and starts clearing the farm.*

Atem *comes in shouting her name.*

Atem   Bonganyi, Bonganyi, Bonganyi!

Bonganyi   Hehehehhe what is it?

Why are you shouting my name out loud?

It's not even six o'clock and you are shouting . . .

Bonganyi! Bonganyi! Bonganyi!

Have you become a rooster?

If names could become extinct today, mine would have been gone a long time ago.

I would really love to preserve the little that is remaining of that name.

Please leave my name for a while, would you?

She walks away from him conspicuously indulges in her farming.

If it were left to you by evening my name would have been finished.

What is your problem?

Eh, I want to work oh . . .!

Atem   Bonganyi my father says all the time,

'If you decide to breastfeed a child that walks, be prepared to rub Manyanga on your nipples.'

Eh eh, see Bonganyi, just go and fix my father's sugar cane!

Bonganyi   Which sugar cane?

Atem   The sugar cane that you just smashed.

Bonganyi   How far are you sure that I am the one who smashed your father's sugar cane?

Atem   See eh,

'Only a blind man will take boiled pepper and put in his mouth.'

Some children told me that you were the first person to pass through my father's sugar cane plantation this morning.

Bonganyi   You are so stupid.

Am I the only one who uses this road to go to the farm?

Atem *gets angry and threatens to go after* **Bonganyi**, *she screams.* **Asong** *rushes to the scene in an anxious manner.*

Asong   Eh eh eh what is happening here?

Bonganyi   Warn him oh!

Atem   Why are you here?

Asong   I was there in my farm and I heard her shouting. I came here to know why she was shouting.

Atem   See eh Asong, Bonganyi has to fix my father's sugar cane.

Asong   Ah. What happened with the sugar cane?

Bonganyi   Massa ask him oh!

Atem   Because she smashed it.

Asong   Bonganyi what happened?

Bonganyi   Well I was on my way to this farm, since I was in a haste to finish work on my master's farm and this good for nothing fool . . .

Atem   What?

Are you calling me a fool?

You are calling me a fool in my father's wonderful plantation?

Bonganyi   Are you not one?

Atem goes forward to catch her and Asong intervenes and stops him.

Atem   See eh Bonganyi I will . . .

'If you put your hand in your anus, be prepared to deal with a smelling hand'.

Bonganyi   A fool.

She sticks out her tongue to him. She knows Asong is protecting her and would not allow Atem to touch her.

Asong   Wait, don't insult him. Just tell me what happened.

Bonganyi   He is a fool.

Atem goes for her again, and Asong stops him. This time Asong screams to both to stop.

Asong   Both of you, wait!

Atem   Did you hear that again?

This girl is very insolent.

No one has ever disrespected me this much and especially not on my father's illustrious plantation.

Bonganyi   Asong, I am sick and tired of people looking at me as a sub human being.

I was born free, but made a slave by my own supposed fellow neighbour.

For a crime I bear no record of.

If not yet for my desire to acknowledge a friendship I didn't know had met the cold hands of death.

I'll be damned if his foot print will mark me from my head right through my body in servitude, because I am a servant and others are heirs.

Just because of common sugar cane.

Asong   How far are you sure that Bonganyi is the one who smashed your father's sugar cane?

Atem   Besides the fact that some children told me that they saw her pass through my father's illustrious sugar cane plantation this morning? Come let me show you something. Look at these footsteps. Look at them. They are tiny, just like Bonganyi's footpints.

Bonganyi   What!!!

Did I just hear somebody say my feet are tiny?

Atem   Yes, and what will you do about it?

What can you do?

'A tortoise is wise only so long as an elephant is not within reach'.

Aren't you even lucky you are to be standing on my father's sugar cane plantation?

How many plantations have you seen in your entire life?

Bonganyi *goes and picks up her hoe and starts running towards* **Atem**.

Bonganyi   By the time I am through with you . . .!

Asong *catches her and picks her up calming her down.*

Atem   You cannot do anything to me, small girl. Small, insignificant girl who smashed my father's precious sugar cane.

Bonganyi   Don't hold me Asong, just let me go and let me teach him a lesson!

By the time I reach him, he will understand that

'Strength does not dwell in the size of an arm but in its ability to lift weight'.

Atem   You cannot do anything, I am the son of the most influential sugar cane merchant in this village, you cannot do anything.

You cannot try anything Bonganyi, you are too small.

'No matter how beautiful a woman can be . . . she has got a price'.

With my father's wealth, I can buy 10 versions of you, Bonganyi.

Bonaganyi *is ranting and hissing.*

Asong   Atem calm down, calm down eh.

'No matter the heat produced by a mountainous eruption, it shall surely get cold.'

Stop this!

Bonganyi   Asong, he says my feet are tiny

That my legs are tiny, wonderful!!!

Tiny eh e h.

Atem   Asong, did she just shout at me?

Asong, she called me a fool, can you believe that?

She called me a fool in my own father's sugar cane plantation.

Me, the only son of the greatest sugar cane merchant of this village.

Asong   You don't have to fight with a girl.

He who fights with a woman fights with his mother.

Atem   Ah Massa leaves man that one!!!

Asong   Girls are very precious things.

The beauty of a girl ought to give you rest from all the troubles in this world.

Please calm down.

Bonganyi   Sugar cane ma head abeg!

She says so and goes away, picking up all her things. **Atem** *and* **Asong** *do not realize that she has gone already.*

Asong   Atem calm down nah, wait!!! Just wait let me go and see her.

He goes towards where **Bonganyi** *was and discovers that she is gone.*

Aha she has gone already.

Bonganyi where are you? Bonganyi?

He calls and goes off stage, still looking for her and calling for her while **Atem** *continues ranting.*

Atem   Yes, call for her, she must fix my father's sugar cane. She must fix it! If not the chief and the council of elders will hear about this.

He waits, hears no sound, then turns around.

Where are they?

So, they think they are intelligent eh?

Ah aha okay the chief must hear about this. The chief must hear this story.

Atem *exits.*

Act Three

Bonganyi *comes on stage with a song, a clay pot on her head. She puts it down. Then she starts dancing, making mistakes and starting all over again.*

Bonganyi Ekati many ma rende
Ma rende mi ye
Ohoh ma rende me niyam quet
Ehehe marende mi ye
Ohoh ma rende me niyam quet.

She stops singing and starts talking to herself as she moves around.

Bonganyi stop joking.

The annual regional extravaganza is tomorrow.

Finally, the day is here.

The dance steps go like this . . .

She does one dance.

This other one.

She does another.

And this . . .

The last dance step is difficult.

I have only three he! I want to be the best dancer, three is not going to be enough.

What is that, my song again.

She starts singing and **Ntem** *comes in, singing with her.*

(Song:) Ekati many ma rende
ma rende mi ye
Ohoh ma rende me niyam quet
Ehehe marende mi ye
Ohoh ma rende me niyam quet.

Ntem Aha, what are you doing here?

Bonganyi You know that since the Annual Regional Extravaganza is fast approaching nah.

Ntem   Yes.

Bonganyi   I counted it and I have just three dance steps.

This style.

She demonstrates a dance step.

That is one nah.

That is other one: (*she counts two fingers*) two.

I made another one and it is not very nice see.

She demonstrates a very clumsy dance step.

Ntem   How can you be preparing for the Annual Regional
Cultural Extravaganza and you did not look for me to come and assist
you?

Bonganyi   Weh Ntem I forgot!

Ntem   See eh Bonganyi!

Bonganyi   Yes.

Ntem   You know that on that day all those other girls will be dancing
like this.

He starts demonstrating by shaking his behind.

Shaking like this, shaking like this, shaking like this . . .
Just only shaking their buttocks.
But you Bonganyi, you know you are my dance queen eh.
You will have to do something extraordinary like . . . see wait let me
show you.

He now comes forward and starts showing her some dance steps.

You have to turn your body like this,
You have to turn again like this,
Then you turn your body like this one more time and go anti clockwise,
You can go right, and you can go left.
Try this one.

Bonganyi   Yes, let me try okay, when you were dancing I was imitating
you, but you did not see.

Ntem   Okay do it.

Bonganyi   Okay sing my song nah.

Ntem   Yes. 1, 2, 3, go!

Bonganyi *starts dancing while* **Ntem** *sings.*

Ntem (*song:*)   Ekati many ma rende
ma rende mi ye
Ohoh ma rende me niyam quet
Ehehe marende mi ye
Ohoh ma rende me niyam quet.

You forgot to go in front.

Bonganyi   I forgot to go in front? But show me again.

Ntem   Yes, you forgot to go like this.

He shows her again.

Bonganyi   Eh okay let me go in front nah.

Eh but this dance step is very technical you said I should go like this.

She beckons to him to shift.

Shift from there nah I need space.

She starts dancing.

Both   One two three!

They start laughing.

Ntem   You know you are my dance queen. I like you very much because you don't take time to learn.

Bonganyi   Thank you.

Ntem   When you finish with the dance steps eh,

Since you have light arms you will just do like this as if you are a bird.

Bonganyi   Like a bird.

Ntem   Yes, stand at the centre so that everyone will see you.

Yes. 1, 2, 3, go!

(*Song:*) Ekati many ma rende
Ma rende mi ye
Ohoh ma rende me niyam quet
Ehehe marende mi ye
Ohoh ma rende me niyam quet.

Bonganyi *is dancing as he sings and both are happy when she succeeds the dance steps.*

Ntem   Ehe that is good.

Bonganyi   Thank you very much.

Ntem   On that day Bonganyi, your dance steps shall make everyone soar in the wind of the melody.

And my eyes, ready and sharp, my hands poised in the air, waiting in applause to the declaration of your victory.

Bonganyi   Do you know what is going to happen to those girls, the ones who will come to shake only their buttocks?

Ntem   Do you know something? When they see you dancing they will look for a place and hide.

Bonganyi   They will run and hide.

Ntem   Yes.

Bonganyi   Hahahahah! Okay come let's try it again.

Ntem   No, no Bonganyi.

Bonganyi   Yes, what is it?

Ntem   It will soon be dark oh. And you know my mother sent me to go and fetch firewood.

Bonganyi   Aha aha, okay you are right.

Ntem   Yes, let me go now.

On my way back eh I will bring you fresh corn eh?

Bonganyi   Yes. How many?

Ntem   I will bring you four.

Bonganyi   Ah no, how many dance styles have we just done just now?

Ntem   Seven dance steps.

Bonganyi   Ehe, seven dance steps for Bonganyi equals seven maize cobs too.

Ntem *exits, leaving* **Bonganyi** *doing the dance step alone on the stage.*

Bonganyi   Ah thank God I have not forgotten them.

Only the way I will go on stage hahahahahhahahahhah!

Those people will know that there are dancers in this balamba village eh.

Asong, *who has been hiding behind a tree, comes out.*

Atem   Yes, I remember!!!

Bonganyi used to pass through this way to go to the stream to go and fetch water.

Let me just hide behind here and wait for her,

So that when she comes out I will step out and catch her and take her to my father's sugar cane plantation.

He stops again and looks round.

But what am I seeing here?

Footprints!!!

Let me follow them. 1, 2, 3, 4, 5 . . .

He stops suddenly, confused.

But this is not the way to the stream. The stream is this way.

Anyway, let me hide here so that when she is passing, I will come out and catch her.

Where will I hide eh.

He looks round and goes to the right side of the stage behind a tree and hides there.

Fru *enters.*

Fru   Okay I remember.

This is the road Bonganyi uses to go and carry water from the stream.

I must wait for her today so that when she is coming I will deal with her.

I can see her footprints.

Let me follow them 1, 2, 3 . . .

But . . . this is not the road to the stream.

Anyway, she must have gone somewhere down the valley.

What I will do, is I am going to hide so that when she comes back

I will come out of the bush and catch her and take her to our compound.

Laughter is heard in the bushes. **Atem** *and* **Asong** *are seen at the extreme ends of the stage, both of them looking for* **Bonganyi** *with their backs to each other.*

Atem   Eh I can hear her voice it seems as if she is coming.

They seemingly have not seen each other.

Asong   Eh I think I hear someone like Bonganyi laughing, maybe she is coming.

And they now turn, thinking it is **Bonganyi** *they have discovered.*

Both   Bonganyi!!!!!!!!

Atem   What are you doing here?

Asong   I am looking for Banganyi.

He starts shouting and calling for her.

Atem   You too.

Asong   Bonganyi!!!!

Where are you hiding?

Atem   Bonganyi, come out oh I must finish with you today.

Asong   Bonganyi, it is better for you to come out because if I meet you there it will be catastrophic for you!

Atem   Bonganyi, come here oh this is the last time I am calling.

Asong   Bonganyi!

Atem   Asong, what are you doing on my father's precious sugar cane plantation, come out of there.

Asong   Ah sugar cane plantation! and you Atem, what are you doing here?

Atem   I am surveying my father's precious sugar cane plantation.

And you what are you doing here?

Asong   I am here hunting, I came to check on my traps that is why I am here.

Atem   Asong, eh yes I remember you were the one the other day who stopped me from squeezing Bonganyi's neck, when I discovered that she smashed my father's sweet sugar cane in his precious beautiful plantation.

Asong   Yes.

Atem   Am I not right?

Asong   Yes, it is true I am the one but how can you Atem, a very young gentle man –

Atem   Eh eh wait, son of the most intelligent, the most handsome, and the strongest business man of the whole of this village.

Asong   – threaten to fight with a young beautiful girl like Bonganyi?

Atem listen, beautiful women are admired. Beautiful women are adorned with gifts and ornaments for the bodies.

Atem   See eh Asong, listen very well.

Atem   In our house, when my father just coughs like this.

He coughs.

My mother just goes on the floor like this as a sign of respect.

He says so by going flat on his stomach on the floor.

A man is master,
a man is king,
a man is power,
a man is feared.

Asong   See eh Atem in our own house,

My mother is the warmth we get in the cold days.

And is the feeling of fresh water on the skin under the scorching sun.

My mother is the spring of water that comes to give plants life in the garden of my father.

Atem   Asong, a man is the head of the family.

Asong   And the woman the heart of the family.

Anyway, Atem let me tell you something, can you imagine my father.

Mr Tata the most powerful hero in the whole of this village,

The hunter who brought the head of a lion to the palace,

Do you know my father?

Atem   So, it was your father who brought the head of the lion to the palace?

Asong   Yes, it was my father; he is even the one who fought with the viper in the forest for three whole days and three whole nights.

Atem   Asong, your father is a brave man eh, a great man.

Asong   My father is a hero, a powerful man, a great man in this community.

Atem   Yes.

Asong   We went to ask for her hand in marriage.

Can you imagine that my father and I brought an antelope, a gorilla, a chimpanzee, an antelope, forty litres of palm wine, fifty kilograms of rice especially cultivated by my mother, fifty litres of red oil . . .

Atem   Is that all?

Asong   No, that is not all. He also brought gin, mirrors, rappas, two bags of salt and shared money to all women in their compound, we brought all these things there to ask for Bonganyi's hand in marriage on my behalf.

Atem   And what did she say?

The boys gather round him in anticipation of his answer.

Asong   Bonganyi refused.

Atem   Wonderful Bonganyi refused?

What?

After all the things you people brought, after your father shared money to all the women in their compound?

Asong   She refused.

Atem   This girl is terrible, even after seeing your father the greatest hunter in this universe, after all the money you shared with all the women in their compound.

Asong   Yes, Atem she refused. That is even why I am here, I want to deal with her.

Atem   You see why I wanted to deal with her?

The other day you stopped me.

Now see what she has done to you.

Bonganyi is very troublesome.

Asong   I must deal with Bonganyi.

We have to do something really drastic.

Atem   Bonaganyi, you smashed my father's precious sugar cane on his plantation which he used all his energy physically, psychologically, intellectually, emotionally to plant.

Asong   Bonganyi, you refused my hand in marriage upon all the gifts that my brave father gave to your family . . . ah no, this is too much.

At this moment **Mofor**, *who is dumb (mute) comes on stage and starts looking for someone.*

Atem   What is wrong?

Who are you looking for?

Then **Mofor** *describes with actions indicating a girl.*

Asong   Is it Beri you are looking for?

Then **Mofor** *indicates: no.*

Atem   Therefore, it must be Lum.

Mofor *still shakes his head from side to side, indicating a no.*

Asong   Who are you looking for, nah?

Mofor *now describes* **Bonganyi** *as a dancer.*

Both   Bonganyi.

Atem   Eh again.

Asong   This girl is not a serious girl.

Atem   Mofor, tell me what has she done to you?

Mofor *starts describing with gestures while* **Atem** *is explaining in words.*

You stole your father's money and gave to Bonganyi . . . yes this is terrible.

Asong   So, you stole all your mother's dresses, her *pincé* [make up kit], her jewelry and gave to Bonganyi?

And she disappeared?

Atem And you haven't yet seen her?

Asong Bonganyi, what are we going to do to this girl?

Atem Come! Come! Come!

Do you know what we are going to do we are going to set up a plan to deal with Bonganyi.

Asong Yes!

Atem just go and check whether someone is coming.

They disperse to the different parts of the stage to check if someone is coming.

Is anybody coming?

Asong No

Atem Come! Come! Come!

Let's go to my father's plantation so that we can set up a plan to deal with Bonganyi.

Okay you people will have the privilege to sit in my father's precious sugar cane,

In fact, the most intelligent merchant you have ever heard in your life eh

Sit, sit, sit.

Asong I am sure we will have a taste of the most juicy sugar cane in this your father's precious plantation.

Atem Yes, so what are we going to do?

Asong No what about the sugar cane?

Atem But can't you wait eh.

Asong Aha but we are supposed to be discussing and chewing some sugar cane.

Aren't we here in your father's precious sweet sugar cane plantation?

Atem Yes nah.

Asong Eh eh and you spend all your time talking about your father's precious sugar cane plantation. Aha give us the juicy sugar cane you talk about, we need some sugar cane to water our throats.

Atem Eh what is it?

Can your father have a sugar cane plantation?

Asong Can your father also catch a lion, a tiger and a buffalo eh?

Atem See here Asong, I don't like it eh. We are not here to talk about your father's lion head, his leopard teeth or his chimpanzee-catching capabilities.

Asong Neither are we here to talk about the prowess of your father's sugar cane plantation.

I am just saying that you should make us have a taste of the precious sugar cane.

What are we going to do now?

Atem Okay it's enough!!

What do we do?

Asong I have an idea.

Atem Yes, tell me.

Asong You know that Bonganyi usually goes to her father's farm down the valley there near the stream. So, we should just go and wait for her on the way, then we will catch her and tie her and take her far away, to another village.

Atem How are we going to do it nah?

Asong You know that I am very strong nah?

I will just come out of the bush and cover her face so that she will not know who is holding her. You will hold her legs. Then Mofor will hold her hands we will carry her away from this village and hide her somewhere and she will never come back again.

Mofor *starts indicating that he is against the idea and that he is leaving.*

Atem Aha Mofor what is it? Came nah.

Where are you going to?

If you don't like the idea tell us Nah.

Why are you going like that?

Mofor *indicates with gestures that he does not like the idea.*

Atem   Okay I know what we will do, on her way from the stream we will just . . . .

Wait let me show you. We will just come out. I will clear her like this.

He indicates by clearing **Mofor** *from off the ground, by sweeping his legs against that of his opponent and making him fall.*

Atem   And then you will just come, and we will carry her away.

Asong   No, no, no.

Have you forgotten that the other day we waited for her on that road she uses to go to the stream?

And she did not finally come.

You know if you catch her like this she will fall down and break her head, what will happen?

So what should we do?

Atem   Mofor do you have an idea?

Mofor *indicates with signs and gestures. He lifts up his forefinger like one who has something important to say.* **Atem** *claps his hands.*

Atem   Ah I did not think about it . . . *(clapping hands in a typical Cameroonian way that indicates negation).* You know that Bonganyi has been preparing for the Annual Regional Cultural Extravaganza and she can't afford to miss it.

So we will just wait for her on the road to the palace and catch her then. Do you know what I will do? I will tie her from her head to her toes and then I will just carry her to my father's precious sugar cane plantation.

Asong   Yes, that is a very good idea. But I don't think we should hide her in your father's precious sugar cane plantation.

Atem   What do you mean?

Asong   He is a very popular man and everybody knows him.

If someone finds Bonganyi in your father's precious plantation, what will the villagers say? I think we should take her to my mother's kitchen.

Atem   Why? Why? Eh!

Why in your mother's kitchen?

Asong   Because there she will have so much meat to eat: dry meat, fresh meat,

Eh cow meat goat meat and all types of meat you can find.

Atem   Okay, okay.

No problem, then let us go nah.

Asong   That is a good idea come to my mother's kitchen let me make you have a taste of my father's precious sugar cane.

Act Four

Asong *is the first to come by their rendezvous site to kidnap* **Bonganyi**.

Asong   Aha where are the others? Anyway, I am the son of a great warrior I am capable of catching Bonganyi alone.

He goes and hides and as soon as he hears footsteps he just leaps out and covers the eyes of the person. Then he realizes it is **Mofor**, *who is angry.*

Aha I thought it was Bonganyi,

Ah why are you angry, you are late nah eh Mofor.

Okay come and let us hide so that when Bonganyi comes we will catch her.

They go and hide but **Ntem**, *who is on his way to call for the village doctor, is also surprised by them.*

Ntem   What is happening here?

Asong   O sorry we mistook you for someone else.

Ntem   Ah ah what are you doing here?

Asong   We are going to the market. Today is the market day have you forgotten?

Ntem   What, at this time of the day?

Asong   Yes, and what about you? Where are you going to?

Ntem   I am going to the village doctor and from the look of things I will go to the palace from there.

He goes in a run. **Atem** *enters.*

Asong   A ha where were you? We have been waiting for you?

Atem   Has she come already?

Asong   Not yet. Anyway, let us hide.

They go and hide themselves waiting for **Bonganyi**. **Ntem** *is on his way back from the village doctor. All three of them pounce on him again. This time* **Ntem** *gets very suspicious.*

Ntem   What is happening here?

Who are you people waiting for with so much anger?

And at this time of the day?

Asong   We are surveying this environment.

Atem   We are on our way to the market.

Ntem   Are you sure you people are not plotting something dangerous here?

'Remember he who eats pepper must be ready to dance to the tune of his anus.'

Asong   We are going to the market

Ntem   At 5 am?

Asong   Have you forgotten that boys from the neighbouring village always come to steal our crops? We are here to track them down.

Ntem   Eh eh okay, no problem.

Asong   So what did the traditional healer say?

Ntem   Come on, get out, are you the one who sent me there?

Anyway, I will go to the palace, the *fon* [chief] must hear this.

Strange things are happening in this village.

Instead of doing something good with your time, you go about gallivanting.

Young boys like you spend time in the bush as armed robbers.

Atem   Hold it there! My father is the most influential, the most intelligent, the most prosperous sugar cane merchant in the whole of this village and region.

Asong   And my father is the one who brought the lion's head to the palace.

Ntem   Whether your father is a . . . a . . . what so ever plantation farmer . . . .

Atem   Sugar cane plantation merchant. The only one for that matter.

Ntem *now turns towards* **Asong**.

Ntem   Whether your father is the friend of a lion or of a gorilla . . .

Asong   Please hold on there!

He is a warrior and a legend.

Ntem Keep it for yourself and look for something serious to do with your life instead of standing here or gallivanting in the village saying arrogant nonsense.

Let me go and leave you to your very busy schedule.

Atem What does he mean by that?

I am a native of this village.

And my father owns hectares and hectares of landed property, plus he is a flourishing sugar cane business man.

Asong This guy is crazy.

Me, son of the greatest warrior, don't I have the right to look at the bush without someone complaining?

Anyway, it looks like Bonganyi is not coming.

Atem Ah this useless Ntem has spoiled our plans anyway. Tomorrow is another day. Let's go to the palace and see the competition.

They all move out, there is complete darkness. There is no sound, and then the same song as in the beginning of the play starts.

Dirge song:

Solo Yondo yondo yondo

Chorus Yondo sélélé

Solo Mama Yondo yondo yondo

Chorus Yondo sélélé

Solo Yondo sélélé

Chorus Yondo sélélé eh yondo sélélé

Solo Yondo eh

Chorus Yondo sélélé eh yondo sélélé

Ntem Bonganyi's mother was devastated. Everybody was in pain.

The sadness was looming in the air.

As if greeting every one of us, seeking to make friends.

Wandering and not knowing where to end.

When I got to their house her mother gave me a letter, and in the letter she explained what had happened to Bonganyi.

Bonganyi   That is how I missed the Regional Cultural Extravaganza.

It was all because of a snake bite.

Fatal, very fatal.

With its poison, ready and quick to lead me to the cold hands of death.

I couldn't plead my cause.

I couldn't plead for my people.

I couldn't stand in the gap for them again . . .

My wish remained my wish and my dreams remained my dreams.

My words of plea travelled right through my throat, stopped in their tracks.

The sound of it stuffed, suffocated, in my throat.

I could feel the hands of a cold breeze

Freeze them all, even before they were born,

How painful it is never to wake up from a dream,

A dream of a people.

Please help me carry a message.

Can you hear me?

Can you take a message?

She moves to stand at the centre.   ·   ·

Tell her,

Tell my mother that I love her very much.

Ah Mama, she used to sing for me to dance.

She used to say I am her dancer.

She would cook my favourite dish.

And after I have eaten she would ask me to dance.

She moves from one end of the stage to the other as if he is struggling to hear something.

Tell my sister that I will always remember her.

Tell her I tried so we could one day live as humans, fully.

Remember that my family and my ancestors have always been slaves.

It is a custom that whomsoever won the Regional Cultural Extravaganza would have their wish granted to them by the *fon*.

I wanted to be the best dancer at the Annual Regional Cultural Extravaganza.

I wanted to be the Best of the Best.

In order to free my people from slavery, in order to free my people from the yoke that bound them to your people, I did not eat nor drink because of anticipation.

On the eve of the competition day,

I was on my way from the stream and since it was getting dark I was running.

I slipped on something and almost fell on the ground.

Then I felt a sharp pain on my right leg at the level of my ankle.

But since it was dark I ran to the house.

Ntem, *who had been moving around, suddenly sits down. Then he speaks out his pain with sadness and solemnity.*

Ntem   I went to check on Bonganyi, to see whether all was ready for the competition the next day.

And when I arrived her mother showed me the wound, saying I should run and look for the traditional healer.

I rushed to the herbalist, but on reaching there I was told he had gone to the forest to harvest some herbs.

By the time I came back it was too late.

The setting is like in the beginning of the play and the dirge continues as they bury the dead. They sing and dance, steps that take them each on their way off the stage.

Chorus   Mama ehe e e

Bato baseh ba tiyana eh mama

Mama ehe e e

Bato baseh ba tiyana eh mama

Solo   Mama a ndedi eh o

Chorus   Mama

Solo   Bato base ba tiyana eh o

Chorus   Mama

From off stage the voice of **Bonganyi** *is heard whispering.*

Bonganyi   I wish I had danced, I wish I had danced, I wish I had danced . . .

They disperse and move offstage.

The End